David A. Lively
March, 1979

→ April 23 - read thru ch. 14
→ April 30 - read thru ch 17, p. 233, Monday
→ May 7 - read thru ch 20, p. 271, Monday
May 21 - last 3 chapters
You lead discussion

Gospel - p. 40

BEHIND
THE RANGES

BEHIND THE RANGES

Biography of
J. O. FRASER *of Lisuland*
Southwest China

By
MRS. HOWARD TAYLOR

moody press
chicago

Printed in the United States of America

CONTENTS

5

INTRODUCTION

BY THE TENS OF THOUSANDS the Lisu tribespeople of southwest China have responded to the Gospel. This movement of God in the villages high on the ridges of the Mekong and Salween canyons is one of the brightest spots in modern missionary annals. This is so, not only because of the number of souls who have responded to the Lord, the many churches that have been established, and the enthusiasm which has been maintained in their Bible schools and mass conferences, but also because of a *continuing* work of grace even now.

The People's Government of China established their regime in that remote area in 1950. But none of the threats and open persecution, the hunger that followed their depredations, and finally the long-term imprisonment and death of many leaders and layfolk moved these Spirit-taught children of the hills. To be sure, some of the weak ones fell away, but these were few compared with the number of faithful who have suffered long in prison, have been tortured to death, or have been killed otherwise for their open witness. These are they "of whom the world was not worthy . . . having obtained a good report through faith" (Heb. 11:38-39).

7

But this is not the end of the Lisu story. *Behind the Ranges* tells the beginning of it in the lifetime of J. O. Fraser. It was his poured-out life and spiritual but very practical wisdom which laid the foundations. Many other missionaries of the China Inland Mission have built thereon, and God has given an ever-increasing harvest.

Isobel Kuhn's books, *Precious Things of the Lasting Hills, Nests Above the Abyss, In the Arena,* and *Stones of Fire,* take the story on to the point where the last missionaries had to flee over the treacherous passes to Burma and freedom. She tells of the Lisu Christians beginning to reach out over the border with the Message of Life for their kinfolk in Burma.

Years have passed. Isobel Kuhn has gone to glory, but the progress of that sturdy missionary operation marches right through history of very recent days to today. And still there is more to follow which some other pen must record.

The Christian Lisu migration over into Burma (30 to 40 thousand of them), their linking up with other Christian villages, making between 60 and 70 thousand baptized Lisu Christians in Burma, and the memory of some 45 thousand Lisu believers still bearing the reproach of Christ in China—these are statistics glowing with triumph because they speak of God's faithfulness through the years in moving men through prayer.

Readers of *Behind the Ranges* will discover that

it was not primarily Fraser's energetic evangelism and wise counsel that made his work so effective. It was his emphasis on prayer in his own life and his gift of fostering prayer groups in the homeland. This constant prayer barrage covered the whole operation, protecting it from the deadly fire of Satan's forces. Surely here lies the secret of a truly successful missionary enterprise.

M.E.A.

Chapter 1

CALL OF THE HEIGHTS

THE MOUNTAINS appealed to something in Jim Fraser that he had hardly known was there—a love of solitude, an instinctive response to the high, the difficult, the forbidding. His inward attitude was the very reverse of today's easygoing wish that all the world were downhill. The heights called him. In climbing, in conquering through long endurance, he found himself. He possessed the mountains and the mountains possessed him by the sternness of their demands and by the riches of their rewards.

Chief among the enjoyments of school and college days were vacations in Switzerland, when Jim and his cousin Aleck Bourne went on walking tours. Perfectly matched in age and tastes, they set their faces toward the snowy heights. They tramped the passes, explored the glaciers, climbed glorious peaks, and sailed the tranquil lakes, taking photographs, meeting with adventures, and drinking in health and happiness.

Some years later, tramping with his guide over more than Alpine heights on the western frontier of China, he wrote:

Long grass, enormous boulders, rocks of every size, streams, and high mountains were all that could be seen, and the mists rolled in upon us in a drizzling rain. We met only one man all day, for the upper slopes afford food and shelter to none but leopards, wolves, and bears. This lofty, wet, wild country— how I revel in it!

Peak and plain alike were invisible, for the mist which hid everything below also hid all above and around us. Oh, the grand, soul-stirring highlands of these mountains! Hour after hour of arduous climbing brought us to the summit—or rather, the pass, for of course no mountain road ever goes over a peak. It was virgin forest, silent but for our footsteps on the cushion of wet leaves and the occasional *spat, spat* of big drops of water falling on the soft, spongy ground. Wet, silent, lonely—not even the call of a bird—the pass must have been 10,000 feet high and most of the year covered with snow.

Then came the steep descent on the far side, hands and feet alike in use as we clambered over mossy tree trunks and through brushwood. For a long time nothing could be seen above or below the mist. Then suddenly—when negotiating such a pass you look up only at intervals—my breath was almost taken away by seeing all the mountains of Tientan and beyond, as well as the plain far below, clearly outspread before me. Such a magnificent view, wide and sweeping, made me pause to take it in—range after range of dark mountains swathed in clouds, and in the far distance the forbidding mass of the Salween Divide barring the way like a solid wall. Down, down, down we went, every now and again stopping to take in the grandeur of the scene, until almost at sundown we reached the Lisu village of Shuichen, wet, bedraggled, and weary—but I was in my element and perfectly happy!

Those summers in Switzerland had been unconscious preparation for the far more strenuous mountaineering that was to come. In ways that often pass unnoticed, God fits His instruments for the work He has in view.

* * *

James Outram Fraser, third son of James and Annie (Palmer) Fraser, was born in 1886. When he was five years old his parents moved to St. Albans (near London, England) to occupy the spacious house they had planned and built. His father was absorbingly busy and saw little of his children, for to his responsibilities as vice-president of the College of Veterinary Surgeons he had added political activities that brought him into prominence and demanded much of his time. To be sure, he conducted evening prayers with his household, but it was the mother who made home for the young people, four boys and two girls, and kept them the united group they were all through school and college days. Few mothers could have had a more rewarding task.

The Fraser children were warmhearted as well as gifted above the average. The breakfast room in the big house was their special domain, and there Mrs. Fraser joined with them in all their interests. She was their first teacher in music and drawing. She read to them and talked with them often about the things that matter most. She studied carefully beforehand for the lessons on the life of Christ which went home to their hearts and, through her own love for foreign missions, interested them in the advance of the kingdom of God. She did not tell them that she had long prayed that at least one of her children might become a missionary. Did she think of James especially in this connection—strong and loving among that promising group? In his pioneer days in China he wrote of his missionary call being due to his mother's prayers. But in the old home at St. Albans he was a somewhat dreamy though venturesome boy.

One day while he was still a child, the foundation stone of a new Wesleyan chapel was being laid just opposite their home. Little Jim could not see the proceedings for the crowd but had an idea for his own place of vantage. He disappeared for a few minutes. Then he was seen standing boldly on the edge of a narrow parapet that ran around the roof of the house, quite unconscious of the dismay his precarious footing brought to the onlookers!

Music was Jim's passion. He knew of his mother's love for the great masters and determined to spend his little all to buy a plaster cast of Beethoven for her pleasure. This he ordered from a music shop in town, not realizing he would have to wait months for its delivery. Five months is a long time for a boy of twelve, especially when it concerns a great surprise. Jim inquired at the shop week after week until at last the beautiful thing came—a small bust of the noble head of the musician. Then patience was rewarded in the loving appreciation of his gift, which adorned that dear mother's desk for more than forty years. The tie between them was always close, though Jim took his full share in the endless interests of all the family.

Out of school hours the children worked hard to produce their little monthly magazine, selling for one farthing (about half a cent), with its pictures, music, puzzles, and serial stories, with a lively Table of Contents on the illustrated cover. To this magazine Jim contributed drawings and musical compositions. His bent of mind appeared also in *The Marvel Twopenny Atlas*, another of their efforts, with ten pages of maps, brightly colored and surprisingly accurate.

When photography became the rage, Mrs. Fraser had no less than five camera enthusiasts about her. Jim and his cousin Aleck established The Imperial Photographic Company, Limited, sending the following letter to all shareholders:

Dear Sir or Madam:
We, the above Company, hereby acknowledge the

receipt of fourpence on January 5, 1900, from which you will receive a dividend of 5 percent.

Signed: J. O. FRASER, *Hon. Sec.*
A. W. BOURNE, *Hon. Treas.*

One of the company's bylaws stated that "persons having ordered photographs are obliged to pay for them." This was hard on one of the household who was more distinguished for good nature than for good looks, and who had allowed herself to be photographed. Dismayed at the result, she would have declined the picture, but Bylaw Number Two was brought into force:

If the Company takes a photo which is perfectly finished but does not give satisfaction because of the fault of the person photographed, he or she will have to purchase the photo.

Another necessary regulation was: "No person shall meddle with or in any way damage the Company's materials." But in spite of all this careful planning, catastrophe was not to be avoided, and the Company's affairs were wound up long before the dividend fell due.

What grand times the young people had with their music on winter evenings and outdoors in summer! The program of one Christmas concert, given at home, shows that all but the youngest took part in violin and piano solos, duets, trios, recitations, and songs.

Cycling was also a family recreation. They would often make excursions together, sometimes riding over to Barnet to visit their maternal grandparents. The welcome that always awaited them and the atmosphere of loving sympathy meant even more to those young hearts than the attractions of the lovely garden and home.

As Jim grew older he developed powers of endurance that were to be needed later in many an emergency. He once walked to London and back, 44 miles in one day. On another occasion he rode 199 miles on his bicycle without dismounting. In his studies he was just as persevering. The teacher at St. Albans had to make a special class for him in mathematics. And, after three years at a school in Sheffield, he passed the London University matriculation examinations, ranking twelfth in all England.

His love of music showed itself from childhood in the pains he took to master its difficulties. He learned under good teachers and made the works he studied so much his own that, even as a boy, he could play the best classical music, hour after hour, with no score before him. He keenly enjoyed the symphony concerts in London. It is not difficult to imagine the eagerness with which he and his gifted sister Millicent would ride up together on their bicycles for those enchanted hours in the great city.

Millicent recalled:

God preparing him

Jim was always good company—so interesting to talk with! He had an alert mind, was sympathetic toward other people's ideas, and had a keen sense of humor. He was also in no bondage to convention.

For a Sheffield concert he once secured a seat in the orchestra. When it was over and everybody was going out, the grand piano—a fine instrument—proved too great a temptation. The orchestra was empty, and he stepped down and began to play. At once the disappearing audience took their seats again —for he had an exceptional touch. But when he found they were listening, he stopped in embarrassment!

School gave place to university, and through it all the inward life was deepening. Not that the Frasers ever spoke much about spiritual things. They were brought up to read the Bible and go to church regularly. James became organist at a small Methodist chapel where he also attended a class meeting and taught in the Sunday school.

But there was an influence deeper than these through all those formative years, an influence that told on life. The reality of prayer and the strength it gave could not be questioned by the thoughtful boy in that St. Albans home. There were trials in the life of his beloved mother that he could not fully understand, but he knew the source of her strength. Sacred to that son was the sense of an unseen Presence when his mother came from the place of secret prayer, renewed again and again in the peace that passes understanding.

Fraser was little thinking, however, of the call that was at hand.

Chapter 2

THE REAL ISSUE

LOOKING FORWARD to his last year at London University, Fraser had just turned twenty. His course in engineering had been difficult, but he was well up in his studies, as was proved when he graduated with distinction. Bright prospects were before him, for he loved his profession and did not lack promising opportunities for its exercise. The goal was in sight, the ambition of years almost attained. He would soon be in a position of independence.

And it was just at that crisis, one of the most important in his life, that the young man was unexpectedly arrested in his plans and the whole course of his life was changed. From what little things the greatest changes often come! A thought, a word, and we are challenged with possibilities undreamed of before. In Fraser's life it was a little paperbound book that brought the challenge—a little book with the strange title *Do Not Say*, given to him by a fellow student.

"Do not say—" As Jim read he found that an attitude of mind was being called into question. It was in fact, the very attitude he himself was taking, had been taking all along by the very tenor of his life.

The writer of the little book, himself a missionary to China, put the matter of world evangelization in a new light. That now, in the twentieth century of our Christian era, the vast majority of mankind should still be in ignorance of the one and only way of salvation is a shocking fact that we as Christians need to recognize, to our own personal discredit. "Do not say," the little book stated, "that this is a matter only for ministers and churches to consider."

Yes, that had been Jim's rational attitude. His call had been to engineering, an honored profession that he intended to use for the benefit of his fellowmen. But now he became conscious of his responsibility for the eternal welfare of others. The China missionary's simple, honest appeal went straight to the heart of things:

Is it right? In the sight of God, in view of the realities of eternity, is it right? A command has been given: "Go ye into all the world and preach the Gospel to every creature." It has not been obeyed. More than half of the people in the world have never yet heard the Gospel. What are we to say to this? Surely it concerns us Christians very seriously, for we are the ones responsible and no one else. The angels are not responsible, for God has not told them to preach the Gospel to the heathen. Neither does God expect unconverted people to carry His Glad Tidings to the heathen. He expects His disciples to do it.

The privilege of carrying the saving message has not been granted to others. The charge has been entrusted exclusively to us. What then can we say if our Master returns today and finds that, after nineteen centuries, more than half of the world is utterly unevangelized? "The Gospel to every creature"—a plain command. Millions have never heard it—a simple fact. What are we going to say? What indeed? I for one am utterly at a loss to conceive what we can say. After puzzling over this question, casting about in all directions to lay hold of something we might reasonably urge as our excuse, I am obliged to give it up. If our Master returned today to find millions of people unevangelized and looked, as of course He would look, to us for an explanation, I cannot imagine what explanation we should be able to give.

Of one thing I am certain—that most of the excuses we are accustomed to make with such good conscience *now*, we should be wholly ashamed of *then*. Oh, we do not think what it means, that our brothers and sisters, so easily accessible, perfectly able to understand the message of God's redeeming love, and so greatly needing it, are still being left in millions to perish.

And among those multitudes were men, women, and children who would believe, to their eternal blessedness, if he, Jim Fraser, went to them.

And then the Man of Galilee, the Master with the pierced hands and feet, passed by. Jesus, looking upon him, said, "Come, follow Me." That was all.

But who, having seen that look, does not know that it was enough!

It does not take long to change the course of a life if the power at work comes from above, if it is high enough and goes deep enough. Fraser's call to missionary service was not primarily a call to China but a simple, unreserved consecration to the Lord Jesus Christ. Concerning the missionary task, Fraser now said, "Christ wants it done. He commands it. He gave Himself for me and kept nothing back. He asks for my fellowship in service, my life, my all."

> Here, Lord, I give myself away,
> 'Tis all that I can do.

And in that act, the young man handed over not the latchkey but the master key of his whole being. Once for all he accepted the leadership—nay more, the *ownership*—of the Prince of Glory who had died upon the cross for him. That cross was taken as his highest privilege, his most binding pledge. The meaning of the words "crucified with Christ" became so real that in his measure he, too, could say, "I live; yet not I, but Christ liveth in me."

Such experiences are sacred between God and the soul. All that even Jim's mother knew was that his life was changed in a most thorough way. He himself looked upon it as his conversion. If he had been a Christian before, it had been a divided allegiance. Now the claims of Christ took the first place—to know

Him, to please Him, to be wholly His. And this brought such joy as he had never known before. Always strong and purposeful, Jim was now under a new control and walked in a fellowship that satisfied his heart.

His mother wrote:

> He did not talk much about it, but I have seen his face shining when he came down from prayer. He said it was that little book which made plain to him his path of duty.
>
> Of course the sacrifice was a real one. He must have known that he had good prospects. He could not but feel the surging power of youth. But he turned from it all without reserve to consecrate his life to God. Conversion should be a real giving of ourselves, should it not? When that takes place, the Holy Spirit fills the heart and there is joy.

The new ownership soon showed itself in genuine concern for the welfare of others. A tramp came to the door one day and Jim not only supplied his needs but before long had him on his knees in the garden, seeking the Friend that sticketh closer than a brother.

Some visitors his own age had come up to London, and he was showing them the sights. They wanted to see a play at the Hippodrome. He left them there, declining to go in, but arranging to meet them again when the entertainment was over. Meanwhile he asked to be guided to anyone whom he could help. His kindly way opened people's hearts and he soon found that one man to whom he was speaking was actually penniless and hungry. After providing him with a meal, Jim found a quiet place where they could be alone and in the simplest way led him to Christ. He heard from the man afterward. He was going on happily as a Christian.

After taking his degree in London with honors (B.Sc. in engineering) Fraser turned from the work he loved to give himself to definite preparation for the life before him. Though only twenty-one, he lost no time in applying to the China Inland Mission. When accepted as a candidate, he went at once to north London for special training at the mission's headquarters. The year he lived there with other young men gave him opportunity for more than Bible study. Daily attending the noon prayer meeting at Newington Green, he came to know the leaders of the mission and many of the workers home on furlough. Appraising the practical outworking of the mission's faith and principles, all he saw and heard confirmed his desire to work on interdenominational lines, without stated salary, avoiding debt in any form, and making no appeals for money. He was encouraged by the experience of the mission, and it was his personal conviction that Hudson Taylor's creed expressed a great and unchangeable reality: "There is a living God. He has spoken in His Word. He means just what He says, and will do all that He has promised."

What need is there for anxiety, when it stands written concerning our temporal needs, "Seek ye first the
kingdom of God and his righteousness, and all these
things shall be added unto you"? Had it not been so
for more than forty years in the experience of the mission which, though numbering over a thousand members, had never been in debt and had never made an
overdraft at the bank?

It was no little strength and comfort to young
Fraser, both then and afterward, that his parents
gave their hearty consent to the step he was taking.
One precious compensation for the parting that drew
near was the new and enriched relationship between
mother and son. Neither of them had anticipated
this. It was one of the glad surprises that come all
along the way to those who follow the Lord fully. In
this connection his mother recalled:

> After Jim's conversion we had such deep spiritual
> fellowship. He was a great help to me. We shared
> spiritual experiences. Indeed, he became my teach-
> er. My progress had been gradual through the years;
> he seemed a mature Christian right away. He had so
> completely given himself to the Lord that he could
> be filled with the Spirit. He emptied himself—and
> so the Lord could fill him.

To part with such a son was a heartache that only
such mothers can understand. Yet it was a willing
sacrifice. "Jim, dear, I am the happiest woman in
London today," she wrote in a little note he carried

with him. And it was a joy that continued, just because the loneliness was for Jesus' sake. "I could not pour out the ointment on His blessed feet, as Mary did," Mrs. Fraser once said, "but I gave Him my boy."

And is He not infinitely worthy?

Chapter 3

MOUNTAIN MEN

A TALL FIGURE in the gown of a Chinese scholar stood in the doorway of a shop in Tengyueh, a city not far from the Burma border. Situated on a main trade route, Tengyueh was a place of call for caravans from far and near. With kindly eyes James Fraser scanned the passersby with interest, for many kinds of people mingled in the streets and inns of the south suburb, and tribespeople in their distinctive dress added color to the marketplace. These stalwart children of the mountains, whether Shan, Kachin, Lisu, or Tibetan, brought mysterious suggestions of unknown habitations behind the ranges.

It was to them especially the young missionary's thoughts tended as he entered upon his life's work. Around him in the city, people were within hearing of the message, but up in those far-reaching mountains thousands upon thousands were waiting still for the words of life that were so long in coming.

But see, a group of strangers were sauntering down the busy street. Could they not be brought in to hear the Good Tidings? Fraser was soon beside them, but only when they responded to his invitation did he

28

realize they were not Chinese coolies, as he had supposed, but Lisu tribesmen from the mountains. This was quite a thrill, for he was especially eager to make contacts like this.

But a greater surprise was in store, for hardly were the four men inside the preaching hall than with one consent they went down on their knees, knocking their foreheads on the ground before him, in token of greatest respect if not worship.

Bewildered for the moment, Fraser managed to raise them up to their feet, then tried to turn their thoughts to the One who alone is worthy of worship. But they understood little Chinese, and he could speak no Lisu. He gathered that they had come from a place six days' journey to the north, where tribesfolk were numerous. No, they could not read, but they took the tracts in simple Chinese that Fraser offered, hiding them carefully in their sash-belts as being of great value.

What they were really thinking would be hard to say. Probably they wondered why this foreign teacher was so kind to them. What was it he so much wanted them to understand? Attracted to him, nevertheless with some shyness and fear, they made for the street before long, but not without first urging their new friend to come and visit them in the mountains.

Encouraged that they should have any wish to see him again, Fraser fell back on his one Lisu sentence. *"Cho ma cho?"* (Is that so?)

"*Cho ma!*" they responded emphatically. (It is, it is!)

At the time of this encounter, Fraser had been in China a little more than a year. Six months at the mission's language school had given him a good start in Chinese, and his designation to the far western province of Yunnan had come as an answer to much prayer. Even before reaching China he had been drawn to work among the tribespeople of that region, so desperately in need of the Gospel. In the whole province, up to that time, only five mission stations had been opened, as much as two weeks' journey apart. Tengyueh, the most westerly, had been occupied by Mr. W. Embery only twelve months previously.

Recently married, after seven years in China, Embery had brought his bride to anything but attractive surroundings. Part of a Chinese house was all he had been able to secure—a separate building in a Chinese courtyard, but damp and rat-infested. Happily Mrs. Embery, a trained nurse, was as true a missionary as her husband, and five years in China had given her a good hold on the language. The women of the city came in throngs to see her, the foreign lady being a great curiosity. Her influence over them was the most encouraging aspect of the work in those early days.

Not a corner being available in the mission house, a room had been found for Fraser in a better-class inn in the same part of the south suburb. Here he enjoyed a measure of comfort and quiet for study. His room, twelve by fourteen feet, was private to himself and situated at the head of a little stairway, over an empty space he could use to store things. A few articles of furniture were made by the local carpenter. Well content with his accommodation, Fraser set to work with his Chinese teacher, going over to the Emberys for meals.

After hours of study it was a relief to plunge into the tides of life about him, especially on market days, when many tribespeople mingled with the cheerful crowds. The quarter-of-a-mile walk to and from the Emberys' quarters afforded opportunities for friendly contacts and brought Fraser into touch with his first Lisu acquaintance. This young mountaineer even ventured to go with him to the mission house and was so interested that he promised to return next time he came to the city. But many market days passed, bringing only disappointment, until Fraser ran into the Lisu unexpectedly on the busy street and learned the reason for his nonappearance. The young man had really intended to come back, but on leaving the mission house had been accosted by a Chinese of some importance who demanded to see the book he carried. This had to be handed over, for the Chinese were the ruling race. The Lisu was angrily rebuked for having anything to do with foreigners and was told that he must on no account read so bad a book! This had effectually scared him away, giving Fraser his first experience of the opposition to be expected from the overlords, whether Chinese or tribal.

Meanwhile, from the east of the province, tidings were coming of a work of grace among the despised tribespeople which no opposition could restrain. Through the conversion of a poor Meo leper, thousands of his own and other tribes were turning to Christ from the grossest immorality and demon worship. Mr. A. G. Nicholls had followed up the work with so much devotion and vigor that it was spreading over a wide territory. The Lisu part of this movement had been committed to Mr. G. E. Metcalf. Fraser had been appointed to Yunnan in order to prepare himself to join them as soon as his knowledge of Chinese should be sufficiently advanced to permit his taking up the study of another language.

Since God was pleased to work in saving power among the tribes in the east of the province, why not also among those in the west? But no one was seeking the Lisu in the Tengyueh district, and Fraser knew that for him to start out as a solitary pioneer was a very different thing from joining others in a successful campaign. But the Spirit of God was working, as he recalled long afterward:

I was very much led out in prayer for these people, right from the beginning. Something seemed to draw me to them, and the desire in my heart grew

until it became a burden that God would give us
hundreds of converts among the Lisu of our western
district.

Little was said about these thoughts and these
prayers. Fraser's nature took things deeply, and
while this fresh spiritual adventure had a strong appeal, it was almost too sacred to speak of, except between the Lord and himself.

So the daily routine of study was faithfully kept
up. It was monotonous of course—the noisy inn, the
busy streets, a glimpse of homelife at the mission
house, Chinese clothes and Chinese food in purely
Chinese surroundings, and back to his books again.
But Fraser was intent on the language. It fascinated
while it almost appalled him. It seemed like two
peaks of one great mountain, as he wrote from the
inn:

> This mountain is called The Chinese Language.
> It is very steep at first, but gradually seems easier as
> you go up. Then, just when you feel you are getting
> on, another peak comes into view, rising up higher
> than the first, but all part of the same mountain. This
> also has to be climbed. It is called Chinese Thought
> and Mode of Expression. You had been told about it
> before you began to scramble up the first mountain,
> but you did not see it then. And the first glimpse
> shows how far it is above you.

And all the while the young missionary was eager
for communication with those about him. He went

with Mr. Embery to the street chapel and nearby villages, but suffered the experience so common to new missionaries—practically dumb and deaf to all but their immediate circle. Members of the missionary's household became adept at interpreting his halting phrases, and Fraser was encouraged to find that before long he could make out the drift of their remarks. But this was not true of those Chinese who had had little contact with foreigners. Shut in thus to himself, his spiritual life was apt to flag.

Realizing the danger, Fraser set himself to watch and pray. Through his letters we find him rising early for quiet over his Bible. He longed to know it better, and was reading every book in order, not once but seven times, before passing on to the next. Prayer was more and more vitally necessary. As soon as the inn woke up each morning there were endless distractions, but out of doors he found quiet places. These became his prayer haunts, whether the hidden gully, the half-deserted temple, or the open hillside. Gradually he found prayer resorts for all kinds of weather. The grand old hymns of the church became increasingly valued—hymns that have expressed the soul's aspirations and longings through the ages. Breadth of outlook was necessary for him—room for God, whether in nature or in spiritual realities. And most of all he was depending upon the personal presence of the One who said, "Lo, I am with you alway."

"What is Christian experience?" wrote an eminent

theologian who humbly walked with God. "What is
Christian experience but the secret history of the
affection of the soul for an ever-present Saviour?"

Secret, steadfast, ever-growing "affection of the
soul"—let that have the first place in practical reality,
and there will be no drifting or decline.

One of the things Fraser most dreaded in those
early days was loss of time and strength on side
issues. He saw that the good may indeed be the
enemy of the best. This applied in his case to correspondence that was not really necessary, to much
photography, to social life with other foreigners, and
even to language study. He wrote:

> I am trying my best to get hold of a good col-
> loquial knowledge of Chinese, but it will take time,
> it will take a long time. I am only at the beginning
> yet. This is more important, I feel, than to become a
> learned Chinese scholar, for after all the chief thing
> is to talk in a way easy to be understood. Mr. Mc-
> Carthy told us of a missionary years ago who was ex-
> traordinarily accomplished as a Chinese scholar, but
> whose own servants could not understand him in
> everyday matters! There certainly is something fas-
> cinating about the study of literary Chinese—which
> must go hand in hand with work on the colloquial—
> but I imagine it would be easy to be too much taken
> up with it.

Notebook at hand, Fraser was always taking down
words and phrases used in conversation around him,

whether he understood them or not. "Jot it down," was his motto, "and then ferret out the meaning, with dictionary and teacher, and learn it by heart."

I have taken down several hundred phrases in this way. The temptation is to be content to use words which *nearly* express your meaning, but not *quite*. For instance, you learn the Chinese expression for "This is badly done," and might make it do duty for clothes not washed clean, a room not properly tidied up, a picture not hung straight, a piece of meat half cooked, a matter unsatisfactorily settled, etc., etc. But the Chinese make distinctions in these things, as we do in English.

To this keen, painstaking student a weak vocabulary would be a confession of neglected duty. His conscientious language study resulted in his becoming one of the best Chinese speakers in the mission.

Young as he was, only twenty-two at this time, he had learned the importance of faithfulness in seemingly trivial duties and of making the most of present opportunities. An earnest letter on this subject, written amid the discomforts of a very poor wayside inn on one of his first journeys, reveals some of the elements of his own self-discipline.

It has come home to me very forcibly of late that it matters little what the work is in which we are engaged, so long as God has put it into our hands; the faithful doing of it is of no greater importance in one case than in another. The temptation I have often

had to contend with is persistent under many forms:
"If only I were in such and such a position," for example, "wouldn't I be able to do a great work! Yes,
I'm only studying engineering at present, but when
I am in training for missionary work things will be
different and more helpful." Or "I am just in preparation at present, taking Bible courses and so on, but
when I get out to China my work will begin." "Yes,
I have left home now, but I am only on a voyage, you
know; when I am really in China I shall have rich
opportunities of service." Or, "Well, here in the language school all my time must be given to study—
how can I do missionary work here? But when I am
settled in my station and able to speak freely, opportunities will be unlimited!"

It is all *if* and *when.* I believe the devil is fond of
those conjunctions. The plain truth is that the Scriptures never teach us to wait for opportunities for
service but do exhort us to serve in the things that
lie at hand. The Lord bids us to work, watch, and
pray; but Satan suggests, "Wait until a good opportunity for working, watching, and praying presents
itself"—and needless to say, this opportunity is always in the future. Since the things that lie in our
immediate path have been ordered of God, who shall
say that one kind of work is more important and
sacred than another?

I believe that it is no more necessary to be faithful (one says it reverently) in preaching the Gospel
than in washing dishes in the kitchen. It is not for

us, in any case, to choose our work. And if God has chosen it for us, hadn't we better go straight ahead and do it without waiting for anything greater, better, or nobler?

More than this, he found need of checking in himself the tendency to chafe against trials which lay in the path of duty.

We often say, "I am looking forward to this, that, or the other." Have we any right to be so dissatisfied with our present condition, which God has ordained for us, that we should hanker after something in the future? I can hardly see that we have. There is one great exception: we are to look forward with earnest expectation to the coming of the Lord. But we have to be patient even in this, for to look for our Saviour's appearing is a very different thing from hankering after enjoyments of which we hope to partake some time ahead. . . . Why should I, in the hot, close, rainy season at Tengyueh, long for the dry months when things are more pleasant all around? Didn't God intend me to put up with the discomforts of heat and mildew? Why should I look forward to the time when I shall be able to speak Chinese more freely? Didn't God intend me to serve an apprenticeship in learning the language? Why should I look forward to a little more time for myself, for reading, etc.? Though it is the most natural thing in the world to have such thoughts, I feel that they are not at all Scriptural. There is much more

of the flesh about them than of the Spirit and they
seem to be inconsistent with the peace of God which,
it is promised, shall guard our hearts through Christ
Jesus. . . . The Apostle Paul said that he had learned,
in whatsoever state he was, therein to be content,
implying that he had reached that attitude through
discipline. And I suppose it must be so with all of
us. The natural tendency is to be always straining
after something in the future.

The resolution with which Fraser lived in the present was rewarded when the great day came for his
first attempt at preaching in the street chapel. After
little more than nine months in China this was quite
an ordeal. He prepared carefully, but when he faced
his audience the written pages were largely discarded. Thoughts and feelings somehow found words
that went home to his hearers. He was well understood, Mr. Embery assured him, and from that time
he took part regularly in the meetings. That this
work was taken seriously is apparent from the study
he gave to it:

In preparing my address I first went through the
Acts of the Apostles and some other passages, comparing them with a view to finding out the actual
Gospel we are bidden to preach. . . . The result was
very instructive to me. I had never imagined the
Gospel was so simple. Why, Peter and Paul both
preached the Gospel in words that would not take
one minute to say! And I found that there are just

Gospel

four things which seem to be essential in preaching the Gospel:

1. The crucifixion of Jesus Christ. No theological explanation needed.
2. The resurrection of Jesus Christ: most important of all. The Gospel was never preached without this being brought in.
3. Exhortation to hearers to repent of their sins.
4. Promise to all who believe on Jesus Christ that they will receive remission of sins.

Beyond these four points others are mentioned occasionally, but they are not many. . . . In teaching Christians, it is quite another matter. To them we are to declare the whole counsel of God as far as they can receive it. But the Gospel, as preached to the unsaved, is as simple as it can be. I should not care to take the responsibility of preaching "another Gospel."

Armed with all these important truths, Fraser was not slow in attempting his first evangelistic journeys. We find him twice on the road, alone except for a friendly coolie, before he had been in China fifteen months. These journeys led to rich results, though there was little promise of it at the time.

Crossing the Tengyueh plain by the main road to the east, Fraser's first journey soon brought him to range after range of mountains on his way to Paoshan. On this journey he was crossing two of the great rivers which, rising in Tibet, wind their long course to the sea through western Yunnan and Bur-

ma. The lesser of these, the Shweili, beautiful in its
deep wooded valley, was reached the first day out
from Tengyueh. Beyond this, majestic indeed, was
the Salween Divide, surmounted after a long, toil-
some ascent in steadily falling rain. The inns at night
were very rough, but the poor food and poorer accommodation were made up for by the beauty of the
mountains rising on every side. From the pass, eight
thousand feet above sea level, was a long descent to
the Salween itself, whose mighty gorges were to
cradle some of the richest results of Fraser's lifework.
As he crossed its turbid waters, he could not anticipate the triumphs of the Gospel he was to witness
among the wild, neglected tribes far up its winding
course. Staying at night among the Black Lisu of the
divide, he noticed that they seemed even poorer and
more unkempt than his Tengyueh people. But they
were kind and brought him eggs to supplement their
coarse food which he ate beside their smoky fires.

The fourth day of the journey dawned bright and
clear, with glorious views of range upon range of
mountains on the east of the divide as they descended
to the Paoshan plain.

To Fraser's surprise, Paoshan was a far larger city
than Tengyueh, with scores of villages spread over
the plain adding to its dense population. Entering by
the south gate, they had to walk quite a long way up
the broad main street before coming to the place
where there were inns. They found one large enough

to accommodate some sixty people, more like a barn than a guesthouse, in which Fraser engaged an upstairs room. He swept the worst of the dust off everything and settled down for a few days.

The advantage of an upstairs room was that Fraser could receive callers with some hope of holding an uninterrupted conversation. Not a few came to see him, including Mr. Wang, a silversmith, who invited Fraser to dinner in his shop on the main street and gave him the use of his premises for preaching and bookselling.

On Sunday he left the crowded city and walked a short distance into the country, preaching and distributing tracts. He found this an encouraging new experience in evangelism:

Coming to a couple of men watching cattle near a small stream, I sat down with them and asked, "Have you heard the Jesus doctrine?"

"No," they answered. "Tell us about it."

I told them the Gospel story as clearly as I could. They listened well and asked questions. A few passersby stopped and sat down, so I had to begin over again. More and more joined us until I had told the same thing four or five times over and about a dozen people were listening. When the sun came out we moved over to a shady spot under a tree and I went on.

Whether they understood all I was telling them I cannot say, but they listened and were friendly. In getting up once I ripped my Chinese gown, and one of them ran home for a needle and thread and repaired it for me. I preached there for about an hour and a half, then two of them led me to other places where I could find people to talk with.

As I entered the city again in the afternoon a man in a teashop saw me distributing tracts and called me to come in. He gave me a cup of tea and asked to see my tracts. A crowd soon gathered and I preached to them as I had been doing all morning. The man who had called me in seemed fairly well educated, for he read the tracts quite smoothly. He listened to all I said and evidently understood a good deal. [This may have been Mr. Chao Ho, a tanner, the first convert Fraser had the joy of winning to Christ in Paoshan.]

The next two days were as busy as could be, for the silversmith fixed up a stall in his open shop-front behind which Fraser sat on a high stool, hour after hour, surrounded by a changing crowd. Scripture portions, calendars, pictures, and tracts, including translations of Spurgeon's sermons, were eagerly purchased, and the willingness of the people to hear all he could tell them moved him deeply. So did the view of the city as he had seen it on Sunday, when he climbed a little hill to rest under a pagoda. He had looked out upon it all for the first time with a burdened heart:

It was a lovely day and I had a clear view of the plain in both directions, as well as of the city. No missionary has ever lived there, and the whole plain, with a population of perhaps 100,000, is without the light of the Gospel. I believe God would be glorified by even *one* witness to His name amid the perishing thousands of Paoshan.

It does seem a terrible thing that so few are offering for the mission field. I can't help feeling that there is something wrong somewhere. Surely God must be wanting His people to go forward. Does not the Master's last command still hold good?

As I think of this little corner of the world here in Yunnan, there seems a strange disparity between its huge districts, large towns, unreached tribespeople, waiting for the workers who do not come, and the big missionary meetings at home, the collecting and the subscribing, the missionary pamphlets, etc., etc. And the need is the same, and in some places even greater, in other parts of the world. Hundreds of millions of people have never yet had the Gospel definitely brought before them—and a mere handful of missionaries are sent out from the homelands to evangelize them!

How glad he was to be where he was, with life before him, lonely and discouraging though the work must have been at times.

On the second journey, long days were spent in preaching and bookselling in another district, south of Paoshan and equally unreached. There, unknown to Fraser, a little boy of six got hold of a copy of Mark's Gospel in its bright, attractive cover. Carried over the mountains to his home in Hsiangta, it was to

fall as seed into good ground—but not until years
later was the young missionary to find and rejoice in
the harvest.

One unknown Gospel portion
planted seed

Chapter 4

MISSIONARY IN CHARGE

IT MUST HAVE SEEMED almost too good to be true when, some months after those journeys, Mr. Embery came in from the market at Tengyueh with a young Lisu who was willing, it appeared, to take the foreign teachers to his home in the mountains. He lived in Pleasant Valley, some twenty miles north of the city, and would return in two weeks to act as guide and carry their load. Fraser's desire to come into close touch with the mountain people was always keen, but there had been several disappointments even when the way seemed to be opening. So now he wrote:

> The matter is in the Lord's hands. If He wants me to go He will send me. It would be very unwise to attempt to rush things or force a door which He has closed. But we shall see. God has done great things for us at the other side of the province, and we cannot but hope that He will work effectively for the tribespeople here as well.

But again, when the time came, the Lisu guide did not appear. They could only assume that he too had been frightened away by the threats of unfriendly

46

Chinese. Fraser did not say much about it, but even the servants realized his disappointment. So it was with satisfaction that the cook appeared, a month later, bringing another tribesman who was ready, then and there, to escort the missionary to his village.

It was a May morning, almost a year after his arrival in Tengyueh, when Fraser, with great anticipation, took the road leading past the waterfall and into the western hills. Crossing the first ridge with its famous temples, he soon found himself on an upland plain backed by higher mountains.

Lisu country at last!

How eagerly he looked for Pleasant Valley, the hamlet to which they were going! Though they were not expected, his guide assured him they would be welcome. And so it proved when, toward evening, they reached the hollow, climbed the fence surrounding a dozen or more houses, and came to the open doorway of the home where they were to stay.

Some excitement seemed to be going on. As Fraser found out later, the family was in the midst of betrothal festivities. His arrival only added to the cheerful bustle, and soon straw mats on which to spread his bedding were dragged up to the fire in the middle of the hard earth floor. A meal of rice, eggs, and cabbage followed, eaten from bowls with chopsticks, and far into the night there were talking and laughter around the smoky fire. Lamps were not lighted:

there were none; but pine chips lay ready for use outside the circle of firelight.

His first days in a Lisu household were memorable to the young missionary. He knew already that they were lovable people, but he was hardly prepared for the natural way in which they made him one of themselves. It was taken for granted that he would join them at the big feast the day after his arrival. This happened to be Sunday. How he longed to give them something better than their drunken revelry! But to them it was a great occasion. Preparations were prolonged, and Fraser had time to take in all the details of the situation.

The dress of the women struck him as picturesque and becoming—dark blue tunics of common hemp made into rough cloth, belted at the waist and reaching to the knees, striped with brightly colored bands of the same material and decorated with a profusion of white shells and other ornaments. A hemp scarf covered the head and hung over the shoulders; feet and legs were bare. By no means shy or embarrassed as Chinese girls would have been, these Lisu maidens joined the group that chatted with their foreign guest. The men wore the dress of the poorer Chinese: short blue trousers and short jacket, with put-tees to protect from the mosquitoes and leeches and brambles of their native hills.

One thing that delighted the crowd was the discovery that the stranger who did not know their lan-

puttee – a strip of cloth worn around the leg from the ankle to the knee

guage could make pencil and paper speak it! The
Chinese, who looked down on them, had always said
that Lisu was a jargon that could not be written.
And of course they were right concerning the impos-
sibility of adapting their complex ideographs to the
phonetics of Lisu. But Fraser was busy at intervals,
jotting down in our familiar roman letters such words
as his musical ear could distinguish. Before long he
had a vocabulary of about 400 phrases which he read
to the amazement and delight of his hearers.

Laughter comes readily to the Lisu, who are as
easy to please as children. So the dark, smoke-filled
rooms resounded with merriment while they waited
for the food being prepared elsewhere.

By the time the feast was spread I was mighty
hungry. Evening had fallen and I had had nothing
to eat all day but rice and cabbage for breakfast. So
they gave me some food before they actually started
themselves—rice and *sanchi* meat (a sort of mountain
goat). This was all they had for themselves except
homemade wine, of which they drank copiously.

There were about fifty at the feast and they sat on
boards on the ground in a rough rectangle, the rice
and meat being set on boards in the center.

The meal was not a sober, ceremonious sort of
business, but more like a family party, with plenty
of jollity. I don't know who the betrothed people
were, but they did not figure especially. After the
eating part—I am afraid the drinking went on all
night—there was a bit of a break, but I could not

make out any order in the proceedings. It was like a game of croquet in *Alice in Wonderland!* I went inside and sat with about a dozen others around the big log fire. One man was recounting an old Lisu legend in a singsong voice, and the rest would break in with a sort of chorus. I could not understand any of it.

Before long I was told that they were ready for the dance, which would be kept up until daylight. What sort of dancing it was to be, I had no idea. My host told me that I could go back to his house whenever I liked, but evidently thought I would want to stay and see it through.

For a while Fraser sat there in the smoke and firelight, watching one of the strangest sights he had ever seen. The dancing proved to be a simple sort of folk dance. Men and women, young and old, held hands in a ring, swaying to and fro to the rhythm of weird reed music, taking two short steps to the right, then to the left, with a peculiar sort of motion. The leader would sing a phrase in solo, to which the others would reply in a sort of moaning chorus, swaying all the while to the constant rhythm. The strangeness and confusion of the scene were Fraser's chief recollection:

I sat in a corner almost unnoticed. Drinking was going on all the time while men and women were gabbling, shouting, and laughing. Some stood up, some were sitting down. They came in and went out incessantly. Everything was smoked and black in the setting of a grimy old room in a Lisu house, the dark shadows of huge grain bins looming here and there, a dog or two now and then running across the earth floor between the legs of the revelers.

Seeing that this was not the time to turn their thoughts to anything better, Fraser went out into the night where the thatched cottages, empty and silent, stood on either side of the mountain stream, and made his way to his host's dwelling.

The scene of the festivities was anything but attractive the following morning. Some of the revelers, still drunk, lay flat on the ground. Others were lounging around eating, drinking, talking, and doing nothing in particular. They were in no mood to listen to what Fraser had to tell them, and he was making up his mind to wait, when a diversion occurred which gave him a better opportunity than he had expected.

A man from Trinket Mountain, six miles away, had come over to invite the foreign teacher to a home where people were eager to learn to read Chinese. Expecting to return in a day or two, Fraser gathered up his belongings and was soon on the way with his new guide.

Through narrow wooded valleys the track climbed westward until it emerged on a mountain slope seven thousand feet high. The surroundings were magnificent—higher peaks enclosing a little plain to the south from which lofty passes led, still westward, toward the Burma border.

In that remote and beautiful solitude Fraser found a surprising welcome, for the place to which he was taken, the best in a hamlet of only seven houses, proved to be the home of the very man whose failure to turn up at Tengyueh some weeks previously had caused so much disappointment. When the young man returned home that night and saw his foreign friend standing there, he hardly knew how to face his unexpected guest. Meanwhile Fraser had made friends with his father and two brothers who brought out the Gospel of Mark which the missionary had given the young man. Fraser learned it had indeed been the threats of Chinese neighbors which had robbed him of his promised guide.

So it was with the Koh family of Trinket Mountain village that Fraser's dream of living in a Lisu household as one of themselves came true for the first time. And how thrilled he was over it all! Sleeping on the ground at night near the log fire and living on the rough fare his hosts pressed upon him, he was initiated into Lisu ways and hospitality. For a whole week he stayed on, finding a real response to his message. When the sons were out at work he had good opportunities with the rest of the large family: sisters, daughters-in-law, the old people, and children. This surely was a happy beginning to the work he so longed to see develop. True, his Chinese was very

limited and he could speak no Lisu, but the simple
hymn and prayer they were learning helped to fix essential truths in their minds by constant repetition,
and they never seemed to tire of singing.

On a dusty shelf at the back of the room lay the
objects used in demon worship: a bowl or two in
which food could be offered, an incense burner, a dry
bunch of leaves regarded with awe as a special haunt
of the spirits, and the Chinese characters for heaven
and earth written on red paper, which in Lisu homes
take the place of idols. Furtive glances turned in that
direction from time to time as the talk and singing
proceeded, until at last, without any urging from
Fraser, a wonderful thing happened.

After some consultation in Lisu, which Fraser
could not understand, the father and his four sons
made it clear that they wanted to pray to the one
true God and to believe in Jesus. So the demon shelf
and other things were torn down and thrown into the
fire, Fraser watching for the first time the burning
that meant so much to him. He was keenly conscious
of how little of the precious truths of the Gospel he
had been able to impart to his Lisu friends. But a
beginning had been made, and he was greatly encouraged.

"It was all very happy and nebulous," he wrote.
Yes, both happy and nebulous.

*   *   *

In the weeks that followed Fraser's return to the

city, he was surprised that none of the family came
to visit him in Tengyueh as he had hoped they
would. He was eager to return their hospitality. But
the rainy season had set in, when mountain tracks
were almost impassable, and he was too pressed with
language study and new responsibilities to do more
than remember them frequently in prayer.

For, not long after his return from Trinket Mountain, Fraser found himself unavoidably promoted to
missionary-in-charge at Tengyueh. He had by this
time abandoned his cheerless quarters in the inn and
moved into the enlarged mission premises. The old
rat-infested house the Emberys first occupied had
been replaced by a chapel and guest hall, behind
which a semiforeign dwelling had been added on
part of the landlord's property. Clean and quiet,
with upstairs rooms opening onto a wide veranda, it
was a change indeed. Facing west, two windows in
Fraser's room looked out toward the mountains beyond which lay the Lisu uplands where he would
fain have been. But on their nearer slopes the Temple of the Winds, famous for its idolatrous pilgrim-
ages, told of needs close at hand. Fraser was still
giving five hours a day to language study:

> I do not weary of it for a moment. Every new
> character I learn and every colloquial expression is
> that much more ground eagerly won. I do not think
> I have ever been so absorbed in any line of study—
> not even parabolas!

Fraser. had been taking increasing part also in guest-hall work, street preaching, and regular services in the chapel, greatly appreciating the fellowship with his senior colleagues, Mr. and Mrs. Embery. And then, when he had been in China only two and one half years, circumstances arose which left him alone, the only missionary in that extensive Tengyueh field.

> Had it been possible for someone else to go to Tali, the Emberys would not have been asked to do so. But the shortage of workers is so great that no other arrangement could be made. As far as matters here are concerned, it means that I am single-handed and must remain so indefinitely. I expect Mr. McCarthy will be coming to stay with me for a time, perhaps next month. I have, however, the responsibility of looking after our comparatively large premises, as well as the much weightier responsibility of preaching the Gospel alone now. So it is no small load which has fallen on my shoulders.

Reading between the lines, one can see how much he felt the parting from his friends.

> I went out with the Emberys seven or eight miles to see them off—and scored a triumph by the way, for I carried the baby some distance up the long hill and she fell asleep on my shoulder.

Fraser's spirit was brave and steady, but from intimate letters to his mother it is evident that he was

often at the end of his own resources. Housekeeping
details were new to him, as was the management of
the servants, whose spiritual welfare he was earnestly
seeking. It was one thing to take prayers every morning with the cook, a married man of forty, and the
houseboy, a nice enough youth when not provoked.
But to still the tempest when quarrels arose was quite
another thing. It was a pleasure to receive callers in
the guest hall when they came at convenient hours.
But to be always ready to set aside other claims and
make the most of such visits at awkward times was
not easy.

I feel, somehow, that my best opportunity for Chinese study is gone forever. Interruptions, visits, and
attention to details absorb a good deal of my time.
Not that I deplore this; on the contrary, I am glad
to be launched into full work as a missionary. It is
what we come to China for. But I am finding out
that it is a mistake to plan to get through a certain
amount of work in a certain time. It ends in disappointment, besides not being the right way to go
about it, in my judgment. It makes one impatient
with interruption and delay. Just as you have nearly
finished a planned piece of work, somebody comes
to sit with you and have a chat. You might think it
hardly possible to be impatient when such an opportunity is presented for telling someone about Christ
—but it is. The visitor has to be welcomed, and I
think it is well to cultivate an attitude of mind which

personal work as important
as teaching
dependence upon prayer

Missionary in Charge 57

will enable me to welcome him *from the heart* and
at any time.

I have also been feeling lately that this personal
work is quite as important as preaching. To have a
man come to see you at your own house and be able
to talk with him plainly and directly about his soul's
welfare—what could be better? Of course preaching
to crowds must be done, but it is not the only way of
bringing men to Christ. It may seem a strange thing
for a missionary to say, but I feel that if God has
given me any spiritual gift it is not that of preaching. I know my own clumsiness very well—but the
Lord has always helped me in the one-by-one work,
and He is giving it to me here.

Interesting details follow in many letters about inquirers with whom Fraser was in touch, each one
being commended by name to his mother's special
remembrance in prayer. More and more he was coming to count upon her as a fellow worker in this way.
He was realizing in a new way his entire dependence
for spiritual results on a power not his own. He
sought to share the burden with his former class
leader at home:

It seems a big responsibility to be the only preacher of the Gospel within a radius of about 150 miles.
I feel my weakness very much, yet the Lord seems
to delight in making His power perfect in weakness.
May I ask you then to remember me specially in
prayer, asking God to use me to the salvation of
many precious souls.

Prayer calls down blessing
Happiness not on outward
circumstances

I am feeling more and more that it is, after all, just
the prayers of God's people that call down blessing
upon the work, whether they are directly engaged in
it or not. Paul may plant and Apollos water, but it is
God who gives the increase; and this increase can
be brought down from Heaven by believing prayer,
whether offered in China or in the homeland. We
are, as it were, God's agents—used by Him to do His
work, not ours. We do our part, and then can only
look to Him, with others, for His blessing.

If this is so, Christians at home can do as much
for foreign missions as those actually on the field. I
believe it will be known only on the last day how
much has been accomplished in missionary work by
the prayers of earnest believers at home. And this,
surely, is the heart of the problem. Such work does
not consist in curio tables, showing of slides, and the
giving of reports. Good as these may be, they are
only the fringe and not the root of the matter. Solid,
lasting missionary work is done *on our knees*. What
I covet more than anything else is earnest, believing
prayer, and I write to ask you to continue to put up
much prayer for me and the work here in Tengyueh.

It was well, perhaps, that Fraser could not know
that it would be three full years before the return of
Mr. and Mrs. Embery, and that for more than half
of that time he would be alone in the work. His enthusiasm was so keen, however, that he could truly
write once and again, "I have never been so happy";
but it was happiness that was not dependent on outward circumstances. Some for whom he held the

brightest hopes backslid in spite of all his care. Indifference and opposition often made his outdoor
work difficult. His inability to do anything for the
women who had been interested when Mrs. Embery
was there often burdened him. Propriety would not
allow them to attend meetings in the absence of any
woman missionary to receive them.

On one occasion this convention was set aside.
Wedding festivities had brought many guests to a
nearby house and some of the women begged their
hostess to take them to the chapel to hear the preaching. Since old Mrs. Li and the landlord's wife could
give some attention to the visiting women, a dozen
of them came with their babies and children. Fraser
took John 3:16 as his text, using a direct and simple
approach.

> I told them the Gospel story and one or two inci-
> dents in our Lord's life, including His blessing little
> children. They listened attentively and Mrs. Li said
> later that they understood me very well. I believe
> the Lord was with me, giving me the promised
> "mouth and wisdom"—I should never have much of
> either otherwise.
>
> It is not easy to stick to one's subject (in a point-
> by-point sense) on an occasion like this. I am re-
> minded of that irregular preacher at home who was
> accused of wandering from his subject. He replied
> that, whether he stuck to his *subject* or not, he
> thanked God that he stuck to his *object*, which was

to bring men to Christ. I hope I shall never lose sight of *that*.

Among the encouragements of those lonely days, Fraser frequently referred to the interest of Mrs. Li, just mentioned, who had been Mrs. Embery's helper and friend. Well on in years, she was able to come to the Sunday services and to do the little laundry work that Fraser needed. With a confirmed opium smoker for a husband, her life had been full of hardship and suffering. Of her eleven children only one had lived to grow up, and he too did nothing but smoke opium. The poor mother had no hope in this life or the next until she found the Saviour. To watch her grow in grace was an increasing joy. Within a year of the Emberys' leaving, Fraser was able to write of her as a bright Christian:

> Listen to what she says: "I used to be anxious and worried about all these things, besides being very angry and resentful at the way I am treated, but it is not so *now*. If I begin to feel that way I just turn to God, and He brings back peace to my heart."
>
> When I exhort her to pray, she replies, "Yes, I *do* pray. I am continually thinking about God and praying to Him as I do my work."
>
> Just a poor, ignorant woman earning her living by washing clothes, despised and jeered at by many and cruelly ill-treated by her husband, yet daily trusting all to her Saviour and praising God! She nearly cries sometimes when she tells me her troubles, but as a rule she is bright and cheerful.

That he was able to do so little for his Lisu friends was one of Fraser's trials at this time. Of the Koh family, about whom he had been so much encouraged, he heard almost nothing. One of the sons came in for eye medicine, and brought sad news of poverty and sickness in the village. Crops had failed and the dreaded evil spirits were cruel. He told of the death of a neighbor, a sick man whom Fraser had visited several times. It was a comfort to know that he had remembered some of the Good News.

He talked about it sometimes, they tell me. Whether he had any real grasp of the truth, however small, or whether it was only a confused impression, I cannot tell. He seemed quite intelligent in spite of his suffering condition, when I talked with him. If the Emberys had not had to leave, I might have gone up again and seen him before he died. I was wanting to go.

When young Koh and others from the mountains came to visit him, Fraser would often enlist the help of his cook, who had come out brightly as a Christian. The joy of hearing him put the Gospel so clearly to his visitors strengthened the young missionary in the conviction that the best way of reaching outsiders was through the Christians themselves, whether tribal or Chinese. His patient Bible teaching was bearing fruit.

Beyond the mission compound Fraser was now a familiar figure in all parts of the city and suburbs.

The preaching shop had been given up in favor of quieter meetings in the new chapel, but open-air work was continued regularly with the help of colored pictures and Gospel posters.

Notable changes were coming in public thought and feeling. The "new learning" in the schools and Western methods in military training were much in evidence. The revolutionary doctrines of Sun Yat-sen were permeating the student class especially, and events were moving steadily toward the fall of the old regime. Questions were posed for the young missionary, and subjects unheard of before were raised for discussion. One gentleman called upon him to talk about Socrates and Aristotle, while others came to improve their English. The active part Fraser had taken in subduing a dangerous fire in the city put him in a new and favorable light, and his increasing fluency in Chinese secured better attention.

Street preaching was still no easy matter, and it required courage to keep on day after day with no one to stand by him. Sometimes, in the evening, the cook would help.

Fraser wrote of such occasions:

> It is dark and, just as at home, people are at loose ends and wander about with nothing much to do. I get an old stool and stand on it while the cook holds the lantern.
>
> If there is one native institution I do like, it is the tea shop. You sit down sociably with others around

a square table and drink your fill of clear, unsweet-
ened tea, leisurely cracking sunflower or melon seeds.
Tea shop people nearly always seem friendly and
let you preach or give tracts to their customers. One
time, after nearly having a fight with one man before I could induce him not to pay for my tea, I
found that the proprietor would not let me pay
either!

That these opportunities were made the most of is
evident from many a letter. More than ever the
young missionary was longing to see men turn to the
living God. He wrote in October, 1911:

I should like you continually to pray not only for
the salvation of outsiders but for blessing on those
who have definitely accepted Christ. I want to be
downright in earnest *myself*, and to be filled with
the Spirit.

"I want an even, strong desire,
 I want a calmly fervent zeal,
To save poor souls out of the fire,
 To snatch them from the verge of Hell,
And turn them to a pardoning God
And quench the brands in Jesus' blood."

It was his last letter before the revolution.

Chapter 5

BANISHED TO BURMA

THE OUTBREAK OF HOSTILITIES was announced to
Fraser, the only missionary then in southwest Yunnan, by the following letter:

October 27, 1911

To Mr. Fu [Fraser's Chinese surname]
Pastor of the Mission Church at Tengyueh

We respectfully inform you that we have chosen
this day as propitious for the overthrow of the present dynasty and the setting up of an independent
China.

We are at the same time apprising all your fellow
nationals in Tengyueh of the fact and beseech you
not to be alarmed. We will without fail protect you
and your property. There is no need for you to send
telegrams to any place, either in China or abroad.
Please rest assured that you will be quite safe where
you are. You will not be molested by anybody.

[Signed] THE UPHOLDERS OF CHINA AS AN
INDEPENDENT NATION

Fraser's only fellow countrymen in Tengyueh were
the British consul and the head of the customs service, with their staffs, so with them he proceeded to
take counsel. The situation proved to be far more serious than the "Upholders of an Independent China"
had indicated. The whole country was seething with
rebellion against the Manchu Dynasty, and foreigners
as well as Chinese were soon to be overwhelmed by
the brief but successful revolution which made the
cities of the Yangtze run with blood.

At the consulate Fraser was urged to go down to
Burma for a time, and it was well that he did so, for
Tengyueh became a storm center. Finally the government troops got out of hand, sided with the rebels,
and murdered their own leader. Meanwhile there
had been a reign of terror.

Before leaving, Fraser had done all he could to
provide for his Chinese teacher and the cook, who
remained in charge of the mission premises. It would
be easy for them, in case of need, to escape the attention which would have been focused on himself; so,
supplying them with all the money he could spare,
he relieved them of the anxiety and the danger of his
presence.

And now began an experience which, though trying at the time, resulted in an enrichment of faith
that made it well worth while.

Arriving in Bhamo after a difficult journey of eight
days, Fraser went straight to the CIM mission house,

Trusting God for money ✓

counting on a welcome from Mr. and Mrs. Selkirk, whose hospitality he had enjoyed some time previously. But the place was silent and deserted. Through ill health the Selkirks had needed to go home for furlough, leaving only the caretaker in charge. In Fraser's position this was serious, but he found written instructions that any visitor who needed them should make use of the few food supplies left in the cupboards. These, with the little money he had in hand, might tide him over until his next remittance, already overdue, could arrive from Shanghai. But would it arrive at all? With communications disorganized all over the country, was it likely that a letter containing a money order would reach so remote a place as Tengyueh and be forwarded from there, safely over the turbulent borderland, to Bhamo? It was not likely, but Fraser committed the whole matter to God in quiet and expectant faith. No one else knew his position, and it was against his principles to borrow money or go into debt of any kind.

Setting to work at once among the Chinese living in Bhamo, Fraser found plenty to occupy his time. He was still wearing Chinese dress and the distinctive queue, which was not generally discarded until the final success of the revolution. In the Chinese quarter of the city there were the usual tea shops in which Fraser could mingle freely with other customers:

Yesterday I went into one of them and purposely refrained from any attempt at preaching. I just sat down on a bench with others, paid a copper coin for a cup of tea, and started cracking pine seeds like the rest. If only you could see a tea shop of this class you would think an East End lodging house clean and comfortable in comparison. Presently I offered tracts to all in the place and went on drinking tea and cracking pine seeds. Soon the customers were chatting with me, asking lots of questions. As many of these were about the Gospel, I had my opportunity quite informally.

Exiled and lonely as he was, Fraser greatly appreciated a kindness shown him by a Burmese Christian woman the first Sunday he was in Bhamo. Coming out of church with her husband, she greeted the young stranger of whom she had heard, and put a little packet into his hand. It proved to be five silver rupees. These she asked Fraser to accept, as she had heard of the troubles in China and feared he might be in need.

He wrote, telling his mother of the gift:

My first thought was to decline it. But she was so evidently sincere about it that I ended up by taking one rupee, not to hurt her feelings, and returning the rest. . . . This was only a little incident, but it cheered me very much to receive such kindness from a Burmese Christian.

It was not long before his supplies began to give out. Visits to the post office were disappointing. No mail had come from China, nor was any expected

under those conditions. Registered letters especially
would be unlikely to reach their destination. Never
before had he been faced with such a test of faith,
completely cut off from any who knew of his predica-
ment; nevertheless he was kept from anxiety. Psalm
37:3-5 took on new meaning:

> Trust in the Lord and do good; so shalt thou dwell
> in the land, and verily thou shalt be fed. Delight
> thyself also in the Lord; and he shall give thee the
> desires of thine heart. Commit thy way unto the
> Lord; trust also in him; and he shall bring it to pass.

Matters reached a crisis when payment became
due to a coolie who had worked for Fraser in necessary ways for a full month. Now, he realized, the
Lord's deliverance must be near—for had He not
said, "Owe no man any thing, but to love one another"? He was subsisting on little save the food left
in the house, but his coolie must be paid at the right
time if debt were not to be incurred.

Needless to say, Fraser was much in prayer about
the matter. On the day in question he felt led to go to
the post office again, for the burden was heavy upon
his heart. To his relief the official seemed pleased to
see him. Yes, mail had just come in from Tengyueh,
bringing one letter, one only. There it was, a registered letter addressed to himself, which had come
safely all the way from Shanghai to the far west of
China, and over the border to Bhamo—just in time!

It was a further remarkable answer to prayer that Fraser was able to get one of the enclosed drafts cashed that very day, through a Chinese friend in the customs service. So the coolie was paid and the young missionary, alone in a strange land, went back to his empty house to pour out his heart in thanksgiving.

He wrote to his mother:

> I have told you all this because it is the most direct interposition of God in providence which I have yet experienced, and it has done not a little to strengthen my faith. No one here knew my circumstances. You can understand how very careful I am in speaking of such things. The Lord, I believe, permitted the trial just to show me how He could deliver me out of it.

Shortly after this another letter arrived which, to Fraser's surprise, also contained money. It was from his mother in England, now a widow and in comparatively straitened circumstances. With a grateful, loving reply, Fraser at once returned the draft, saying:

> It is literally true that you need it, Mother, more than I do, for the Lord has not forgotten me but has abundantly supplied all my need—even though affairs out here are so upset at present.

Another experience which made this time in Burma memorable was a visit to an American Baptist Mission station among the Shan and Kachin tribespeople. Fraser traveled with a Chinese-speaking letter carrier as guide through deep jungle which gave place on the second day to the mountain ranges dividing Burma from his own province in China.

Here the views were really magnificent. In open spaces one could look out over great sweeps of the Irrawaddy valley, a vast area of jungle. The winding road was full of interest. For the first time I saw monkeys, good big ones, jumping about among the trees. A green parrot found here could be taught to speak . . . and there are gorgeous pheasants, exquisitely beautiful birds.

Fraser arrived to find the missionary absent on a preaching tour, but the local Christians were all the more ready to show him hospitality.

It was this welcome from the Namhkam church leaders and fellowship with them in spiritual things that made the visit one long pleasure. On the hills above the plain were Christian villages, both Shan and Kachin, which Fraser was able to visit, and in the station itself he found evangelists, schoolteachers, and others eager for quiet talks over the Word. Although he was young and hampered by having to speak through interpretation, they felt and responded to the sincerity of his prayer life, faith, and devotion, while he was greatly cheered by their love and prayers.

Mr. Sam Bwa, principal of the high school, and his wife cared for him more like a son than a foreign guest, and the whole experience was a happy foretaste of the fellowship yet to be among his own tribespeople.

Before leaving I spoke a few words to my host's family and household and had prayer with them. When I had finished, Mrs. Sam Bwa and others were nearly crying. I really did feel sorry to leave them.

You can hardly understand until you come into touch with them what simple, warmhearted people the Shan Christians are. Sam Bwa told me that I could be of help to them even if I could *say* nothing. The mere fact of your coming to see them, showing yourself genuinely pleased to sit with them in their houses, attend their services, share their food, and generally make yourself one of them is enough to endear you to them. If I sing or pray in Chinese, they cannot understand a word, but that makes no difference. They like me to do it. They do not judge you by the learning or eloquence of your discourse, but by what they see of you personally. If they see that you love them and like to be with them, they love you in return.

And it was love that showed itself in practical ways, as Fraser long remembered. For when his load was being packed for the return journey, a shower of good things was added, including twenty eggs, a roast chicken, two pieces of cooked beef, a packet of tea and one of sugar, as well as cookies and a drinking mug—most of which Mrs. Sam Bwa herself provided. She had not failed to notice how little the missionary had with him. Knowing well the hardships of the road, she planned to improve matters for his return journey. So a little pillow found its way in with the other gifts, also an embroidered shoulder bag to hold things for handy use. More than this, the letter carrier was charged with the load of enameled plates, knife, fork, and spoons, to supplement Fraser's chopsticks. And it was all done with a simplicity that called no attention to the givers.

Fraser wrote to his mother:

I think I can see her now, carefully packing all these things into the courier's baskets, just as you would have done it yourself. I almost felt like sinking through the ground at such kindness!

After this, they trooped out to see me off, including the boys and girls from the school. At the brow of the hill leading down to the Namhkam plain we shook hands once more. Some of the old folk from the Shan village said to me several times, "We will pray for you." When I tried to tell Mrs. Sam Bwa how grateful I felt for all her kindness, she made no reply but turned her head away to hide her tears. Dear old soul! Of all the people who have been good to me out here, none has been so like my own mother. Mr. Sam Bwa then struck up, "God be with you till we meet again." We all joined in the first verse, and they stood and watched us for a while as we set out for the plain.

On the way back to Bhamo, Fraser stayed a night

among Kachin Christians and spoke through interpretation in their little chapel.

Afterward, we all sat around the log fire. Talk
about your Grand Hotel! I had rather sleep in a
simple, homey place like that, among such people,
than in the grandest of hotels at home. But our Kachin friends did not stay on indefinitely. They said
I had walked a long way and must be wanting rest,
which was thoughtful. So they went away and left
us in silence, with the fire dying down. I turned in
and soon fell asleep beside the dull red logs.

Chapter 6

LISULAND AGAIN

IT WAS NOT LONG AFTER THIS that the way opened for
Fraser's return to Tengyueh. He was glad to be in
China again after four months' absence. He had been
not a little concerned about the Christians, few in
number, whom he had had to leave amid the upheav-
al of the revolution. Outward order had been restored after the inauguration of the republic, but
Tengyueh with its mixed population and commercial
activity was a ferment of new ideas. Still the only
missionary in the city and district, Fraser was thankful that his prescribed course of language study was
almost completed, for there were many calls to other
work. A Bible class for young men was claiming his
attention. And several, though not themselves Christian, were seeking his help in starting a YMCA.

Fraser wrote in July, 1912:

I have at last finished my six sections of Chinese
language study, the consummation of three and one-
half years of work, and a load is off my mind. What
a perfect ocean of knowledge Chinese opens to you
when you have been at it a few years. If I were to be

mainly engaged in work among Chinese-speaking people, rather than the tribes, I would never give up the study of this language, spoken and written, as long as I live.

Another world of living interest was opened up to him in the coming of a fellow worker. It was good that Fraser's mind was hospitable to new ideas, for Carl G. Gowman, a graduate of the Moody Bible Institute, came fresh from a responsible position in the head office of Ford Motor Company, Detroit. Fitting in admirably with his senior missionary (as to age, senior by only five days), Gowman was such a live wire that Fraser's outlook was considerably brightened.

Those summer days (Gowman arrived in August) saw them down at the river for a good swim before six o'clock prayers with the household. Gowman had seen Niagara but was nevertheless impressed with Tengyueh Falls. He was still more enthusiastic about the beauty of the mountains and soon became interested in the tribespeople who frequented the markets.

More than this, Gowman was engaged to be married, and a new interest attended the arrival of mail from other parts of the province. His prospective bride was at Tali, with Mr. and Mrs. W. J. Hanna, only eight days' journey away. The rule of the mission, that new workers must be in China two years before marriage, worked some hardship on this couple, for their engagement had already been prolonged on account of college and Bible studies. But the bride-to-be was as truly a missionary as Gowman himself, and saw in the waiting time a needed opportunity for becoming adjusted to the climate, language, and ways of the people.

Fraser wrote of his new colleague:

> He was a bright, delightful companion, just the one I was needing. He caught on to my interest in the Lisu and joined me in prayer for fresh openings among them. I was more burdened about these people than anything else in the world, though the duties of the station, the claims of Chinese study, and the upheaval of the revolution had kept me from further contact with them.

A visit from a young tribesman, almost a stranger, seemed to come as an answer to these prayers. He was from the Lisu village of Six Family Hollow and brought with him a surprising gift—a live silver pheasant, caught in the mountains. Unsuspectingly Fraser accepted the beautiful bird, whose brilliant plumage he was sure would attract visitors to the mission compound, only to find that it laid him open to an equally surprising request. The youngest son of the Tsai family was about to be married and Ah-do had come to ask for a loan of ten dollars for wedding expenses. Ten dollars! And the missionaries had made it a rule not to lend money.

About to decline, Fraser was arrested by the thought that he had not asked for specific guidance.

Excusing himself, he went straight to his study and spread the matter before the Lord. The result was perhaps the greatest surprise of all. Ah-do returned with the ten dollars to the rejoicing family and Fraser received an urgent invitation to the wedding!

Always hospitable, the mountain people excelled themselves on this occasion in doing honor to their foreign guest. Slender bamboos were cut and plaited into matting for the walls of a lean-to attached to the Tsai home. The roof was well thatched with grass and the indispensable recess dug in the middle of the earth floor for the fire. Plenty of logs were gathered, as well as pine chips to take the place of lamps at night. There was no furniture beyond a few wooden stools, and straw mats were provided on which to spread the bedding and whatever else their visitors might bring.

At the appointed time the bridegroom arrived with his best man to escort Fraser, Gowman, and the baby organ (specially requested) to the scene of the festivities. It was a charming spot amid high hills and surrounding mountains, not far from the villages Fraser had visited two years previously. Gowman was disappointed to find the hamlet so small—only three families, two of whom were Chinese—but that one Lisu household later became the pivot upon which a great movement was to turn.

Arriving several days before the wedding, Fraser was able to make friends with his hosts, including the daughters-in-law and children, before the general hubbub began. He soon discovered that the old mother was very much the head of affairs. Left a widow with land as well as children, she had secured help by marrying a good farmhand. The family had prospered through her unusual strength of character, until now they were taking a wife for the sixth son, the youngest. Busy as they were, Mother Tsai found time to sit by the fire now and again, listening to the talk of her foreign guests. She was interested in the prayers and singing in a way that revealed a real hunger of heart. Needless to say, Fraser made the most of this opportunity, both before and after the bride arrived. Of the wedding itself he wrote in some detail.

The bridegroom looked something like a Highlander in full dress, but neither he nor the bride figured largely in the proceedings except for their waiting on other people.

The only real ceremony was when the girl actually entered the house. Brought from her own village in the company of a score of her relatives, she and the other girls had to stand off a little distance from the bridegroom's home for some time. Then her mother-in-law and another old dame went down and escorted her, one on each side, up the steps and into the house. There was a bridesmaid with her too. Just as they were going in at the door, four musket shots were fired, this being *the* moment of the whole occasion.

After this there followed a lot of drinking in an orderly kind of way, which seemed to be drinking to the health of the new couple. Two people at a time came forward, each took a big bowl of native wine, made a low bow which was returned by the officiating people, bowed around to a few others, then drank the wine, returning the empty bowls with another low bow.

The bridegroom and his best man stood nearby all the while, bowing every time the others did. This went on for a long time, but it was not as monotonous as you might think, for other guests were walking about, chatting and laughing.

Along with the bowls of wine a lump of cold pork was presented to each guest. We took our pieces like the rest (though not the wine, by previous arrangement) and were supposed to eat it there and then. Imagine taking a chunk of greasy fat pork to eat in your hands! Gowman ate his, but they brought me a plantain leaf in which I wrapped mine.

About a hundred guests had assembled, and two nights and days were given up to the revelry that followed. With the usual ring-dancing Fraser was already familiar, but on this occasion the bride's relatives led off with new steps, including a sort of clog dance in which she took part.

Three girls, one boy, and a man stood in line, the girls with their arms around each other. Farther away stood another boy, the bride's brother, with a kind of guitar, and beyond him another man. They all faced the same way and, without turning, kept step with the music. I should like you to have seen it!

The dress of the girls beggars description. Indeed, all the women wear gorgeous dresses on such occasions. Some of them look very handsome. They go in for loud checkerwork with large squares of all sorts of colors. They wear big headdresses, too, and a great variety of beads, bangles, necklaces, bracelets, and what not.

The confusion increased, with more and more of the crowd becoming intoxicated. Fraser asked a middle-aged woman whether she thought so much drinking was a good thing. "Oh, yes," she said, surprised at the question. "It's so much more fun when you get tipsy!"

It was not possible to do much under those circumstances except to talk to changing groups around the portable organ. Fraser had brought with him some sheets on which hymns were written in large Chinese characters. As both he and Gowman had good voices they were able to sing and explain the old, old story in a simple but effective way for hour after hour.

It was no less a relief to the Tsai family than to their foreign visitors when the last wedding guests departed and they could gather in the living room at night, the great occasion over and only cheerfulness within. Snow had fallen on the distant Salween

Range and the tang of winter in the air made them
seek the fireside—dogs, chickens, children and all—
despite clouds of smoke until the logs burned red.
Then, with the organ in the circle around the glowing embers, they sang hymns and choruses and talked
over the Good News far into the night. Mother Tsai
had many questions to ask and Fraser was glad that
his Christian cook was there to help them make clear
to her mind the great truths she was drinking in for
the first time.

The missionaries stayed on for a whole week after
the wedding, visiting other villages in the daytime,
including one where Fraser found an empty house
which fitted in with his desire to visit the district
frequently without being dependent on the Lisu for
hospitality. Up there at Valley of Ease village the
headman of some twenty Lisu families showed real
interest in the Gospel.

One longer expedition was made to Trinket Mountain, to visit again the Koh household, of whom
Fraser had not heard for some time. It was disappointing to find only the old father at home. He was
glad to see his missionary friend again and wanted
the party to stay overnight, but he was suffering so
from his eyes that it seemed kinder not to prolong
their visit.

Fraser had already been absent from Tengyueh
for ten days, and Gowman was not too well after his
first experience of roughing it in the mountains. So a

last night was spent at Six Family Hollow, to confirm the Tsai family in their newfound faith and show them how to bring all that was in their hearts to God in prayer. They did not know how to pray in Lisu, they said, but Fraser explained that the Lord understood Chinese quite as well as their more familiar language. So they parted, cheered to think that they would often meet in the city.

How clean and spacious the mission house looked, for all its simplicity, when Fraser and Gowman returned to Tengyueh! They had come back to a new and heart-moving experience. Years of faithful seed-sowing had borne fruit at last, and the time had come to inaugurate a Christian church in that southwest corner of China. Tengyueh was to witness its first baptisms. Though the number to confess Christ was not large, they were precious trophies of His grace.

The spirit of it all was very beautiful, as it comes out in letters written at the time. One can almost see the quiet stretch of river near the falls, where the water was a convenient depth and an arched bridge provided a place, just above, where onlookers could stand and hear every word of the service. The four to be received included Mrs. Li, though she was not baptized until Mrs. Embery returned. The three men went down with Fraser into the river, a cultured teacher taking his place gladly beside the Christian cook and Tang, the water-carrier, a humble soul who loved the Word of God.

Fraser wrote of that Sunday, April 20, 1913:

> It all went off without a hitch. After the baptism I stood where I was in the middle of the river and preached to the onlookers on the bridge. It struck me afresh what a beautiful and simple ceremony baptism is—God's open air and God's flowing water seemed far more fitting and natural than any indoor baptistry.

At the Communion service which followed, Mrs. Li joined the others in remembering the dying, never-dying love of Christ at His table. The care of this little flock and of his beloved Lisu filled Fraser's heart in those days, but not to the exclusion of the crowds in the city streets. Open-air work was no easier than it had been, but he was more than ever conscious of the deep inward compulsion, "Woe is me if I preach not the Gospel." He writes of this so naturally that one can see the true missionary impulse, born of the Spirit.

> When utterly disinclined to go and stand up on a stool in the street and preach to an indifferent crowd, I have felt an inward urging which I could not resist. It is like so much pent-up Gospel inside you, which must have an outlet.
>
> Last Friday I was prevented from going out as usual to preach and tried to satisfy myself with the resolve to do so the next day instead. But on Saturday the very same thing happened, and, by the time for the evening prayer meeting, I had let another day

go by without having given this witness. I felt just as ill at ease as could possibly be. All my peace of mind was gone and I was impatient for the meeting to be over.

When it ended, I could stand the conflict no longer, but *had* to go out on the main street, late though it was, get up on a bench, and give my message to the people. This done, I was happy again! It is a good thing to have God call you to work with Him, isn't it? But better still, I think, to have Him make you do it!

Chapter 7

A CHALLENGE

THESE LISU! I cannot get them out of my mind," Fraser had written shortly before the baptisms at Tengyueh. If he could only have doubled or multiplied himself it would have been more possible to meet their need and make the most of other opportunities. As it was, he was thankful that the rains did not hinder his Lisu from Six Family Hollow coming down from the mountains. Often on market days they would turn up at the mission house, sure of a welcome, bringing news their missionary was eager to hear.

I enjoyed the evening they stayed here immensely. Their simple ingenuousness attracts me tremendously. They take you into their confidence as if you were an old friend of the family. The boy who was married while we were up there learned a new hymn this time, one of Pastor Hsi's, which they like very much. This brings their repertoire to the grand total of three. For devotions they religiously rattle through these hymns each evening, after which all the family stands up to pray. They tell me they can pray in Lisu now. On Sunday evenings—dear, simple souls—they try to hold a special kind of service. There is nothing much extra they can do except to sing a little more than usual and try to make out what the hymns are all about. Crude, isn't it? But I wonder if the Lord is not just as pleased with their simple, groping attempts to worship Him as He is with our elaborate services at home. "Out of the mouths of babes and sucklings thou hast perfected praise."

Old Six, as the bridegroom is called, stopped in the middle of learning this hymn to remark, "I say, Teacher, it has been fine since we became Christians! The evil spirits don't get after us now the way they used to."

They say that most of the Lisu up at the Valley of Ease are waiting to see if anything happens to our Tsai family. If not, many of them will want to become Christians, too.

Fraser was finding this fear of demons to be a great reality among the mountain people. Evidences of it were always cropping up. An older brother of the bridegroom had told him of one occasion after the wedding when they were all much alarmed. They were talking about the hymns they had been singing when the old father, looking across at the incense bowl still on the shelf, said timidly, "Well, what of *that*, if Jesus is our Saviour?"

"Take it down," responded the others. "We have no more use for it."

The suggestion was forthwith acted upon. But that very night the old man began to suffer from a strange, unaccountable pain in the back, which soon spread to his whole body. All the family were up, trying such remedies as they could think of for his relief. At last, toward midnight, someone said, "Why not pray to God about it?"

They did this, and soon there was peace in the little home in the mountains. The pain passed away and by daylight the old father was himself again. "Such an experience," Fraser wrote, "goes a long way toward strengthening their faith. But the fear still lingers that the demons will get them if they are not propitiated as they always have been."

Perplexed himself by such happenings, the young missionary could only assure his Lisu friends that the Lord Jesus, who died for our sins, is indeed exalted over all principalities and powers and every name that is named. As we put our trust in Him, we need have no fear, even of demons.

But there was much that he also had to learn. One need that pressed upon him was that of closer contact with the mountain people through a knowledge of their language, so he sought to be out among them more often and set himself to master Lisu as he had Chinese. Happily his heart was in the matter. He loved the rough and tumble of pioneer journeys, the hardships of gypsy life and, above all, the response of open hearts to his message. Of one place he visited with Ah-do at this time we find him writing:

> I had a good time at Little River. It is only a tiny village of six families, the simplest people you ever saw. We were there for four days. I had the luxury of a room to myself—oh no, not private! Privacy is a thing almost unheard of out here. The walls of these houses, made only of bamboo laths, let in more than the free, fresh air! People come around you all the time, asking endless questions, wanting to see your things and spitting their red betel-nut juice all over the floor. You think it is blood the first time you see it. I think I like almost everything about them except this habit, but I do not let even this bother me. They are just like children and you love them as such.

Picture the scene—the friendly group around the fire, the merry jests and laughter, the women with their babies, girls in gay colors, the often dirty and ragged old people, the flow of chatter on all sorts of things, and the lively curiosity about their foreign guest.

Of course they could not understand his being twenty-six and still unmarried. They wanted above everything else to see an Englishwoman. One of them had once beheld such a being and readily re- told her experience. She had gone down with her vegetables to Tengyueh as usual and was there at the marketplace when two foreign men passed by with a lady between them. How strange and wonderful her dress was, and what a small waist she had!

Shining eyes around the fire were turned on Fraser with understanding. They seemed to sense his loneliness and soon in all seriousness offered to help him find a wife. Even though his country was so far away, the situation could be remedied, they assured him. They would act as go-betweens (quite indispensable to the Lisu as to the Chinese) and would arrange for him to wed "the nicest Lisu girl to be found anywhere"!

The genuine kindliness of their concern touched the young missionary and opened the way for more important things. Putting up a hymn sheet, he soon had them singing, and Ah-do held their attention with an earnest Lisu presentation of the Gospel. How it rejoiced Fraser to hear this man witnessing and praying in his own language! Day after day it went on, until the boys and girls knew the hymns by heart and the older people talked about building a chapel in their village, for they all wanted to become Christians. But there on the hillside above the hamlet stood the demon shrine that held them all in awe.

It was a poor, wretched little structure with a thatched roof and open on all four sides. There were no idols in it, for the Lisu are not idolaters. In fact, there was nothing in it but a rough shelf on which they put offerings of food when the spirits came and harassed them. Ah-do and I inquired whether or not they would be willing to give this up. After consultation they said they would give up anything which was inconsistent with their becoming Christians, so we could do what we liked with the shelf.

So Ah-do and I went up, and it did me good to see him wrench from its place the demon shrine and fling it away, crying, "What have we Christians to do with fear of demons?"

A leader was then appointed to conduct morning and evening worship, Ah-do being careful to explain that the true God, to whom we pray in the name of Jesus, is able to understand Lisu just as well as Chinese.

"What shall we do, Teacher," called an old lady in parting, "when we go out on the mountains to watch our cattle and stay out on the hills all night? Can we pray out there, too?"

Fraser took time to explain to her that the God we worship is the One who made all their mountains and valleys, the great Father with whom we can be at home anywhere.

It was hard to leave Little River and, as he returned over the hills with Ah-do, the missionary's heart went out in prayer for these new friends. He was bound for Trinket Mountain, the district in which he had first tasted Lisu hospitality, to look up the Koh family of whom he had not heard for some time. The surroundings were beautiful as ever, but after climbing the steep ascent to the village, Fraser felt a change had come over the familiar homestead. The old father was cordial in his welcome but the household was reduced in numbers and the place looked shabbier.

When Third Son came in that night he was quite hospitable and the big room filled up, as before, for evening devotions. But something was lacking in the atmosphere and before long it became evident that there was opposition.

Third Son seemed to have something against what Fraser was saying. A controversy arose inside the house, but, as it was in Lisu, the missionary could not understand much of it. He gathered that something had happened to the family since he had been among them.

Next day all was made plain when, on their way to Pleasant Valley, Ah-do was more than ready to unburden his heart. And a strange, sad story it was.

Ah-do said that when I was up there the first time, the Koh family believed all I told them and decided to pray to God and to the Lord Jesus. At that time there were four sons living at home. Not long afterward the youngest son fell ill. In accordance with my teaching they prayed for his recovery— some of them, at least—but the sickness only became worse. Apparently they continued praying, though whether or not they also resorted to any of their old ways I do not know. The boy continued to sink until in desperation they felt something else must be done.

So they stopped praying and sent for a diviner, who told them that the illness was due to spirit seizure. He told them what to offer to appease the spirit—a pig, a chicken, or whatever it was. They offered it and from that time the boy began to recover.

But that was only the beginning of the story, and Fraser was little prepared for the sequel. Things went smoothly for a while but the storm broke before long.

Third Son is a timid, mild kind of youth. You would never expect anything unusual or violent from him. But one evening he and his younger brother went mad. He got a big winnowing basket and beat it as if it were a gong, raving all the time and scaring everybody. Then these two scrambled up onto the *chia-tang* [a long, narrow table occupying the place of honor under the ancestral tablet shelf], raving like madmen. To his aged father Third Son shouted, "I am going to die! Come over here and kowtow to me!"

The younger brother began to stuff his mouth with rice—only done when people are at the point of death, to give them something to eat in the next world. Frightened out of his senses, the old man went up and made humble obeisance before his sons, who continued their raving.

Then Third Son seized a clay incense bowl and shouted in demoniacal fury, "I'll show you earth-people whether I have power or not!" Whereupon

Paroxysm - sudden outburst of emotion or action

he flung the bowl violently to the ground, but it did not break.

After this paroxysm had passed, the younger brother fell ill again and in spite of all they could do he gradually sank and died.

Later, Second Brother went out into the fields one day and in anger for something or other scolded his wife, upon which she went back to the house and committed suicide by taking opium. Second Brother ran away and has not been heard of since.

All these calamities descended upon them, they believe, because they forsook the worship of the spirits and turned to God and Jesus. "Do you not remember," Ah-do questioned, "what a big family this used to be? There seems nothing left of them now." And when I realize their point of view on such things my wonder is not that they have come in so seldom to see us but that they have come at all.

It was a crucial hour in Fraser's experience, face to face as never before with the stark reality of demon power. He wrote:

Thinking over the whole matter, it seems to me that it is explained by Luke 11:24-26: "When the unclean spirit is gone out of a man, he walketh through dry places, seeking rest; and finding none, he saith, I will return unto my house whence I came out. And when he cometh, he findeth it swept and garnished. Then goeth he, and taketh to him seven other spirits more wicked than himself; and they enter in, and dwell there: and the last state of that man is worse than the first." After a lifetime of service to the evil one, these people tried, in a blundering way, to break free and worship God through Jesus Christ. Then came the trial of their faith. Satan raged. He got his knife into those who dared to question his authority in his Lisu kingdom. He was successful. Old habits and superstitions got the better of feeble faith. His rebels gave him back their allegiance. First, the bait, to show how kind a master he is: the boy got better. Then, with sevenfold fury, the whip! And he gave them a time of it.

In spite of these convictions growing upon him, Fraser was still slow to believe that demon possession can be as real today as when our Lord was on earth.

You may call it imagination if you like, but from the Scriptures we know that Satan is the god of this world, now as much as ever he was. "The whole world lieth in the evil one." The thing that made it so painful to me was that the Lisu, in their ignorance, put all the trouble down to their attempt to become Christians instead of attributing it to the very opposite, their reversion to demon worship. And the finishing touch, to me, was the way it shook the faith of Ah-do to hear about it all.

And still deeper testing was to follow. It was early summer and the mountain people were so busy that Fraser had returned to Tengyueh and was giving himself to the city work. For some weeks no tribespeople had come in, not even from Six Family Hollow. And then Ah-do appeared with heavy tidings.

I cannot tell you all of it, but the evil one has been terribly busy. The result is that all the Tsai family, with the exception of Ah-do, have gone back to their old life and superstitions.

While I was away, their oldest grandson was taken ill with fever. A little quinine would probably have put him right, but instead of coming to us for medicine, as I had urged them to do in case of need, they listened to their neighbors and called in a wizard. It was the spirit, he told them, outraged by their pulling down that bunch of leaves, who had come to take his revenge. Thereupon they put up a big bunch of leaves again and promised to sacrifice a pig to the spirits. This they will do as soon as they can afford it. Down came the hymn sheets and Christian posters, and the Christian books were put away. They have stopped singing and praying.

Of the whole family, only Ah-do holds fast. The others have made a complete renunciation, at least for the present.

They do not object to his still being a Christian if he likes, but they are going to bide their time—perhaps later on, if it seems safe. This, of course, is Satan's argument. I cannot tell you how I feel about it—you must use your imagination. But I am going to pray for them as much as ever. Will you?

This was the reaction shared with his mother whose understanding he could trust: "I am going to pray for them as much as ever. Will you?"

Chapter 8

A DECISION

How often the work of God seems to hang by a single thread! But that thread will hold if it is of God's weaving and held in His hand. More was at stake than even Fraser realized at this time. He was thinking in tens; God was thinking in thousands. He was cast down and yet upheld, perplexed but not in despair, sorely tried but not forsaken. He wrote this to his mother:

> I have no further news from Six Family Hollow. We must do our patient best to repair the damage done by the false step they have taken. I very, very much hope that they may be won back soon. Quite apart from the damage to themselves, this sort of thing does a lot of harm to the cause of God among the Lisu. I desperately want to see the foundation of a real work among them before I leave.

For one element of his trial was that he knew his opportunity in that field might be drawing to a close. He was still designated for work among the Meo at the other side of the province and, when the Em-

berys returned from furlough, he might be called to
the relief of the reapers there, who could not over-
take the harvest. His own seed-sowing, meanwhile,
seemed fruitless.

They tell me that the people at Little River, who
were so responsive when I was there, have gone
back too. They say that after I left, a lot of them fell
sick, so they all veered over to demon worship again.
Whether this is wholly true I do not know. If it is
so, may God forgive them, for they know not, or can
hardly know, what they do.

Meanwhile a letter was on its way to the general
director of the mission, telling of Fraser's recent visits
to Six Family Hollow and other places. He was almost sorry, now, that he had written of encouragement, for his tendency was always to understate
rather than to paint too bright a picture. But the
cheering aspect of the work had also been true. The
death of Mr. McCarthy having left the province
without a superintendent, it was necessary for the
young missionary to send his reports direct to Mr.
D. E. Hoste. Was he conscious, in the darkness of
those hours, of the upholding of Mr. Hoste's unfailing remembrance in prayer?

Carl Gowman, with increasing experience, was a
helpful companion in those days. Always bright and
cheery, he was more so in prospect of his approaching marriage. The two years of preparation over, his
bride would soon be on her way to join the bachelor

household. The women among the Christians eagerly anticipated her coming, and there was much to do and plan.

Another element that relieved the situation was the visit of a young Karen from Burma, recently set apart as a missionary to the Lisu and other tribespeople. Though only twenty-three, Ba Thaw was an experienced Christian and a man of education. He had traveled widely, spoke excellent English, and had begun to translate hymns and a simple catechism into the Lisu language. Best of all, he was spiritually minded. Little wonder that his coming seemed providential and was made the most of for the Christians at Tengyueh! More than this, Ah-do and other Lisu inquirers spent some days with him in the city, after which they escorted him to their mountain homes on his return journey. There he was used of God to help the Tsai family and others to see how they had been misled, so that before he returned to Burma things were more hopeful.

And then came a letter from Mr. Hoste that opened the way for further developments. Always ready for advance, he suggested that Fraser should follow up his recent work by making an exploratory journey to ascertain the number and location of the Lisu and other tribespeople throughout his district. Could it be that the hopes and prayers of the young missionary were to be fulfilled? Eagerly he embraced the opportunity, leaving the results with Him who work-eth all things after the counsel of His own will.

Such an exploration was more easily planned than carried out. It meant serious census-taking as far as the Burma border, west and north to begin with, and later through the wild Kachin country to the south. But Fraser was cut out for a pioneer. He loved the freedom and strenuousness of frontier life, the silence and simplicity of the wilds. Yet even his endurance was to be tested by the six weeks of pioneer explora-tion that lay before him, for the region was almost unknown as far as Europeans were concerned.

Starting from the already familiar district of Trin-ket Mountain, he traveled Lisu fashion, walking in sandals and burdened with as few belongings as pos-sible. Ah-do, his only companion, was able to carry their slender outfit, consisting chiefly of literature for distribution and blankets for the night. Fraser wore Chinese dress after his own pattern: jacket and trousers of dark blue cotton, well tucked into socks of the same material for some protection against voracious leeches, mosquitoes, and other pests.

They expected to face cold and hunger at those high altitudes, remote from markets or shops. A spe-cies of weasel afforded a feast at times; and when a Sunday could be spent in some larger village, eggs and even pork might be available.

As it was the rainy season, swollen streams often had to be crossed, some of them on submerged planks

or makeshift bridges that called for the nerve of a
tightrope walker. At other times it was a case of
plowing through mud fully a foot deep, but on mountain trails it was "clean mud, very different from the
slimy stuff around cattle pens and pigsties" in many
a village at night. The deodorizing if blinding smoke
of log fires was welcome on these occasions. Fraser
loved it all, or most of it.

Coming in from one long day on the heights, in
view of ranges mightier than the Alps, he wrote of
"sitting down in that poor little place among utter
strangers, thousands of miles from home and several
days' journey from the nearest white person, warm-
ing my wet clothes and looking out on a silent world
of mist, rain, and mountains, feeling just as happy as
could be—even thrilled with pleasure to think of it!"

But smoky fires, Lisu hovels, and mountain grandeur only formed the setting for the human contacts
of those days. Fraser knew that the Lisu were a lighthearted people, but his first visit to the Tantsah district was strongly impressed on his mind. More than
a hundred Lisu families were congregated in the
villages of that little upland plain, and he was glad
to be detained by their ready welcome.

People came in and out all day. In the evening we
had splendid services. The room was jammed to
overflowing with men and boys, and women with
their breast ornaments, beads, and babies, all squeez-

ing in to listen. Attention was often rapt and response hearty.

"Yes, yes," they would break in, "we all want to
become Christians!"

Then, after the meeting, there would be a veritable Babel—a crowd around the table trying to read
Chinese Gospels, and another group around the fire,
all laughing and talking. To add to the confusion,
someone would bring out his guitar and start up a
dance! And I would fall asleep at last, dead tired,
with more people around the bed examining my
mosquito net.

But it was not all merriment in that Tantsah district, even among the Lisu, for it was there Fraser
came across a cruel manifestation of demon power.
He was more and more impressed with the sinister
meaning of what we lightly dismiss as mere animism,
with its seemingly childish observances. "The things
which they offer to idols, they offer to demons" was
written by inspiration long ago, and the same dread
power is found today even behind the worship of
sticks and stones.

In a village to which Fraser was taken in that district, the local priests had established a custom that
held the people in awe. At times "a great spirit,"
which had to be propitiated to avert disaster, was
said to descend. This was done by a sword-ladder
ceremony. A dozen or more swords were honed razor-
sharp and set in parallel poles to make a ladder of
upturned blades. Several men meanwhile were pre-

pared for the ceremony by mystic performances, including abstinence (for ritual "purity") and bathing for three days. Great excitement was worked up and, when the time came, the performers, stark naked and with unearthly mutterings or shoutings, ascended the ladder on their bare feet.

Fraser commented:

> They all tell me that no man so "prepared" is ever injured, though they frequently suffer from fear beforehand. They say too that no one ritually unprepared would dare to attempt the feat, for the blades would surely cut his feet in pieces. When the sword-walkers reach the top of the ladder, they stand on a small platform from which they glare down at the crowd and in unearthly tones give messages from the spirit.
>
> At times they make a huge fire in which they heat iron chains red hot, then in a paroxysm pick them up and throw them around their shoulders without suffering burns, so they say.
>
> You might suppose that the onlookers regard these rites as a kind of entertainment, but that is not so. They all say they wish they knew how to get rid of the burden, but they *must* do it whether they want to or not.
>
> Last year only one man was found "pure enough" to go through with the rite. I saw his father and the little home up on the mountainside where they allow themselves to be drawn into this diabolical vortex.

"The dark places of the earth are full of the habi-

tations of cruelty." To read of such happenings, as
we do, in the shelter of a Christian land is very different from being under the actual oppression of demon power "where Satan's seat is." What that oppression can be, only those who have known it by
experience and have found its darkness lift and pass
away at the name of Jesus—only those can understand.

The joy of telling of the Great Deliverer to those
who had never heard was quickened, here and there,
by the response of prepared hearts. Talking with a
few men in a poky little shop one day, Fraser was
surprised by the entrance of a bent and suffering
woman who addressed him. She had caught the drift
of his preaching out on the village street, and ventured the question, "If idols are false and cannot help
us, *then what is true?*" Very simply Fraser told her
of the living Saviour and how to put her trust in Him.
It was a joy to hear her say, as she left him, that her
heart was now "ten-tenths at peace."

"Teach me to pray," was the plea of another, a busy
innkeeper, who had listened while serving her guests.
She too seemed to grasp the way of salvation and
went over and over the simple prayer Fraser had
taught her. It was still dark the following morning
when she came to him as he was preparing to leave
the inn. "Tell it to me again," she said earnestly, "for
there will be no one to teach us when you are gone,
and I do want to remember how to pray to Him."

From the far north of his district, where great rivers flow down from the highest plateau in the world, Fraser returned by way of the Kachin country to see what access could be gained to that tribe.

They are the wildest people around here by a long way. Inveterate robbers, their hand is against every man and every man's hand is against them. Unkempt and ignorant, they are despised as savages by everybody else.

Yet the way was open and, with his Lisu companion, Fraser was able to approach their villages, though not without danger. The first Kachin they met were a ferocious-looking group, crudely armed, seated around a wayside fire, decocting opium. With quiet friendliness Fraser and Ah-do came up and joined them. There was some excitement and loud talking but, not knowing the Kachin language, they could only make out from the occasional interspersed Chinese words that they were discussing some question of taxes. And that might mean they would be robbed of all they had! Happily, at this juncture, another Kachin who seemed to have influence appeared and was soon chatting with Fraser in Chinese. He had been in the service of a British official down in Burma, and in friendly asides he enlightened the rest of the group about their visitors. After this Fraser and Ah-do were permitted to proceed without being molested.

decocting — to extract (the flavor or active principle of) by boiling; to concentrate by boiling

"But, Teacher," said Ah-do anxiously, "what if they rob us of all our things farther down the road?"

"Just let them take them," was the quiet reply.

"But what would you do without money?"

"Trust in God to help us. He would not let us starve."

And this confidence was genuine. Far from robbing them, however, the Kachin received them into their strange houses at night and treated them with real if rough hospitality—so much so, in fact, that Fraser's love for the Lisu was shared with their despised neighbors from that time forward, to be as truly returned before long.

Fraser wrote his fourteen-page report of this journey from a full heart. He had explored only the northern half of his district, but he had seen or located some three hundred towns and villages with a total population of more than ten thousand Lisu, not to speak of still more numerous Kachin, on their barren uplands, and the wealthier Shan occupying the hot, low-lying plains. It was a great appeal: "souls for whom no man cared."

The hope that he might be able to remain and devote himself to this district moved the young missionary deeply. Yet his confidence in the judgment and prayerfulness of those at the head of the mission withheld him from pressing his own point of view. He knew that Mr. Hoste had the whole field to consider and, while burdened about the needs around Tengyueh, Fraser sought to leave the issue in higher Hands and to a greater Love.

In the weeks which followed his return to the city, a time of physical reaction set in. Even Fraser's powers of endurance had been severely tested. Ulcerated feet and legs from a dog bite and the bites of leeches and other pests laid him up for weeks, while recurring fever also sapped his strength. Under these conditions he had to fight against depression, and occasional visits from his eager, loving mountain friends were a great help. Market days generally brought some of them in to see him.

This evening Ah-do has come in again. He brings good news of his family. They all seem to want to stand firm now, with the exception of his elder brother. They have thrown away the bunch of leaves put up some months ago and again have devotions every evening. And he tells me the sick people at Little River have both recovered. These are the ones for whom I have been praying constantly, hoping very, very much that they might be spared. . . . We have been talking over our recent trip together and how the Lisu gave us ready hearing everywhere.

And last but not least, Ah-do himself seems to be holding fast and growing in grace, so that he has played the part of an angel in banishing gloom from my spirit. Like Paul refreshed by the coming of Timothy with good news of the Thessalonians, I too

*Authority says move on, — Fraser
perplexed but plans to be obedient
and pray*

A *Decision* 107

can cry, after a season of despondency: "Now we
live, if ye stand fast in the Lord."

It had been hard to wait for Mr. Hoste's reply. It
was harder still to take it as from the Lord. For, to
Fraser's surprise, the facts he had reported had not
modified the director's point of view. Mr. Hoste still
felt that the prior claim was among the Meo at the
east of the province and that Fraser should move as
soon as possible to Sapushan, the field of his first designation. The disappointment was too deep for
words, yet he could later write:

> I was not staggered by unbelief. I did not know
> what to make of it, for God had given me such a bur-
> den for the Lisu and a growing conviction that He
> was leading. So I just went on praying about it—as
> much and as happily as before—though a good deal
> perplexed.

So the autumn days drew on, bringing the long expected wedding. The arrangement was that on the
return of the Emberys, Fraser should travel with the
bride and bridegroom, who were also to take up work
in the east of the province.

The preparations for the great occasion can be better imagined than described—the first European marriage in Tengyueh. It had to be in that city, as there
was no British consul any nearer to Tali, even though
it meant an eight-day journey for the bride with her
Chinese escort.

Before dawn on November 28, 1913, Gowman and

Fraser were hastening across the plain to meet the tired bride-to-be coming down the road from Tali in a sedan chair. But weariness was soon forgotten. She was transferred from the ordinary sedan chair to the festal bridal chair with its red silk hangings and four bearers.

A mile or so from the city Mrs. Li and a number of others were waiting to receive the bride. It must have been a surprise to see her looking so young and happy—no sign of the tears demanded by Chinese etiquette for such an occasion! But she made an excellent impression and won their hearts right away by her bright friendliness. There was time only for a belated breakfast and a quick change into her wedding gown before they had to go to the consulate. The marriage ceremony in Chinese and the feast came next, followed by a short journey to the hills, where arrangements had been made for a perfect honeymoon.

Left alone in the mission house, Fraser awaited the return of his senior missionaries. They had been away three years, memorable years which had seen the inauguration of the Tengyueh church and of a spiritual movement among the Lisu. And now.... But is it ever in vain to wait upon the Lord in quiet trust? The single thread that seemed about to break was still in His hands.

Before the Emberys arrived, the unexpected happened. Fraser did not know how God had been working behind the scenes. The leader of the Meo work, in conference with Mr. Hoste, had generously approved of steps which changed the situation. The result was the sending of a telegram to far-off Tengyueh. Fraser read it twice before he could take in its meaning. Yes, it was from Mr. Hoste, and it said in substance: "If you feel distinctly led to stay on for Lisu work, I would not press your going to Sapushan."

A week later the Emberys were welcomed home and in charge once more. The house was full and busy, for it was the Christmas season. Fraser, in search of quiet, had gone out that winter night to one of his prayer haunts in the city, a deserted temple. He was aware of the serious nature of the decision before him. To go east, to a work already in full swing by the blessing of God, would be the easier path. But love held him to his needy field. "The love of Christ constraineth us." Years later, when his "Lisu children" were numbered by the thousand, he said:

I walked up and down in the moonlight, praying aloud in the silence, until prayer was turned to praise. There was no longer any question. Committing myself to God for whatever might be His purpose, I decided to stay on in my Tengyueh field.

Chapter 9

POWERS OF DARKNESS

CALLED TO THIS NEW FORWARD MOVEMENT, Fraser realized the first thing to do was to strengthen the spiritual base of the work. Not only was his dependence to be upon the divine Leader but in a sense he had to lean on the support of fellow believers, one with him in Christ. He might be the hand reaching out into the darkness, but not a hand cut off and thrown ahead of the body. The vital union must be maintained. He was about to start on an exploratory journey to the Lisu of the upper Salween, a district until then wholly untouched by missionary effort. But before doing so he felt he must give expression to a desire which had long been growing. In January, 1914, he wrote his mother:

> I know you will never fail me in the matter of intercession, but will you think and pray about getting a group of like-minded friends, whether few or many, whether in one place or scattered, to join in the same petitions? If you could form a small prayer circle I would write regularly to the members.

110

This was the first suggestion of a fellowship which was to become in a very real sense the power behind his work. His mother at once responded, prayerfully seeking friends to act with her in this commitment. Even before Fraser could return from the Salween she had written of one and another who felt definitely led to work with him in this way for the Lisu of the Burma border. It was a small group at first, but very earnest, as Fraser soon realized. And the encouragement of their prayers was timely, for the journey to the upper Salween proved afresh the sternness of the task.

Happily, in this undertaking Fraser was not alone. He was joined by his nearest missionary neighbors, the Reverend J. G. Geis of the American Baptist Union and his valued Karen helper, Ba Thaw of Myitkyina. He also had the help of Major Davies' new map of Yunnan and Mr. Forrest's report of an exploration in the Salween district, published by the Royal Geographical Society.

Even so, the ordeal was serious enough. Setting out in winter to avoid the rainy season with its landslides and slippery mud, the party encountered stormy weather at high altitudes. Though nearing fifty, Mr. Geis was a good companion, full of life and fun. But let your imagination fill in the following notes, made in a talk with Fraser over their experiences:

Spent the night on top of a range 10,000 feet high after seeing no human habitation for two days. Darkness came on and snow began to fall. Our Lisu made a sort of booth for us to sleep in. Snow was thick on the ground next morning, obscuring the track. The Lisu were wet through and shivering with the cold . It was *ku teh liao-puh-teh* [extreme suffering]. Ba Thaw stubbed his foot, leaving blood marks all along the way. He had never been in snow before. We had to find our way over the pass. No food until late in the afternoon when, below the snow line, we could make a fire. We saw some armed robbers but they did not attack us. The scenery was magnificent and I enjoyed it—after a fashion.

The following two weeks were spent in Black Lisu country, traveling up the Salween gorge. Little could the travelers anticipate the work of God that was to spring up in that wild, inhospitable region. Nor did they dream that one day Fraser and his fellow workers would be translating the whole New Testament into Lisu on those very mountainsides, amid a Christian community numbering thousands! As it was, they found it difficult to get in touch with the people because of the great difference in dialect. Even the Lisu who had come with them could hardly be understood, and it was only Fraser's excellent Chinese that carried them through.

North of Luchang, where government officials and a post office were found, the road was increasingly perilous, sometimes a mere ledge across the face of a precipice, the river winding like a thin green ribbon far below. Branches of trees were stuck in cracks here and there to steady passersby. Great stones might be dislodged at a touch and crash down on the pathway, carrying all before them. Yet hamlets were to be found wherever a water supply was available, the houses of log-cabin style with floors of broad planks laid right on the earth.

As their object was to gain impressions of the people rather than of the country, the travelers turned back when three days north of Luchang. They had seen enough to convince them that the Lisu of the district were sufficiently numerous and distinct in language and customs to require missionaries of their own, whether tribal or foreign. A people waiting, accessible, and in desperate need of the Gospel—this was a call indeed, though they could see no way at the time to meet it.

On Fraser's return to Tengyueh, he wrote:

What a number of earnest, spiritually minded Christians there are at home, and how correspondingly rich are the prayer forces of the church! How I long for some of this wealth for myself and the Lisu here! Yes, I have had it in measure already, but I should very, very much like a wider circle of intercessors.

Our work among the Lisu is not going to be a bed of roses, spiritually speaking. I know enough about

Satan to realize that he will have all his weapons ready for determined opposition. He would be a missionary simpleton who expected plain sailing in *any* work of God. I will not, by God's grace, let anything deter me from going straight ahead in the path to which He leads, but I shall feel greatly strengthened if I know of a definite company of pray-ers holding me up. I am confident that the Lord is going to do a work, sooner or later, among the Lisu here.

That spring Fraser made his home at Little River, "a village on a very steep mountainside," as he wrote. "A foaming river roars along 2,000 feet below, and the mountains all around run up to 11,000 feet and more." His room in this beautifully situated hamlet was not much to boast of.

It is really an outhouse made of bamboo and thatch, all tumbling to pieces. But it has not come down on top of us yet! It leaks badly, but Ah-do has patched it up by putting plantain leaves over the rotten roofing. The floor is as usual plain earth trodden hard, and there are a lot of old bins, baskets, logs, and other things cumbering the ground. But such as it is I am very comfortable in it and do not hanker after anything better.

The "comfort" consisted chiefly in Fraser's books, for he had gone to the lavish expenditure of about fifty cents for coolie hire to bring some of his treasures, including study books and his Greek New Testament. He also had an enamel plate and mug, a few cans of condensed milk, some cocoa, and "all the bedding I want, instead of the irreducible minimum." His hosts supplied the ordinary food they had themselves, and Ah-do was there to help in various ways. A bath could be obtained by a descent to the swift, turbulent river, involving a climb of 2,000 feet back up again. As far as externals were concerned, he felt his supplies were sufficient for a prolonged stay.

Fraser was tested along another line at this time. In the ardor of his faith he had taken for granted that God's time had come for the blessing he longed to see among the Lisu. Now that he was giving himself wholly to them, he thought they would surely respond and gather around him in larger numbers. They would appreciate his learning their language and be eager to hear more of the Word of God.

But the very opposite was true. The people at Little River, though as hospitable and friendly as ever, showed no deeper interest in spiritual things. At Six Family Hollow he was always welcome, Ah-do's old mother being especially real in her love for the Saviour. A few others, scattered in three villages, gave some evidence of a change of heart, but beyond that the work seemed to have come to a standstill. Where was the great and growing interest? He had been so happy in the expectation that the walls of his Jericho would soon come tumbling down. "We thought this was the seventh day of our compassing," he re-called many years later, "but it was only the first."

The children of the hamlet loved him and were full of fun and curiosity. Indoors or out they hung about him, watching his every movement and trying to help him learn to speak their language. Pioneering in the new realm of tackling a language not reduced to writing was proving to be a tough job. So Fraser welcomed the interest of the children, who never tired of repeating words and phrases until he had them written down, tones and all. For his musical ear insisted on correct reproduction of the sounds.

It was not lack of interest in his surroundings that led to the depression of spirit that now began to assail him. He did not know at first what to make of it. Was he lonely in that isolated hamlet, remote from contact with the outside world? Was it the poor food that left him undernourished? Was it the struggle with the language or the deadlock in the work? Rain and mist in the mountains might be depressing, but as the days and weeks wore on he realized there were influences of another kind to be reckoned with.

A strange uncertainty began to shadow his inward life. All he had believed and rejoiced in became unreal. Even his prayers seemed to mock him, as they seemed unanswered. "*Does* God answer prayer?" loomed larger and larger as a tormenting doubt. "Does He really know and care? Your faith, your expectation—what do they amount to?" In his soli-

tempted even to suicide

tude, depression such as he had never known before closed down upon him. Was he right in the course he had taken? Five years in China and so little to show for it! Was there any purpose after all in his burden of prayer for the Lisu? How he dreaded the coming of some letter of misplaced sympathy with the tone of "Perhaps you were mistaken" or "Are you sure you are in the will of God?"

Deeply were his foundations shaken in those days and nights of conflict, until Fraser realized that behind it all were powers of darkness seeking to overwhelm him. He had dared to invade Satan's kingdom which had been undisputed for ages. At first, vengeance had fallen on the Lisu inquirers, easy prey. Now he himself was attacked, and it was to be a spiritual war to the death. No one knew what the lonely pioneer was facing. No one imagined that in his extremity he was even tempted, and that persistently, to end it all.

No one, did we say? Then how was it that succor reached him just at that time and in the very way to help him most? For it was then, when the rainy season was at its dreariest, that a messenger came from Tengyueh with letters and papers, one of which brought him light. Someone had sent him a copy of *The Overcomer,* a magazine with which Fraser was not familiar. Its arrival at the poor little shack in those Lisu mountains was surely timed by omnipotent Love, for it set forth the very truth he needed in that strange conflict, the truth that would make him free.

As he pored over the pages of the magazine, reading and rereading every word, the fact came home to Fraser that Satan is indeed *a conquered foe*. Christ, our risen Lord, in very truth "bruised his head" upon the cross of shame. "Having put off from Himself [through His death] the principalities and powers, He made a show of them openly, *triumphing over them in it*" (literal translation). This he had believed, as a matter of doctrine. Now it shone out for him in letters of light. Victory was his in Christ. Satan had desired to have him, determined to wreck the life and work of this missionary then and there. No words could tell what the long struggle in the dark had been like. But now the Mighty Victor took him by the hand. What other voice could have said it as He said it? "Triumph thou because of Me. Overcome, even as I also overcame" (see Rev. 3:21).

Long years before, Fraser had responded in obedience to the claims of that glorious One who, for him, had died upon the cross. Now, in the Lisu mountains, he responded again to the liberating power of the same cross. "They overcame him [the great enemy] by the blood of the Lamb and by the word of their testimony." There, in that poor shack, the victory was won that was to mean life to thousands. More of this experience was told by Fraser long afterward,

resist on the grounds of the cross
different truths for different times
resisted depression

as far as words could tell it, in conversation with the writer.

I read it over and over, that number of *The Over-comer*. What it showed me was that deliverance from the power of the evil one comes through definite resistance on the ground of the cross. I am an engineer and believe in things *working*. I had found that much of the spiritual teaching one hears does not seem to work. At any rate my apprehension of other aspects of truth had broken down. The passive side of leaving everything to the Lord Jesus as my life, while blessedly true, was not all that was needed just then. Definite resistance on the ground of the cross was what brought me light. I felt like a man perishing of thirst, for whom some clear, cold water had begun to flow; for I found that *it worked*.

People will tell you, perhaps after a helpful meeting, that such and such a truth alone is the secret of victory. No—we need different truth at different times. "Look to the Lord!" some will say; but "Resist the devil" is also Scripture (James 4:7), and I found it worked! The cloud of depression dispersed. I found that I could have victory in the spiritual realm whenever I wanted it. The Lord Himself vocally resisted the devil: "Get thee behind me, Satan!" In humble dependence on Him, I did the same, talking to Satan, using the promises of Scripture as weapons. *And they worked!* Right then, the terrible oppression began to pass away. I had to learn gradually how to use the newfound weapon of resistance. I had so much to learn. It seemed as if God were saying,

God wanted to work in his heart
before he worked among the Lisu
Spoke out loud to God and the enemy
told him of his defeat

120   *Behind the Ranges*

"You are crying to Me to do a big work among the
Lisu; I am wanting to do a big work in you yourself."

This aspect of truth opened up more and more.
The enemy does not retire at the first setback. Some
time later Fraser was tried by the persistent recur-
rence of evil thoughts which almost came to be an
obsession.

> These thoughts were present with me even when I
> was preaching. I went out of the city to a hidden
> gully on the hillside and there voiced my determined
> resistance to Satan in the matter. I claimed deliver-
> ance on the ground of my Redeemer's victory on the
> cross. I even shouted my resistance to Satan and all
> his thoughts. The obsession collapsed then and there
> like a house of cards, to return no more.
> James 4:7 is still in the Bible. Our Lord cried
> "with a loud voice" at the grave of Lazarus. He
> cried "with a loud voice" from the cross. In times
> of conflict I still find deliverance through repeating
> Scripture out loud—appropriate Scripture brought to
> my mind through the Holy Spirit. It is like crashing
> through opposition. "Resist the devil, and he will
> flee from you."

Another attack of the enemy at Little River came
through the serious illness of Ah-do, the Lisu friend
and companion from whom Fraser had hoped so
much. His personality and gifts fitted him for leadership, and he had always been earnest about making

the Gospel known. High temperature and delirium
indicated typhoid fever, and Fraser did his best to
care for him in those primitive surroundings, fearful
and distressed for the sake of the work should he not
recover. Prayer was answered and Ah-do's life was
spared, but mental symptoms persisted even after he
was taken to Tengyueh for medical treatment and for
a long time he was quite unlike himself.

Fraser wrote to his mother:

> It is painful for me to see him in this condition.
> He has a peculiar expression at times, such as I have
> never seen in his sane moments—sometimes a worn,
> harassed look, like a suffering old man, sometimes
> a dull, hard aspect of defiance. These moods of his
> are uncanny and distressing. He needs prayer, be
> sure of that.

Ah-do was to have accompanied Fraser on a journey to Tali, to meet one of the leaders of the tribal
work in the east of the province. This was out of the
question now, and it was doubtful if he would ever
be the fellow worker Fraser had longed for. But
comfort was at hand in this trial also. Just as he was
setting out on the eight-day journey to Tali, mail arrived from home telling of the formation of his Prayer
Circle. This greatly cheered his heart, so that he
could write in cold and rain from an utterly wretched
inn:

> When things seem to go wrong I try to keep my
> mind in the attitude of Romans 8:28 and my heart

in the attitude of I Thessalonians 5:18—good wings
on which to rise! "All things work together for good
to them that love God," and "In everything give
thanks: for this is the will of God in Christ Jesus concerning you."

Time would fail to tell of all the help Fraser received from the visit to Tali and the fellowship with
Mr. Metcalf, who had come two weeks' journey to
meet him. Much was to be learned from this quiet,
gracious man whom the Lord was using among the
Lisu of the eastern district. His experience was generously made available to the younger missionary,
whether regarding language study, methods of work,
or spiritual effectiveness. They had good times together, enjoying the snow-capped mountains with
their outlook over the far-reaching lake and distant
ranges, and refreshed by the hospitality of Mr. and
Mrs. Hanna and the Chinese Christians.

On his return journey, Fraser was further encouraged by definite answers to prayer with regard to the
important city of Paoshan. Five years previously he
had found a hearing for the Gospel there, on his first
evangelistic journey, but no one had been able to
follow up the work. Now he was prospered in renting
a shop on the busy street, in which he preached every
evening to more people than could be crowded in,
many standing outside the open front to listen. It
was a joy to be using Chinese again and to have part
in the opening of Paoshan as a permanent mission

station. The work thus begun was carried on by a
devoted Chinese evangelist. The expense of renting
and furnishing the preaching hall—the first to be
opened in that large heathen city—was met by a gift
from Fraser's mother.

Renewed in vision and courage, Fraser again
worked at his main task. Five strenuous weeks were
spent in visiting the Kachin and Lisu villages in
which he was already known, and in making friends
in a number of other villages. Everywhere the feeling seemed to be the same—the little places must
take their lead from the larger centers. "If the people
of Tantsah become Christians," was the refrain, "we
would all turn with them."

It seemed clear that Fraser must have some sort of
home from which to carry on settled work. After
much thought and prayer this upland plain with its
considerable Lisu population was decided upon. So
to Tantsah Fraser went in the early autumn, as the
rains were giving place to clear, cold winter. And
cold it was up there, 6,000 feet above sea level! But
the forests supplied abundant fuel, and the headman
of the Tsai family with whom Fraser had stayed before was warm in his welcome.

A two-room shack made available to him supplied
all the comfort that was needed. Ah-do was with
him, recovered from his long illness. With more than
forty villages within easy reach, Fraser felt well in
touch with his work. Wearing everyday Chinese gar-

ments, living on the people's level, and eating the food they provided, he was available to the family and neighbors at all times. Language study filled all spare moments, so that to his Lisu friends it must have seemed that "he was always praying, always preaching, always visiting, always catechizing, always writing and studying" (as Rutherford's flock at Anworth said of their pastor). Though making progress with the spoken language, he was keenly feeling the need of books from which to teach the inquirers. This influenced him to go down to Myitkyina to settle the much discussed question of a Lisu form of writing by conferring with Mr. Geis.

But before leaving Tantsah for several weeks, Fraser called together the chief Lisu of the district to ascertain their willingness to receive him and his message. After talking it over for hours, the majority said they would like to become Christians if Fraser would stay and be their teacher. A simple meal together ratified this conclusion and sent him happily on his way to Burma.

After six years in that remote corner of China, it was a relief to exchange the crudities of pioneer life for a brief touch with the comforts of civilization. British government outposts were found as soon as the border was crossed. From the 6,000-foot altitude it was a glorious descent to the plains of the Irrawaddy.

Fraser's spirits were rising. The beauty of Burma

fascinated him. Unflinching as he was in enduring hardness when necessary, he had not lost his capacity for enjoyment. Several nights in Kachin hovels heightened his appreciation of the government rest house at Sadon.

> You could not wish for a better place—so roomy and comfortable! You have it all to yourself and feel quite lordly. I have had a sort of light European meal which was nice, and a hot bath too—quite aristocratic! One enjoys things by contrast, you know. Excuse all this trivial stuff, dictated by the exuberance of the moment!

The two weeks spent at Myitkyina, in the large mission compound and among the Lisu of the jungle villages, were full of interest. Mr. Geis and Ba Thaw gave themselves to collaborating with their guest in working out a Lisu script and preparing an enlarged catechism. This accomplished, Fraser was eager to return to his promising field at Tantsah, where the prayers of years seemed about to be answered. Before leaving he wrote of the charm of Burma:

> The air is balmy, the sunsets are rich and beautiful, and the evening colors in the sky and on the hills are wonderfully soft, reflected from the lake-like surface of the Irrawaddy. I look up from this letter to a fine extensive view of wooded heights, bathed in sunset glow, stretching perhaps sixty miles in some directions, abounding with sharp peaks and lofty ridges. Burma, beautiful Burma!

A six-day journey lay before the missionary, up and up to the rugged frontier of his adopted country. It was good to be facing China again, though rumors that reached him from the first day out were not encouraging. Bad news travels fast. It appeared that his friend and host at Tantsah was in serious trouble. Reports were vague at first, but Fraser's apprehensions increased as the journey proceeded, until at last messengers appeared who begged him to turn aside and on no account return to Tantsah. This he would not consider, but it was with troubled heart he came again to his Lisu headquarters. He had been away barely a month, but the enemy had been busy. The situation is best explained in his own words:

> The very day I left for Burma the Chinese of Tantsah, who outnumber the Lisu, began to circulate wild stories about me. They said I had come to the district with the intention of turning it over to the British government for money, and that Mr. Tsai was my accomplice. Also that Tsai's going with me to Myitkyina to buy salt was a blind; his real purpose was to fetch the load of money the British government was paying him! Some of them were for confiscating his house and property right away. Milder counsels prevailed, however, and they agreed to wait until his return.
>
> When he got back they held what could only be called an intimidation meeting. They summoned Tsai and all the Lisu who had eaten the meal with me that day and, after much argument, made them

all discouragement from devil to be resisted like sin

sign an agreement that they would on no account turn Christian or allow me to come and live among them. Otherwise they would have their homes and property confiscated. Tsai, as a kind of leader, was made to stand the cost of a meal for all present. The Lisu, overawed and alarmed, gave way entirely and sent word to me, like the Gadarenes of old, and besought me "to depart from their borders" (Mark 5: 17).

One comfort in the sorrow of it all was that, as far as Fraser could judge, the attitude of his Lisu friends was not unfavorable to him. It was simply that they dared not receive him, or become Christians, in the face of the opposition of the Chinese neighbors. If Fraser could obtain permission from higher authorities to return and live among them, they would like to do as they had said before he left for Burma. The really vital thing, however, was not this hopeful element, but the way in which Fraser reacted to the whole situation:

If such a thing had happened a year ago it would have driven me to the depths of depression. I have given way to discouragement, dark discouragement, far too much in the past. Now I know better and thoroughly agree with the assertion that all discouragement is of the devil. Discouragement is to be resisted just like sin. To give way to the one is just as bad and weakens us as much as to give way to the other. God has wonderfully sustained me through this trial, and to Him be all the praise when I say that not for one instant has it disturbed my peace or radiant faith in the risen and ascended Lord. God has enabled me to rejoice in Him more than ever before, and to believe more than ever before for a work of grace among the Lisu.

Chapter 10

A FRUITFUL INTERLUDE

BEFORE LEAVING BURMA, Fraser had unconsciously been prepared for this very situation. For years he had been praying for a spiritual ingathering among the Lisu. For this he had lived and worked, regardless of cost. For this he would endure any hardness. With the deepening of his own spiritual life, faith had grown and become more definite. He had come to see that what was needed was the liberation of whole families from bondage to demon worship. The clan system was so strong that, unless the elders approved, the family spirit-altar and sacrifices would not be effectively done away with. So it was for the turning to Christ of whole households—men, women, and children—that he prayed with increasing longing. The crisis came while he was still in Myitkyina, praying that hundreds of Lisu families would put away their demon worship and turn in faith to Christ. Then it was that the thought came with conviction: "You have been asking for this long enough. When are you going to believe that your prayer is answered?"

The difference between asking and receiving shone out with startling clearness. The burden became not so much the condition of the Lisu as his own lack of faith in dealing with God about them—the faith that *obtains* mercy and *finds* grace to help in time of need (Heb. 4:14-16).

"Now ask in faith!" came the urge of the Spirit.

Then and there the vital change was wrought. Fraser wrote soon afterward:

I knew that the time had come for the prayer of faith. Fully conscious of what I was doing and what it might cost me, I definitely committed myself *in faith* to this petition: hundreds of Lisu families for Christ. The transaction was done. I rose from my knees with the deep, restful conviction that I had already received the answer.

So great was the change in his own outlook that, even before leaving Burma, Fraser had written to the members of his prayer circle:

The Lord has taught me many things lately about the spiritual life. In fact, my own spiritual experience has undergone some upheavals during the past twelve months. Not the least important thing I have learned is in connection with *the prayer of faith*. I have come to see that in past years I have wasted too much time over praying that was not effective prayer at all. Praying without faith is like trying to cut with a dull knife—much labor expended to little purpose—for the work accomplished by labor in prayer depends on our faith: "According to your faith"—not your labor—"be it unto you."

I have been impressed lately with the thought that people fail in praying the prayer of faith because they do not believe God *has* answered, but only that He *will* answer their petitions. They rise from their knees feeling that God will answer some time or other, but not that He has answered already. This is not the faith that makes prayer effective. True faith glories in the present tense, and does not trouble itself about the future. God's promises are in the present tense and are quite secure enough to set our hearts at rest. Their full outworking is often in the future, but God's word is as good as His bond and we need to have no anxiety. Sometimes He gives at once what we ask, but more often He just gives His promise (Mark 11:24). Perhaps He is more glorified in the latter case, for it means that our faith is tried and strengthened. I do earnestly covet a volume of prayer for my Lisu work—but oh, for a *volume of faith* too!

Prepared in this way for the shock which awaited his return to Tantsah, Fraser was enabled to stand his ground unshaken. It clearly was wise to give time for the opposition to quiet down in that neighborhood. After consultation with Mr. Embery he decided to go on "a Lisu hunt" in another direction.

It might appear to be an incident of small consequence that he occupied this interval with an evangelistic journey, but could the outcome have been foreseen, the young missionary might well have regarded it as one of the most important developments of his life. He was thinking only of the unreached Lisu in a district visited five years previously, on his first evangelistic journey. But the One who had been watching over the seed sown in "good ground" at that time saw that it was now ready for the harvest. So He guided His waiting servant to a waiting soul.

It was early in February when Fraser started on this itineration, a six-week journey to the southeast of Tengyueh. Many Chinese towns and Lisu homesteads were visited, and the diary Fraser kept is full of graphic touches. He never let a day go by without preaching somewhere—in the open air, in tea shops, in Chinese inns at night, or by Lisu firesides. As it was the Chinese New Year season there were plenty of holidaymakers about. "Small market but very good time in the evening," is one brief entry. "Preached by moonlight, standing on big, high table in the street, with a smoky lantern. Unusual attention."

But the waiting soul was not there.

Though strong and accustomed to mountain climbing, Fraser found the long stages, poor food, and disturbed nights quite tiring. On the seventh day of his journey he came to the city of Longling, on the southern reaches of the Salween Divide, a district in the bend of the great river where it turns westward into Burma. From this place he did not follow his former route but left the main road to find a Lisu settlement of which he had heard.

The town of Hsiangta lay on this track over the mountains and was reached too late at night to allow his going farther. New Year decorations were much in evidence and promised good audiences next day, but Fraser was tired physically and needed spiritual refreshing. So the following morning, instead of plunging at once into the work awaiting him, he slipped out early with his Bible and found a quiet place where he could be alone for a time. Such seasons were needful for him. Without them he could not have continued a life so taxing and devoid of outward help. And there at Hsiangta, as his journal shows, he was especially cast on God:

> Spent the day mostly in Bible reading and prayer, alone on the mountains. Felt I needed it. Asked God to give a blessing in the evening—my first visit to the place. A stranger in a strange land, I knew no one at all.

With this sense of loneliness still upon him, Fraser reentered the town, hungry no doubt but spiritually strengthened. The prospect was none too hopeful, for a theatrical company had taken possession of the marketplace. The performance had not yet begun, however, and Fraser soon had a crowd around him. His accordion and singing aroused interest and, though there was some heckling, a hundred or so listened well as the evening shadows gathered about them.

Earnestly Fraser reasoned with them of the one and only way of salvation, inviting any who wished to hear more to follow him to his inn. Then, as his custom was, he closed his address by drawing in the net. Would any of his hearers respond to the love of God by receiving the Lord Jesus Christ as their own personal Saviour?

Immediately a hand shot up, and a youngish man stepped forward with obvious eagerness.

It was impossible to satisfy the hunger of that seeking soul in one interview, though it lasted far into the night. Moh Ting-chang had much to tell. It was with wonder Fraser learned that the little book which made the inquirer long for light had come from his own hand.

Moh Ting-chang had never heard the name of Jesus until five years previously. His son had gone down as usual to the great Shan plain, ten miles away, to sell the cakes for which his father was famous. Moh was a baker, an especially good one. The boy had one of his cousins with him and they arrived to find the market at Mangshih full of excitement. A white-faced foreigner had come and was actually giving away, not selling, books to all who could read! The boys couldn't read, but in the scramble some of the books fell to the ground, and Moh's nephew hid one in the sleeve of his gown. He carried it back up the mountain that night, produced it for his uncle to see, and that is how Moh had come into possession of his treasured Gospel of Mark.

A treasure indeed it had proved to be, opening to him a whole world of new thought and feeling. The thing Moh could not account for, however, was the response of his own heart to the One who moved and spoke through its pages. Why was he so drawn to this great Teacher who must have been more than man? Why did His sufferings and death seem to have something to do with himself?

Years had passed and Fraser had known nothing of the work the Spirit of God was doing in that remote spot. Now he was face to face with the man to whom he had unconsciously been the bearer of the Glad Tidings. How full Moh was of eager questions and how unwilling to allow his friend to go on his way the following morning! But word had been sent ahead that Fraser would be at a certain group of Lisu villages that day; the people were expecting him and he must go.

"Come back. Come back soon and be my guest," urged Moh as they parted, an invitation which was gladly accepted.

Turning south from Hsiangta, Fraser had plenty to think over as he tramped the lonely mountain road to seek out this Lisu settlement. His face was now set toward a region never before visited by a preacher of the Gospel—one vast expanse of mountains stretching away to the frontiers of Burma and Thailand, occupied by large populations of Shan, Lisu, and other tribesfolk. He was turning the first page of a new chapter in his experience, though as yet he little dreamed of the answer to his prayer of faith which he was to see in that very region.

Tasiaho was the hamlet at which Fraser was received that night with characteristic Lisu hospitality, cheery folk crowding in to keep him company around the big log fire. His hosts set before him the best they could provide and would not hear of accepting payment. Best of all, they listened with lively interest to all he had to tell, singing over and over again the simple hymn he taught them and learning by heart a few sentences of prayer.

"Go farther south," they urged, when they found they could not keep him. "In all those mountains beyond you will find many Lisu."

This Fraser had decided to do. But he shortened his first visit so as to return to Moh Ting-chang as soon as possible, explaining to his new friends that for some weeks he would still be within reach of them.

It was something of a shock, on being received into the home behind the baker's shop, to find all the implements of idolatry and ancestral worship still there and in use. Wondering greatly, Fraser said nothing about it, while fitting into the family life.

Moh's welcome was unmistakable. He had prepared an upstairs room for his guest and, laying aside business claims, spent every moment with him, even sleeping on the floor beside his bed at night— the height of Chinese courtesy. But, Fraser questioned within himself, if Moh were really converted, how could he still be burning incense to that prominent brass idol?

As the next day wore on, Fraser felt increasingly assured of the reality of Moh's conversion and spiritual life. They went through the catechism together, talking fully over each question and answer. This brought up the matter of idolatry, but still Fraser made no direct application, waiting for God to work. At length, in the afternoon, Moh was so obviously eager to follow Christ in all things that his new friend quietly called attention to the worship of ancestors and idols in his home.

Faced with this issue, Moh frankly confessed he had not dared to touch these household gods. It was a serious matter. He feared for his family—his aged mother, his wife and children.

With full understanding, Fraser suggested that they should go to God about it, asking Him for strength to do the right thing and for His protection from all the powers of evil. Never could Fraser forget the prayer that followed, the first outpouring of a newborn soul in broken words and deep reality. He too prayed and Moh was strengthened.

When we rose from our knees he went straight to the stand where there was water and a basin, took a cloth, and was about to approach the family altar when again he hesitated.

"Come over here and let us pray once more," I said, seeing the conflict.

We did so and that settled it. Without a word he tore down the strips of red paper with the characters for heaven and earth, also the incense, paper money [like children's play money but used in demon worship], and the idol itself. Silently he burned all that could so be destroyed. I had never seen it done before in so summary a fashion. Later Moh said more than once: "If I have done right, I shall have good dreams tonight!"

My first question in the morning was, "How did you sleep last night?"

"Good dreams, good dreams!" he answered heartily.

And I could see that he was set at liberty.

That very day Moh went out preaching with Fraser in the marketplace, and the news spread all over the town that his idol and ancestral worship had been discarded. "I never knew a braver man in his witness for Christ," Fraser commented later. "Persecution assailed him from all sides just because he was so bold and bright. He has had his ups and downs, but never has denied his Lord."

When Fraser had to leave the district a month later, his parting from the interested Lisu who would have kept him was made easier, for he assured them: "Come to Mr. Moh on market days or at any time. He will teach you more about the Lord Jesus. And if you decide to become Christians and want me to come over again and help you, he will write to me for you."

Chapter 11

THE PRAYER OF FAITH

ON RETURNING TO TANTSAH Fraser made his home in
the loft of a headman's house in the lower part of
the village. Opposition had died down and better
quarters were in view, but all through that spring
and early summer he shared the dusty attic with its
original inhabitants, the rats.

If the arrangement left something to be desired, it
also had its advantages. Smoke and smells came up
from below, between the loose boards of the floor,
but so also did the cheerful clatter and chatter of
family doings—a lively lesson day and night in the
language he was so eager to acquire.

Here Fraser was again among the people he loved.
He shared the family meals, cooked in primitive style
over a log fire and served at irregular hours. Rice,
cabbage, and potatoes usually made up the menu for
the paying guest, supplemented with eggs, pork, or
sinewy chicken on occasion. With bowls and chopsticks as utensils, the hard earth floor for a table,
and a few low stools and straw mats for furniture
and furnishings, life was simple. He did not even

object to the incursions of the donkeys, pigs, and chickens that sought shelter from the cold nights in dusky corners and extensions of the living room. "Give me Lisu converts," he wrote that summer, "and I can be truly happy, even in a pigsty!"

How Fraser longed to see a movement of the Spirit of God right where he was! Interested as they were, his Lisu host and neighbors could not be called converts. He had come back with renewed hopes and a wider outlook. The conversion of Moh at Hsiangta had quickened the missionary's faith in the power of the Gospel, and the Lisu population of that southeastern district had opened a new vista to faith and prayer.

It was fear that kept his Lisu neighbors in bondage —a fear which he knew was not unfounded. He was learning that only in a close walk with God and a life of prayer could the powers of darkness be overcome, either in his life or in those around him. It did seem as if some especially sinister power of evil held sway in Tantsah and the neighborhood. In his loneliness Fraser was often conscious of the opposition of unseen foes and fell back with increasing thankfulness upon the prayer cooperation of his small but growing prayer circle at home. The relationship was a close one, for he wrote to them all individually (they numbered only eight or nine at the time) and received detailed letters telling of their interest.

Sometimes he went down to Tengyueh and was helped by the unfailing sympathy of Mr. and Mrs. Embery. After months up in the mountains without seeing another European, the change to their happy family life brought just the relaxation he needed. The children were a joy to him, and Mrs. Embery noticed the hunger of his whole being for music. Before they could get him to take a meal or even a cup of tea, he would sit down at the portable organ and play, if not interrupted, for hours. Bach, Beethoven, Schumann, Chopin—without a note before him. What music he brought out of that little instrument, and how revealing it all was!

From Tengyueh Fraser wrote his prayer circle concerning the things most upon his heart:

> About twelve men at Tantsah have professed their intention of becoming Christians. Few or none of these come regularly to the services, nor do I know of any who have definitely renounced demonolatry (that is, those who are responsible members of their families). They are too afraid of the demons to turn to God as yet. Still, God is leading me onward and I am quite hopeful. I do not intend to be in too much of a hurry, and yet I will cry to God for a blessed work of grace among the Lisu as long as He lends me breath.

More and more he was coming to depend on prayer, as did the Master Himself in His earthly service.

"If two of you shall agree . . ." I feel, even when praying alone, that there are two concerned in the prayer, God and myself. I do not think that a petition which misses the mind of God will ever be answered (I John 5:14). Personally, I feel the need of trusting Him to lead me in prayer as well as in other matters. I find it well to preface prayer not only by meditation but by the definite request that I may be directed into the channels of prayer to which the Holy Spirit is beckoning me. I also find it helpful to make a short list, like notes prepared for a sermon, before every season of prayer. The mind needs to be guided as well as the spirit attuned. I can thus get my thoughts in order and, having prepared my prayer, can put the notes on the table or chair before me, kneel down, and get to business.

One month later Fraser was writing again to his praying friends, this time from a place of his own at Tantsah. One big bare room with its packed earth floor afforded more privacy than the loft, though it yielded little more comfort. Carried over the mountains to Tengyueh by his Lisu runner, there to be mailed to the homeland, the letter may help us, too, in praying the prayer of faith.

TANTSAH, YUNNAN, CHINA
October 9, 1915

MY DEAR FRIENDS:

The Scriptures speak of several kinds of prayer. There is intercession and there is supplication; there is labor in prayer and there is the prayer of faith; all perhaps the same fundamentally, but they present various aspects of this great and wonderful theme. It would not be unprofitable to study the differences between these various scriptural terms.

There is a distinction between *general* prayer and *definite* prayer. By definite prayer I mean prayer after the pattern of Matthew 21:21-22 and John 15:7, where a definite petition is offered up and definite faith exercised for its fulfillment. Now faith must be in exercise in the other kind of prayer also, when we pray for many and varied things without knowing the will of God in every case.

In *general prayer* I am limited by my ignorance. But this kind of prayer is the duty of us all (I Tim. 2:1-2), however vague it has to be. I may know very little, in detail, about the object of my prayer, but I can at any rate commend it to God and leave it all with Him. It is good and right to pray, vaguely, for all people, all lands, all things, at all times.

But *definite prayer* is a very different matter. It is in a special sense "the prayer of faith." A definite request is made in definite faith for a definite answer.

Take the case of a Canadian immigrant as an illustration of the prayer of faith. Allured by the prospect of "golden grain" he leaves home for the Canadian West. He has a definite object in view. He knows very well what he is going for, and that is wheat. He thinks of the good crops he will reap and of the money they will bring him—much like the child of God who sets out to pray the prayer of faith. He has his definite object too. It may be the conversion of a son or daughter; it may be power in Christian service; it may be guidance in a perplexing situation, or a hundred and one other things—but it is *definite*. Consider the points of resemblance between the cases of the prospective Canadian farmer and the believing Christian:

1. *The breadth of the territory*. Think of the unlimited scope for the farmer in Canada. There are literally millions of acres waiting to be cultivated, No need, there, to tread on other people's toes! Room for all—vast tracts of unoccupied land just going to waste, and good land too. And so it is with us, surely. There is a vast, vast field for us to go up and claim in faith. There is enough sin, enough sorrow, enough of the blighting influence of Satan in the world to absorb all our prayers of faith, and a hundred times as many more. "There remaineth yet very much land to be possessed."

2. *The government encourages immigration*. Think also of the efforts of the Canadian government to encourage immigration. All the unoccupied land belongs to it, but settlers are so badly needed that they are offered every inducement—immigration offices established, sea passages and railway fares reduced, and grants of land made free! And God is no less urgently inviting His people to pray the prayer of

faith: "*Ask—ask—ask*," He is continually saying to us.
He offers His inducement too: "Ask, and ye shall receive, that your joy may be full." All the unoccupied
territory of faith belongs to Him. And he bids us to
come and occupy freely. "How long are ye slack to
go in to possess the land?"

3. *There are fixed limits.* Yet this aspect of the
truth must not be overemphasized. Blessed fact
though it be that the land is so broad, it can easily be
magnified out of due proportion. The important
thing is not the vastness of the territory but how
much of it is actually assigned to us. The Canadian
government will make a grant of 160 acres to the
farmer-immigrant, and no more. Why no more? Because they know very well he cannot work any more.
If they were to give him 160 square miles instead of
160 acres he would not know what to do with it all.
So they wisely limit him to an amount of land equal
to his resources.

And it is much the same with us when praying the
prayer of definite faith. The very word "definite"
means "with fixed limits." We are often exhorted,
and with reason, to ask great things of God. Yet
there is a balance in all things, and we may go too
far in this direction. It is possible to bite off, in
prayer, more than we can chew. There is a principle
underlying II Corinthians 10:13 which may apply to
this very matter: "According to the measure of the
province [limit] which God apportioned to us as a

Faith like a muscle, exercise strengthens it.

measure" (A.S.V.). Faith is like muscle, which grows stronger and stronger with use, rather than rubber, which weakens when it is stretched. Overstrained faith is not pure faith; there is a mixture of the carnal element in it. There is no strain in the "rest of faith." It asks for definite blessing as God may lead. It does not hold back through carnal timidity, nor press ahead too far through carnal eagerness.

I have definitely asked the Lord for several hundred families of Lisu believers. There are upward of two thousand Lisu families in the Tantsah district. It might be said, "Why do you not ask for a thousand?" I answer quite frankly, "Because I have not faith for a thousand." I believe the Lord has given me faith for more than one hundred families, but not for a thousand. So I accept the limits the Lord, I believe, has given me. Perhaps God will give me a thousand; perhaps He will lead me to commit myself to this definite prayer of faith later on. This is in accordance with Ephesians 3:20: "above all that we ask or think." But we must not overload faith; we must be sane and practical. Let us not claim too little in faith, but let us not claim too much either. Remember the Canadian immigrant's 160 acres. Consider, too, how the Dominion Government exercises authority in the matter of location. The government has a say as to the *where* as well as the *how much* of the immigrant's claim. He is not invited to wander all over the prairie at his own sweet will and elect to settle down in any place he chooses. Even in regard to the position of his farm he must consult the government.

Do we always do this in our prayers and claims? Do we consult the heavenly government at the outset, or do we pray the first thing that comes to mind? Do we spend time waiting upon God to know His will before attempting to embark on His promises? That this is a principle upon which God works He has informed us very plainly in I John 5:14-15. I cannot but feel that this is one cause for many unanswered prayers. James 4:3 has a broad application, and we need to search our hearts in its light. Unanswered prayers have taught me to seek the Lord's will instead of my own. I suppose most of us have had such experiences. We have prayed and prayed and prayed, and no answer has come. The heavens above us have been as brass. Yea, blessed brass, if it has taught us to sink a little more of this ever-present self of ours into the cross of Christ. Sometimes our petition has been such a good one, to all appearances, but that does not insure its being of God. Many "good desires" proceed from our uncrucified selves. Scripture and experience agree that those who live nearest to God are the most likely to know His will. We are called to be "filled with the knowledge of His will" (Col. 1:9). We need to know more of the fellowship of Christ's death. We need to feed on the Word of God more than we do. We need suffering

Good

more holiness, more prayer. We shall not, then, be
in such danger of mistaking His will.

The wonderful promise of John 15:7 is prefixed by
a far-reaching "if." I wonder if that verse might not
be paraphrased: "If ye abide *not* in me, and my words
abide *not* in you, *do not* ask whatsoever ye will, for
it shall *not* be done unto you." Perhaps if we ex-
amined ourselves more thoroughly before God we
might even discover, in some cases, that the whole
course of our life was not in accordance with His will.
What right would a man have, in such a case, to expect his prayers to be answered? But is not this the
fact with regard to much "good" Christian work?
"Get your work from God" is a good injunction. How
often Christian leaders make their own plans, work
hard at them, and then earnestly seek God's blessing
on them. How much better, as Hudson Taylor felt,
to wait on God to know His plans before commenc-
ing! Much Christian work seems to have the stamp
of the carnal upon it. It may be "good," it may be
successful outwardly, but the Shekinah glory is not
there. Now all this applies to the prayer of faith.
We must have the assurance that we are in the right
place, doing the right work. We must be sure that
God is leading us, when we enter upon specific
prayer.

It does not follow that because a thing is the will
of God, He will necessarily lead *you* to pray for it.
He may have other burdens for you. We must *get*

our prayers from God, and pray to know His will. It may take time. God was dealing with Hudson Taylor for fifteen years before He laid upon him the burden of definite prayer for the foundation of the China Inland Mission. God is not in a hurry. He cannot do things with us until we are trained and ready for them. We may be certain He has further service, further burdens of faith and prayer to give us when we are ready for them.

4. *The claim endorsed.* Turn to the immigrant again. He has come to an agreement with the Canadian government. He falls in with their terms, he accepts their conditions, he agrees to take over the land allotted to him. So he presents his claim at the proper quarter, and it is at once endorsed. Could anything be more simple? Nor need our claim in the presence of God be any less simple. When we once have the deep, calm assurance of His will in the matter, we put in our claim, just as a child before his father. A simple request and nothing more. No cringing, no beseeching, no tears, no wrestling. No second asking either.

In my case I prayed continually for the Tengyueh Lisu for over four years, asking many times that several hundred families might be turned to God. This was only general prayer, however. God was dealing with me in the meantime. You know how a child is sometimes rebuked by his parents for asking something in a wrong way—perhaps asking rudely. The parent will respond, "Ask me properly!" That is just what God seemed to be saying to me then: "Ask Me properly! You have been asking Me to do this for the last four years without ever really believing I would do it—now ask *in faith.*"

I felt the burden *clearly.* I went to my room alone one afternoon and knelt in prayer. I knew that the time had come for the prayer of faith. And then, fully knowing what I was doing and what it might cost me, I definitely committed myself to this petition *in faith.* I cast my burden upon the Lord and rose from my knees with the deep, restful conviction that I had already received the answer. The transaction was done. And since then (nearly a year ago now) I have never had anything but peace and joy (when in touch with God) in holding to the ground already claimed and taken. I have never repeated the request and never will: there is no need. The asking, the taking, and the receiving occupy but a few moments (Mark 11:24). It is a solemn thing to enter into a faith covenant with God. It is binding on both parties. You lift up your hand to God, you definitely ask for and definitely receive His proffered gift—then do not go back on your faith, even if you live to be a hundred.

5. *Get to work.* To return once more to the Canadian farmer. He has put in his claim, the land has been granted, the deed made out and sealed with

the official seal. Is that the end then? No, only the beginning!

He has not yet attained his objective. His objective is a harvest of wheat, not a patch of wasteland, and there is a vast difference between the two. The government never promised him sacks of flour all ready for export—only the land which could be made to yield them. Now is the time for him to roll up his sleeves and get to work. He must build his homestead, get his livestock, call in laborers, clear the ground, plow it and sow his seed. The government says to him in effect, "We have granted your claim— now go and work it!"

And this distinction is no less clear in the spiritual realm. God gives us the ground in answer to the prayer of faith, but not the harvest. That must be worked for in cooperation with Him. Faith must be followed up by works, prayer-works. Salvation is of grace, but it must be worked out (Phil. 2:12) if it is to become ours. And the prayer of faith is just the same. It is given to us by free grace, but it will never be ours until we follow it up, work it out. Faith and works must never be divorced, for indolence will reap no harvest in the spiritual world. I think the principle will be found to hold in any case where the prayer of faith is offered, but there is no doubt that it always holds good in cases where the strongholds of Satan are attacked, where the prey is to be wrested from the strong.

Good

Think of the children of Israel under Joshua. God had given them the land of Canaan—given it to them, notice, by free grace—but see how they had to fight when once they commenced actually to take possession!

Satan's tactics seem to be as follows: He will first of all oppose our breaking through to the place of a real, living faith by all means in his power. He detests the prayer of faith, for it is an authoritative "notice to quit." He does not so much mind rambling, carnal prayers, for they do not hurt him much. This is why it is so difficult to attain to a definite faith in God for a definite object. We have often to strive and wrestle in prayer (Eph. 6:10-12) before we attain this quiet, restful faith. And until we break right through and *join hands with God* we have not attained to real faith at all. Faith is a gift of God—if we stop short of it we are using mere fleshly energy or willpower, weapons of no value in this warfare. Once we attain to real faith, however, all the forces of hell are impotent to annul it. What then? They retire and muster their forces on this plot of ground which God has pledged Himself to give us, and contest every inch of it. The real battle begins when the prayer of faith has been offered. But, praise God, we are on the winning side! Let us read and reread Joshua 10 and never talk about defeat again. Defeat, indeed! No. Victory! Victory! Victory!

Please read II Samuel 23:8-23. All I have been saying is found in a nutshell in verses 11 and 12. Let Shammah represent the Christian warrior. Let David represent the crucified and risen Christ—and note that Shammah was "one of the mighty men that David had." Let the "plot of ground" represent the prayer of faith. Let the lentils, if you will, represent the poor lost souls of men. Let the Philistines represent the hosts of wickedness. Let "the people" represent Christians afflicted with spiritual anemia.

I can imagine what these people were saying as they saw the Philistines approaching and ran away: "Perhaps it was not the Lord's will to grant us that plot of ground. We must submit to the will of God."

Yes, we must indeed submit ourselves to God, but we must also "resist the devil" (James 4:7). The fact that the enemy comes upon us in force is no proof that we are out of the line of God's will. The constant prefixing of "if it be Thy will" to our prayers is often a mere subterfuge of unbelief. True submission to God is not inconsistent with virility and boldness. Notice what Shammah did—simply *held his ground.* He was not seeking more worlds to conquer at that moment. He just stood where he was and hit out, right and left. Notice also the result of his action and to whom the glory is ascribed.

6. *Praying through to victory.* I repeat that this does not necessarily apply to every kind of prayer. A young Lisu Christian here is fond of telling an experience of his a few months ago. He was walking

through the fields in the evening when his insides began unaccountably to pain him. He dropped on his knees and, bowing his head down to the ground, asked Jesus to cure him. At once the stomachache left him. Praise the Lord! And there are no doubt multitudes of such cases—simple faith and simple answers.

But we must not rest content with such prayer. We must get beyond stomachache or any other ache and enter into the deeper fellowship of God's purposes. "That we henceforth be no more children" (Eph. 4:14). We must press on to maturity. We must attain to "the measure of the stature of the fulness of Christ," and not remain in God's kindergarten indefinitely. If we grow into manhood in the spiritual life we shall not escape conflict. As long as Ephesians 6:10-18 remains in the Bible, we must be prepared for serious warfare—"and having done all, to stand." We must fight through and then stand victorious on the battlefield.

Is not this another secret of many unanswered prayers—that they are not fought through? If the result is not seen as soon as expected, Christians are apt to lose heart and, if it is still longer delayed, to abandon it altogether.

We must count the cost before praying the prayer of faith. We must be willing to pay the price. We must mean business. We must set ourselves to "see things through" (Eph. 6:18, "with all perseverance").

Our natural strength will fail: and herein lies the necessity of a divinely given faith. We can then rest back in the everlasting Arms and renew our strength continually. We can then rest as well as wrestle. In this conflict-prayer, after the definite exercise of faith, there is no need to ask the same thing again and again. It seems to me inconsistent to do so. Under these circumstances, I would say let the prayer take the following forms:

a. A firm standing on God-given ground, and a constant assertion of faith and claiming of victory. It is helpful, I find, to repeat passages of Scripture applicable to the subject. Let faith be continually strengthened and fed from its proper source, the Word of God.

b. A definite fighting and *resisting of Satan's host* in the name of Christ. As direct weapons against Satan I like to read in prayer such passages as I John 3:8: "For this purpose the Son of God was manifested, that he might destroy the works of the devil," and Revelation 12:11: "They overcame him by the blood of the Lamb." I often find it a means of much added strength and liberty to fight in this way. Nothing cuts like the Word of the living God (Heb. 4:12).

c. Praying through every aspect of the matter in detail. In the case of my Lisu work here, I continually pray to God for a fresh knowledge of His will, more wisdom in dealing with the people, knowledge of how to pray, how to maintain the victory, how to

Don't make definite prayer unless God gives it

instruct the people in the Gospel or in singing or in prayer, help in studying the language, help in ordinary conversation, help in preaching, guidance about choice of a central place to live in, guidance about building a house (if necessary), guidance in my personal affairs (money, food, clothes, etc.), help and blessing in my correspondence, openings for the Word and blessing in other villages, for leaders and helpers to be raised up for me, for each of the Christians by name, also for every one of my prayer helpers by name. Such detailed prayer is exhausting, but I believe effectual in ascertaining the will of God and obtaining His highest blessing.

I would not ask anyone to join me in the definite prayer for the turning to God of several hundred Lisu families unless God gives him individual guidance to do so. Better offer prayer in a more general way than make a definite petition apart from His leading. I should, however, value highly the prayer cooperation of any who feel led to join me in it. What I want, too, is not just an occasional mention of my work and its needs before the Lord, during the morning or evening devotions, but a definite time (say half an hour or so?) set apart for the purpose every day, either during the daytime or in the evening. Can you give that time to me—or rather, to the Lord?

About a fortnight ago I baptized two Lisu women at the little village of Six Family Hollow, the wives of two young Lisu men I baptized last January. I have now baptized six Christian Lisu altogether, all from that one family. It was my painful duty, however, only the next day, to exclude Ah-do from church fellowship. It appears that he has been continually breaking the seventh commandment, not only in his own villages but also in other places where he has been with me. The Lisu are a very immoral race in any case, but in spite of his Christian profession he has been even more promiscuous than most of them. He seems quite penitent and never attempted to deny his guilt. We must pray for his restoration.

I have no other special news of the work just now. I am thinking of visiting Six Family Hollow again in a few days, as well as other villages.

Hoping to write again next month, and with earnest prayers for you all,

Yours in the Lord's service,
J. O. Fraser

THE SWORD-LADDER
FESTIVAL

WHILE STILL GIVING TIME to the study of the language, Fraser was out on the road a great deal (if mountain paths and tracks almost lost in the jungle could be called by that name). In tiny hamlets over the Burma border, he had the joy of seeing several families turn to the Lord, and from south of Tapu Pum (a frontier giant 11,000 feet high) invitations began to reach him from districts as yet unvisited. Yet the trial of his faith was great as month after month went by and the larger ingathering he was prayerfully expecting seemed as far off as ever.

Six Family Hollow was always a bright spot, because of the steadfast faith of Mother Tsai and most of her family.

The old man is nearly seventy and his wife is over sixty. Her two sons and their wives all believe and have been baptized, though Ah-do has had to be disciplined (as I mentioned before). As far as I can see, he is turning over a new leaf. They have been

159

Christians for three years now and seem to be growing in faith and courage. The old lady is firmest of all. It is probably owing to her that they are now believers. When they first turned Christian, they underwent some severe trials for a time, and very nearly fell back. They had considerable sickness and were taunted by their neighbors, Chinese and Lisu, with having offended the demons and incurred their wrath. Everything seemed against them, but the old lady held on and they finally pulled through. She has a very practical faith and can tell you of many answers to prayer.

As an instance, she tells you that her pig (a most valuable possession) has run away three times, but has come back every time in answer to prayer. When a pig runs away to the mountains it is almost sure to stay there. Up here, people do not keep them in sties, but let them roam in and around the houses for whatever they can get. Mrs. Tsai has a sense of humor, too. Her pig has a peculiar habit of leaning its head on the side of the trough, shutting its eyes, and grunting a little while before eating. So she tells the people that even her pig knows how to pray!

Not far from the Tsai home lived three other families of whom it was encouraging to hear. They too had become Christians and Fraser lost no time in going over to see them at Bamboo Hut and Artemesia Plain. Mr. Fish of Bamboo Hut was half blind, had suffered much pain in his eyes, and had made costly offerings to the spirits without effect. At last he grew desperate and determined that, since the spirits would not help him, he would renounce them all and turn to the God of his Christian neighbors.

So he actually took a sword and hacked down his family altar, refusing to burn any incense or paper money, though it was Chinese New Year. He had heard the Gospel previously, but this is the first case I have come across of a man's definitely discarding idolatry on his own initiative. I did not visit him until nearly three months after that, during which time he had gone down to my colleague, Mr. Embery, and obtained some eye lotion, and was quite relieved of the pain. I stayed three days in his home and found him, his wife and children, as well as his old father and mother singularly wholehearted in their determination to worship God.

A cheering answer to Fraser's prayer for whole families of mountain people to turn to Christ!
He continued:

This case has been noised abroad throughout the district and has made a favorable impression. The one thing many of the people are waiting for is to know whether or not it is really safe to throw the evil spirits overboard and turn to Christ. It is important to pray for those who have already turned Christian, that their faith and constancy may be equal to all the tests, and that the Spirit's power for the healing of sickness may be with them. For a man to turn Christian and then be smitten down with sickness at once discredits the Gospel in the eyes of the Lisu.

The two families at Artemesia Plain were not quite so out-and-out, but Fraser felt that they too, by God's blessing, would hold on.

> Mr. Fish of this village is an opium smoker, but he intends to break it off, if we will help him. He says he is not afraid of "house demons" (the ancestral spirits worshiped in the central room of every home, Lisu as well as Chinese) but only of the "outside demons." He cleared his home of demonolatry without demur, while I was there, but said that the proof of the efficacy of the Gospel will come out in its power to ward off evil influences when he is out on the hills. Evil spirits are believed to lurk in certain spots and, when anyone passes their lair, they may attack them, causing severe pain in some part of the body. I assured him that the Lord Jesus is able to protect all who really put their trust in Him, and he said that he would give the Gospel a fair trial. I stayed with the family two or three days and taught them to pray.

From that little mountain home Fraser's thoughts must have turned sadly to a very different experience he had met with some weeks before. He had had high hopes of a group of inquirers in a place near Tantsah, where the far-famed Sword-ladder Festival was held from time to time. The demon priest of Cold Horse Village, though refusing to have anything to do with the Gospel himself, had not sought to hinder Fraser's influence among the people, "No," he said, "it is impossible for me to become a Christian. The gods have entered right into me and I belong to them. You may exhort the other people of the village. If they turn Christian, well and good— but I cannot."

He had even invited the missionary to come to the next great occasion, when he was to wash his hands in fire and mount the ladder of swords. This brought Fraser to the village early in 1916 full of hope for a number of inquirers, both there and in the nearby hamlet in which he was hospitably received. But it proved to be a plunge into abysmal darkness, not only in the manifestations of demon power but also in the suffering of his own spirit.

Hundreds of people were gathered in and around the temple, where the spirits were to be propitiated for the protection of the district. A fellow missionary, Mr. Goby, had come up from Tengyueh, the first European person Fraser had seen for three months. Together they moved among the excited crowds watching the proceedings.

The sword-ladder had about three dozen rungs and was fixed vertically. It stood right out in the open place and was some forty feet high. The evening before the ascent, the devil-dancer, a man over sixty years of age, was supposed to wash his hands and feet in a fire of red-hot cinders. Goby and I went to the temple to witness this. There was a whole lot going on.

Sacrifices, which included one of two chickens which the devil-dancer killed by biting through their necks with his teeth, were being offered to some hideous idols. With the beating of gongs and drums they were trying to work up some kind of frenzy, but with only partial success. At length the devil-dancer emerged from the temple and just swept the red-hot coals about with his bare hands and feet. We both noticed, next day, that his hands showed signs of being burned.

This was despite the fact that he was supposed to be immune from harm, either from sword or fire. The formidable ladder also was more or less of a deception. For, while some of the swords could have sharpened a pencil, many had lost their edge. Still, to climb it was a feat which neither Goby nor Fraser would have cared to attempt!

The old devil-dancer did not emerge from the temple until about two o'clock the next afternoon and, after more incantations, proceeded slowly and cautiously to ascend the ladder. After more talk and carrying-on at the top, he slowly came down again. Then two younger men made the ascent and descent. A woman also very nearly did so. She has fits of demon possession in her home, they say, and was to be cured by mounting the ladder of knives through the power of her god. But she apparently could not get hold of the spirit power necessary for the feat, so after carrying on in a wild kind of way for a while, she gave up the attempt.

The excitement meanwhile was intense, the faces of the people expressing the horrible fears that kept them in bondage. It was no wonder that the good seed Fraser had been sowing should fail to take root in ground so overgrown with tares. The whole experience impressed upon him afresh the need for truly supernatural power in meeting such conditions. With a bleeding heart he wrote to his prayer helpers at home, pleading for deeper fellowship in the work to which he was called—the always costly work of redemption (Heb. 9:11-12).

I was very severely disappointed about the attitude of the Lisu of that district to the Gospel. They received the Word with joy at first, as they so often do. Several announced that they were going to turn Christian, one old man and his son seeming specially earnest. Then the spirit of fear seemed to possess them, and one by one they dropped off, until no one would take a stand at all. We had to leave them as heathen as I first found them. It was a very painful experience and seemed almost to stun me for a while.

Goby left him the next day, and from his loneliness at Tantsah Fraser wrote to his prayer partners of the deeper experiences into which he was being led. The record of Hannah's grief and faith in the opening chapter of I Samuel was speaking to his heart.

How much of our praying is of the quality we find in Hannah's "bitterness of soul" when she "prayed unto the Lord"? How many times have we ever "wept sore" before the Lord? We have prayed much, perhaps, but our longings have not been deep as compared with hers. We have spent much time upon our knees, it may be, without our hearts going out in an agony of desire. But real supplication is the child of heartfelt desire, and cannot prevail without it: a desire not of earth or issuing from our own sinful hearts, but wrought in us by God Himself. Oh, for such desires! Oh, for Hannah's earnestness, not in myself only but in all who are joining me in prayer for these poor heathen aborigines!

And is there not sufficient reason for such earnestness? We have our Peninnahs as surely as ever Hannah had and as God's saints have had all down the ages. David's eyes ran down with rivers of water, because the ungodly observed not God's law (Ps. 119:136). Jeremiah wept with bitter lamentation because of the destruction of the holy city. Nehemiah fasted, mourned, and wept when he heard of the fresh calamities which had befallen Jerusalem. Our Lord wept over it, because of its hardness of heart. The Apostle Paul had "great sorrow and unceasing pain" in his heart on account of his brethren according to the flesh (Rom. 9:2).

Yes, and *we* have our "sore provocations," or should have. How else ought we to feel when we see all the ungodliness and unbelief around us on every hand? Would a lighthearted apathy become us under such circumstances? No, indeed! And I want you, please, to join me—or rather share with me—in the "provocation" which is daily with me in my work among the Lisu. Let the terrible power of evil spirits among them be a provocation to *you*. Let their sinfulness, their fears, their pitiful weakness and instability be a provocation to *you*. Ask God to lay the burden upon you, and that heavily—that it may press you down upon your knees. My prayer for you is that God will work such sorrow within you that you will have no alternative but to pray. I want you to be "sore provoked" as I am.

Such a state of mind and heart is of avail, however, only as it is turned into prayer. Desire, however deep, does nothing in itself, any more than steam pressure in a boiler is of use unless it is allowed to drive machinery. There is a spiritual law here. A strong spiritual desire does harm rather than good, if it is neglected. An earnest desire in spiritual things is a bell ringing for prayer. Not that we should wait for such desires. We should pray at all seasons, whether we are prayer-hungry or not. If we have a healthy prayer-appetite, so much the better. But if this appetite be unnoticed or unappeased, a dullness will come over us and we shall be weakened in spirit, just as a lack of sufficient food weakens us in body. See, in I Samuel 1:15, the way in which Hannah dealt with her God-given desire. Her soul was bitter, and she "poured it out" before the Lord. Blessed bitterness! But it must be poured out.

Chapter 13

"WHO TEACHETH LIKE HIM?"

(Job 36:22)

BEFORE THE WRITER lies a rather large brown book, bound in half-calf and bearing signs of much use. It is a heavy 150-page book, feint-ruled and filled almost to the end with small, clear writing. A line a day is all that is given to most of the entries and there are but few blank spaces. One line a day—the amazing record of Fraser's missionary activities, beginning at Tantsah with New Year's Day, 1916, and abruptly ending at Paoshan, twenty-two years later. "Thirtieth anniversary of sailing from Tilbury" is almost the last entry, a few days before his swift translation to higher service.

As time went on, life became too full for any record save the barest facts, but in the Tantsah period the opening pages of the journal are rich in revealing thoughts and experiences. Here we company with Fraser in his loneliness, tramp with him on his preaching tours, share his inner life amid joys and sorrows, and enter into the deeper communings of his heart with God. Truly the place is holy ground.

The journal adds meaning to the correspondence he kept up so faithfully with his mother and the praying friends she gathered around her. She was the heart of his prayer circle, the one who originated and tended it with all a mother's love. She lived, toiled, and suffered with her boy so far away, and when he was hard pressed in his Lisu trenches, instead of worrying she gave herself the more to prayer and getting others to pray.

As the prayer circle grew, Fraser was distinctly conscious of a change both in himself and in his surroundings. A new spirit of expectancy began to stir within him and there seemed new power with his message. This made him long for more such prayer help, and in his practical way he set to work to obtain it. Writing to thank the members of the circle for their faithful intercessions, he made this plea:

> You will know how, sometimes, a passage of Scripture comes to mind with such insistence and such an obvious application to present circumstances that you can hardly doubt its being a direct message from God. It seems as if God's word to me at present comes in a passage from Isaiah which spoke to me powerfully a few weeks ago and still seems to ring within me: "Enlarge the place of thy tent . . . spare not, lengthen thy cords, and strengthen thy stakes; For thou shalt *break forth* [spread abroad] on the right hand and on the left" (Isa. 54:2-3).
> Knowing as I do the conditions of the work, its

potential magnitude, its difficulties, and the opposition it meets with, I have definitely resolved, with God's help, to enlarge the place of my tent, to lengthen my prayer cords and strengthen my intercessory stakes. I have resolved to make a forward movement with regard to the prayer circle.

Up to that time Fraser's occasional letters about the work had been forwarded from one to another, around the group of eight or ten prayer helpers. Now, at his own expense, he was to send a separate copy to each one, as well as taking steps to add to the membership.

I am persuaded that England is rich in godly, quiet, praying people, in every denomination. They may not be a great multitude, but they are "rich in faith," even if many of them be poor and of humble station. It is the prayers of such that I covet more than gold of Ophir—those good old men and good old women (yes, and not necessarily old, either) who know what it is to have power with God and prevail. Will you help me, prayerfully and judiciously, to get some of these to join the circle? The work for which I am asking prayer is preaching and teaching the Word of God, pure and simple. I have no confidence in anything but the Gospel of Calvary to uplift these needy people.

How much Fraser's heart was in this work comes out in both letters and journal. Oh, those endless journeys over the mountains, tramping around his districts, new and old! How widely he scattered the precious seed, how fervently he watered it with his prayers. Of one journey on the Burma border there is no record save in penciled notes to his mother:

> In this poor, mountainous part of Burma, the people put up very rough shanties. They live practically —sitting, eating, and sleeping on their earth floors. For a bed, they lay you a lath-mat, near the fire in the center room, on which you spread your bedding. So you lie only an inch above the ground. And the people, often a whole roomful of them, are much interested in the process of dressing and undressing. They give you little or no privacy if they can help it, from the moment you enter the village until the moment you leave it. Bathed in dashing mountain stream, among the big boulders. Less tired in the evening; preached and talked to the people.

But in those tiny hidden hamlets, overshadowed by mountains 11,000 feet high, there was a response to the message Fraser brought that made the effort worthwhile.

> At the village of Six Families we put up in a "Black Hole of Calcutta" kind of house. As this was not one of the places to which I had been definitely invited, I was preparing to leave in the morning, when my Lisu helper came to say that the villagers were asking us to stay on, as some of them wanted to turn Christian. So of course I stayed. I am at their beck and call whenever they want to turn to God. More preaching in the evening.

Quite a little is involved in this "turning." First, a good talk with the family around the fire, explaining the meaning of the step they are taking. Then prayer with them all, standing up, followed by the removal of all objects used in demon worship. This takes quite a while. All that will burn is thrown on the fire, and we have a fine old blaze. The joy of seeing this done is second only to the joy of baptizing.

At Chop River, the Bear family also gave cause for encouragement—an old lady with her son, his wife, and three children.

A delightful family. None on the whole trip turned Christian more wholeheartedly. The son made a clean and bold sweep of all demonolatry, both inside and outside the house, leading me around to see that all was O.K. Someone suggested that it would be enough to remove only the things used in spirit worship, leaving the shelf for other purposes.

"No, no!" he exclaimed. "We will get rid of the whole lot while we are about it!"

His young wife, an unusually bright, intelligent woman, plied me with all sorts of questions about the Gospel.

But such joys were none too frequent. The reaping time had not yet come for the lonely pioneer, and his hopes for Tantsah especially were far from being realized. Yet he had no liberty at all about moving to another center. From January to May he held on, waiting for guidance. Turning the early pages of his journal, one is awed to see the depths of soul exercise involved, the height and length and breadth of his prayers. His experience at this time seemed full of failure, checkered with defeat. And in a sense it was just that. But to those who knew him in later years this experience goes far to explain the spiritual level on which he lived—a plane many of us know little about and never reach. In these long-closed pages we see him climbing, undeterred by the cost.

TANTSAH, Saturday, Jan. 1, 1916: Must watch against getting up too late these intensely cold mornings. The indwelling Christ is my successful weapon against all sin these days—praise Him!

Sunday, Jan. 2: An earnest desire to save souls is on me, but prayer is rather unstable. I must regain my equilibrium in the prayer life. I must maintain, also, my abiding in Christ, by prayer without ceasing (silent), which I am now finding blessedly possible. Romans 6 is not now my weapon so much as John 15.

Tuesday, Jan. 4: Finished Finney's autobiography; much help received from it. Finney's strong point is the using of *means* to an *end*. My own leading is not a little along that line also. I do not intend to be one of those who bemoan little results while "resting in the faithfulness of God." My cue is to take hold of the faithfulness of God and *use the means necessary* to secure big results.

Saturday, Jan. 8: Prayer out on the hill, from noon until about 3:30 P.M. Much drawn out for the Lisu work generally.

Sunday, Jan. 9: Discussion with Ku's family about his removing the household's demon altar and also about the betrothal ceremony of his son tomorrow.

Monday, Jan. 10: Nearly all the Christians were away at Ku's betrothal ceremony, where there would be the usual drinking and dancing. I spent most of the evening in prayer. Nothing will give me lasting joy on this earth, now, but the salvation of large numbers of Lisu. To hear of Lisu turning to Christ anywhere, or even intending to turn, rejoices me in a way nothing else does.

Sunday, Jan. 16: Not a single Lisu came to service in the morning.

The walls of Jericho fell down "by faith" (not the faith of the walls, though!). Of all the instances of faith in Hebrews 11, this corresponds most nearly to my case, for it was not only faith that was necessary. The wall had to be compassed about for seven days. Seven days' *patience* was required, with the diligent march around the city every day, which seems to typify the need to encompass the situation by regular, systematic *prayer*. Here then we see God's way of success in our work, whatever it may be—a trinity of prayer, faith, and patience.

Tuesday, Jan. 18: Prayer today was rather on general than particular lines; patience the chief thought. Abraham was called out by God and went in blind faith. When he got to the land of promise he found nothing but a famine—much like me with the Lisu these two years. But Abraham—or his seed—possessed the milk and honey of the whole land, later on. God's time had come for Abraham, but not for the Amorites. God's time has come for me, but perhaps not, this month or this year, for the Lisu.

I am impressed, too, that I do not yet know the channels which the grace of God is going to cut out among the people here. Hence general prayer has its place, until God's plan is revealed a little more fully.

It appears that Fraser was assailed at times by the uprising of what he calls "fierce impatience" with a very trying helper, a man from whom he endured not a little rudeness and inefficiency. He was usually able to control any manifestation of annoyance, but the inward perturbation left him with a deep sense of defeat. He had not yet learned by experience the meaning of victory in Christ, which is so much more than outward self-control.

"How *can* thee be so calm and pleasant?" exclaimed a young Quaker girl, seeing the way an older lady responded to great annoyance.

"Ah, my dear," was the quick reply, "thee doesn't know how I boil inside!"

It was just that *boiling inside* from which Fraser sought deliverance—sought and found it in the blessed fact, "I live, yet no longer I, but Christ liveth in me." In the details of everyday life he increasingly found that the indwelling Christ was his successful weapon against all sin. "Claim more; claim victory," he quoted from a book by S. D. Gordon he was reading at the time. "I do not mean, ask God to give you the victory, but claim His victory to overshadow you.

When in the thick of the fight, when you are the object of attack, plead less and claim more on the ground of the blood of Jesus Christ." But the conflict was real, for the journal continues:

Tuesday, Feb. 1: Prayer in the afternoon for about three hours, but not enough grip or intelligent method—as if I have arrears in prayer to make up.

Thursday, Feb. 3: Depressed after defeat this morning, from which no real recovery all day (last day of the Chinese year).

Friday, Feb. 4: No meal until 2 P.M. Thoroughly depressed about the state of work in Tantsah. No one to count on in matters demanding an earnest spirit. The evil one seems to have the upper hand in me today, as well as in the Christians. Fighting between Gu and Ku in the evening, also between Ah-do and O-lo-si. Ku off to the dances. Several visitors during the day. A little prayer in much distress of soul, on top of hill. Feel much inclined to "let Ephraim alone." But just here I am torn between two alternatives—for I seem to have no leading to leave Tantsah, any more than the Lord had to leave Jerusalem (Luke 19:41). My prayer is not so much, "Lord, lead me somewhere else," as, "Lord, give me a solid church here in Tantsah."

Saturday, Feb. 5: Yesterday's attack of depression and defeat almost over, but not quite. Such times are not easy to recover from, I find. Enabled in large measure, however, to adopt the attitude of combined common sense and restful faith.

O-lo-si and his wife came in this evening. Had a

useful talk with them and also with Ku. Still much distressed, however, over the condition of things. The majority of the Christians have gone in for the whiskey-drinking which is customary at the New Year season. The outlook here in Tantsah at present seems less hopeful than at any time since I first set foot in the place.

I am not, however, taking the black, despondent view I took yesterday. The opposition will not be overcome by reasoning or by pleading, but chiefly by steady, persistent prayer. The *men* need not be dealt with—it is a heartbreaking job, trying to deal with a Lisu possessed by a spirit of fear—but the powers of darkness need to be fought. I am now setting my face like a flint. If the work seems to fail, then *pray*. If services fall flat, then *pray still more*. If months slip by with little or no result, then *pray still more and get others to help you.*

Sunday, Feb. 6: B—— and Va announce that they will become Christians if their parents will allow them to. Four young men say they will follow Christ whatever happens. I adopt an entirely new attitude with them, concealing my earnest desire for them beneath a calm, almost indifferent exterior. I now think that this is the best way after all. It will give them more confidence.

If you wish to make headway among the Lisu people you must let them take the initiative to a large extent, carefully avoiding the least suspicion of pressing or urging them to turn Christian. Such a thing as pressure or even earnest exhortation on the missionary's part tends to create fear and misgiving. They are, one and all, friendly to the missionary (many even warmly so), but they are excessively timid and, like very small children, have to be treated with extreme care. They are possessed with a spirit of fear—fear of demons, fear of the Chinese, fear of me because of what the Chinese tell them. Very many are afraid I am going to *compel* them to turn Christian, as well as compel them to do other things (such as pay taxes to me!), and nothing reassures them more than to insist they are free to become Christians or not, as they please.

Tuesday, Feb. 8: Mo-la-pa turned Christian this morning! Gu, Va, and T—— all at his house. I am full of joy and praise.

But there was fighting, drinking, and dancing that New Year season even in "Christian" households. The dancers came up to Fraser's courtyard one night and he awoke to find people in his room and revelry going on outside.

An evangelistic trip took him away for a time, and before long he was able to write:

Clouds seem to have lifted considerably—perhaps because the prayer burden was fought right through. After much pressure, even agony, in prayer for Lisu souls, I was enabled to break through into liberty, and to pray the definite prayer of faith for signal blessing among the Lisu during the next few months. . . . Real, prevailing prayer for the first time for a week or more, and well worth the travail that led up to it. . . . Much peace and rest of soul after making that definite prayer, and almost ecstatic joy to think of the Lisu Christian families I am going to get.

Perhaps you will wonder why I say *families*. It is only when the responsible members of any particular family turn to God that the household idolatrous implements may be removed. Until that is done the real commitment has not been made. A definite committal of some kind is of first importance among these people. If a man turns to God but shrinks from burning the bridge behind him by discarding his idolatrous utensils, he will as likely as not slip back again into his old life. But if he once removes all idolatry from his home, you may feel fairly certain of him afterward. It is seldom that a man who takes this step reverts to demon worship again. Strong as is the hold of demonolatry on the people, one such blow seems to break its power forever.

When these tribespeople turn to the Lord *en famille* it does not necessarily mean that every member of the family is wholehearted about the matter—indeed this is seldom the case—but it does mean that the responsible members of the family turn from Satan to God with a definiteness otherwise lacking. So when I speak about so many Christian "families," I mean families where those responsible have removed all vestige of demonolatry from the home. Much, of course, remains to be done after this, but you feel that you have, in a sense, already landed your fish when this step has been taken, and you thank God for the haul. In some cases a younger member of the family will turn Christian while the others hold back. He cannot by himself tamper with the household demonolatry. He may be quite sincere, and of course you receive him, but such converts are apt to be unstable. At present I have a total of about ten families, in five different villages, who have turned to God.

A few days later Fraser was writing in reference to one who was causing anxiety:

O-lo-si here in the evening. After he left, was enabled to strive for him in prayer, with the result that I now hear of his redecision to be a Christian. He must be held onto in faith, however. Much helped by Mrs. Penn-Lewis' bringing out the point, "*Say* to this mountain . . ." Was enabled to *say* this evening. Retired strong in spirit.

In his loneliness, as often before, Fraser was helped by articles in *The Overcomer*. Quotations made toward the end of March show the lines along which he was thinking.

March 20: Each time your spirit goes under and faints in the testing and trials which come to you, you lose mastery over the powers of darkness; that is, you get below them instead of abiding above them in God. Every time you take the earth standpoint—think as men think, talk as men talk, look as men look—you take a place below the powers of darkness. The mastery of them depends on your spirit's abiding in the place above them, and the place above them means knowing God's outlook, Gods' view, God's thought, God's plan, God's ways, by abiding with Christ in God.

You may be so entangled with the things of earth that your spirit cannot rise above them. The devil knows this and pours earthly things upon you to *keep you down,* so that you go under and not over when the battle comes.

Romans 8:11: You must know the quickening of the body to a very great extent if you are to be able to endure the conflicts of this present hour. Your natural strength would go under, so God quickens your mortal body to make you able to endure what no flesh and blood could endure, and live. One of the temptations in the spirit-warfare is to say, when the body begins to flag, "I must give up," instead of casting yourself upon God who raises the dead and can quicken the mortal body to endure and triumph in and through all things (Rom. 4:17; 8:11).

Ephesians 6:10: Oh how we need *strength,* for often we can hardly hold our ground!

In every battle there are crucial spots. Get near and stay near to your divine Chief until He turns and points them out. And at those points face and force the fight. And though the conflict be keen, though defeat seems certain, though the battle should continue for hours, for days, for months, even for years, yet *hold* on, HOLD ON; for to such Jeremiah 1:19 is written: "They shall fight against thee; but

182 *Behind the Ranges*

they shall not prevail against thee; for I am with thee, saith the LORD, to deliver thee."

The aim of satanic power is to cut off communication with God. To accomplish this he *deludes the soul with a sense of defeat,* covers him with a thick cloud of darkness, depresses and oppresses the spirit, which in turn hinders prayer and leads to unbelief— thus destroying all power.

Any position you have really taken with God's help *may be retaken at once by faith* after a temporary lapse.

It is one of the most subtle wiles of the foe to get us occupied with superficial and surface concerns, such as selling books, language study, running a mission station, writing reports, correspondence, accounts, building operations, repairs, making purchases, and reading. The enemy is delighted to have us so occupied incessantly with *secondary concerns,* as to keep us from attacking and resisting in the true spirit of the conflict. *Weigh these words!*

So true

Times of defeat are frequently noted in the journal and traced to their true cause. "I am needing more form and order, more diligence, definiteness, and dispatch in my prayer life," Fraser wrote at this time. Laziness in spiritual things he found to be one of his chief causes of failure, and he was startled to note how quick the enemy was to attack when he was off guard, and to gain ground not in himself only but also in others. One experience of this kind, which

The truth

caused him much distress of mind, is faithfully recorded in the journal.

It had been a day of failure and slackness of spirit. He had tried to pray as usual, but had been baffled by listlessness and wandering thoughts. "No grip," he wrote, "no power"; only a sense of sliding down and beating the air, the cause of which must be "mercilessly investigated." But efforts at recovery had only left him the more conscious of defeat. Matters came to a climax in the evening, as some of the inquirers came in for Bible reading and prayer. They were three of the most hopeful, his Tantsah inner circle, but that night they did not seem themselves. The experience that followed was so humiliating that we confine ourselves to Fraser's own notes, made at the time:

A very definite sense of spiritual weakness—aggravated, no doubt, by further defeat in the evening with Ku, Va, and O-lo-si. The latter seemed almost as if possessed by a laughing demon, so entirely foreign to his usual demeanor. Insane giggling during study, followed by a burst of laughter (the first I remember here from any Christian) as soon as I commenced to pray. Va follows him, more or less. I stopped praying and burst out at him in carnal anger, which quite failed, of course, from almost every point of view. But I felt quite incompetent to deal with it, unequal to the situation, master neither of myself nor of anyone else. I felt weak, lazy, and semipassive and had lost my grasp of things. O-lo-

si's unnatural flippancy seemed only a reflection of
my own condition. I almost felt as if a demon were
laughing at me through him because of my power-
lessness, defeat, and spiritual inertia.

I refused, however, to be discouraged, but got
down on my knees at once and got right with God.
I have had many such experiences of failure before,
but have made the mistake of giving way to depression instead of calmly investigating the cause of
things. This time, however, the thief was not going
to escape!

Formerly it used to take me a few *days* to recover
from such defeat. Then, when I began to know better, it took a few *hours*. But now I know even that
to be too long, and only allow a few minutes for complete recovery. The sooner the better, and there is
no time limit (I John 1:9).

Praise God!

The lessons learned from this experience were unexpectedly practical. Seeking the explanation of his
defeat, Fraser came to see that it was due to physical
as well as spiritual causes. He had confined himself
too much to his room—the only place in which he
could count on privacy—and had neglected exercise
and the mental balance of good hard study. Loneliness and the pressure of surrounding darkness had
driven him to his knees too exclusively. The laws
of nature are also the laws of God, and he had to
learn that ignorance or forgetfulness of either the
one or the other does not save us from the penalty
of breaking them. "I now think," he wrote quite

simply, "that a long healthy walk was indicated, or wholesome Lisu study, rather than the forced 'knee drill' I had practiced with such signal failure."

I will still continue to test before God this new-found explanation, but a practical rule I may well go by is this:

1. Do not imagine that success and blessing in the work are absolutely conditional on one's spending a few hours daily on one's knees with unfailing regularity. Cast-iron methods in spiritual matters are never free from objection. Let regularity be tempered by Spirit guidance, even in such matters. For example, one's mind or body may be genuinely tired and require a little relaxation. Also, one may have prayed through a thing a day or so previously, and now have simply to hold on in expectant faith. But it is more than probable, when there is no liberty in spirit, that a change is needed, or a spell of study, as I have found.

Wisdom!

2. Always remember, "I will pray with the spirit, and I will pray with the understanding also" (I Cor. 14:15). Let the spirit and the understanding work in about equal proportions. First, think over the needs, taking into account any consciousness of spirit burden. Pray tentatively along that line, asking God continually to *focus* your prayers. If, after covering such ground in prayer, no "grip" comes anywhere, it is probably best to close at once. Do not be in a hurry to do this, but don't press on in the energy of the flesh.

Yes, passivity—or, to call it by an uglier word,

laziness— is the cause of half my defeat. I need never be defeated, as I know quite well. Victory all the rest of the day. This bears out what I have been learning.

When you are weak and feel unable to free yourself from the power of sin, just up and sing a song or shout a determined note of defiance against the enemy, then roll up your sleeves and do some good Lisu study. Lack of this spirit brings defeat. Moral: *Try to find God's balance between work and prayer.*

* * *

Temptation again overcome by virile activity.

Oh, yes, we Christians need never be overcome. One weapon at least will always be found to work, if others fail. When we are defeated there is a cause. We should not pass it over as inexplicable. Cast about to find the cause, with the help of the Holy Spirit. Then put the thing away and avoid it in the future.

Spent most of the morning in prayer, very peacefully—drawn out especially for O-lo-si, or against the powers of darkness, rather, that hold him back. This prayer continued in power until, apparently, it was fought through. I spent the rest of the day in Lisu study, thoroughly wholesome. Friday's lesson is being burned still deeper into me. Yes, God teaches, all right!

* * *

Today I saw the biggest victory ever since I set foot in Tantsah. O-lo-si's demonolatry came down. Ku very helpful. Oh, to learn more about coopera-

tion with God in all things! This is coming home to
me now as never before.

Turning from these arresting experiences we leave
a spirit on its upward way.

> My soul thirsteth for thee . . .
> My soul shall be satisfied . . .
> My soul followeth hard after thee.
> —Psalm 63:1, 5, 8

Three stages of experience, successive yet ever
present—thirsting, satisfied, following hard after our
upholding God.

Chapter 14

THE LETTER NEVER WRITTEN

BEFORE LEAVING TANTSAH in the summer of 1916 to
visit a new district on the Burma border, Fraser came
to a costly decision. The lack of converts in any number weighed heavily on his heart. Whatever the reason, it seemed as if God's time had not yet come for
the answer to his prayer of faith. What should he do?
Was it right to stay on, waiting and praying, when
workers were urgently needed in other, more fruitful
fields? The outcome of much thought and prayer
was that he decided to write to the mission headquarters in Shanghai, cost what it might, and offer
to go elsewhere for a time if Mr. Hoste approved.
But first, this evangelistic journey must be made in
response to recent invitations—a journey which led
to unexpected developments.

In this district under the shadow of Tapu Pum,
however, even Fraser's powers of endurance gave
way. Coarse food and Lisu cooking did not usually
trouble him, but in the lofty region there was little
or nothing to eat, just then, but the poorest of red

188

rice, without even turnip or cabbage to help it down.
Fraser did his best, and so did the village folk who
welcomed him. As long as he could hold out, he responded to their eager interest—teaching, singing, explaining the Glad Tidings they had never heard before. But after a week or so, the coarse food simply
would not go down. His digestion went on strike.
Illness followed and, in a state of semistarvation,
Fraser had to make for Tengyueh as best he could.
There, in the care of Mr. and Mrs. Embery, he rallied
after a time and was at hand to meet a demand that
arose for help on the Chinese side of the work. A
visit had to be paid to the city of Paoshan. Having
been the pioneer in that district, Fraser was the one
to undertake it.

The four-day journey, once so formidable, was
more like a pleasure trip after the rigors of the Lisu
mountains. It was a joy to be preaching in Chinese
again and to see the influence of the young evangelist
in charge of the work.

> Chao is really a splendid fellow. He lacks in edu-
> cation and in scriptural knowledge, but has such an
> earnest spirit and the heart of a shepherd in looking
> after the converts. He has also a kind of shrewd
> wisdom in dealing with people. . . . I sometimes
> refer to you, in speaking of prayer for the work, and
> Chao and his wife wish to be remembered to you.

After some weeks spent with the inquirers, three
of these were baptized and a communion service held

for the first time in Paoshan. Before leaving the city, Fraser had the joy of seeing a Buddhist leader come out boldly for Christ, breaking her vegetarian vow. On the return journey a detour was made to revisit Moh Ting-chang, the baker at Hsiangta. What a joy it was to be in his home again and find him matured in spirit, though as enthusiastic as ever!

Moh is a remarkably earnest Christian. It is a treat to stay with him and see the way he witnesses for Christ down in the shop. He is the kind of man who takes the initiative in a bright, natural way . . . arguing with much ingenuity.

Just now I am writing at his table in a big upstairs room, littered with all sorts of things—for order and neatness are not among his virtues. There are three beds, just the usual planks laid across a couple of benches and covered with straw mattresses. On the floor stand big earthenware jars as high as your waist, piles of firewood, bales of cotton brought from Burma, supplies of dried fruit, and all kinds of odds and ends. Moh is watching me write and is asking all about you: "Is your mother a Christian too? What is her venerable age? And can she read, like Mrs. Embery?"

The persistent opposition of Moh's mother had been one of his biggest trials in leaving all to follow Christ. She was an opium smoker and lived with her older son, so that the younger son's change of faith did not materially affect her. However, she keenly felt the social disgrace he had brought upon her and all his ancestors. In vain he explained the message of redeeming love and all that it meant to have a living Saviour. No, he was bewitched and casting off the family!

"Take me up, then, and throw me into the river," was her bitter retort. "But no, you need not even do that—I will jump in myself!" And in such a mood she might indeed have done so.

With all his brightness, Moh deeply felt the alienation of his family, and Fraser's fellowship was so welcome that for a whole week he would not let him go. To his visitor, the hours spent in prayer together were no less helpful, in view of the uncertainty of his own immediate future. Out on the hillside, or in the barnlike room over the shop, they strengthened one another's faith.

> Leave God to order all thy ways,
>   And hope in Him whate'er betide;
> Thou'lt find Him in the evil days
>   Thy all-sufficient strength and guide:
> Who trusts in God's unchanging love
> Builds on the rock that naught can move.

Autumn tints were already glowing on the Teng-yueh ranges when Fraser set out again for his Lisu home. One more journey around the familiar district to see if everything was as barren as before, and then the letter must be written upon which he had decided at Tantsah. His heart was heavy, facing all

that it would mean to leave his well-loved work, even
for a time. He knew that he had prayed the prayer of
faith for his tribespeople. He knew the blessing so
definitely asked, and received, would be given. But
as of old, the promise was delayed in its fulfillment.
He must be willing for God's time as well as God's
way—"even God, who quickeneth the dead, and call-
eth those things which be not as though they were."
In his journal there is a brief entry for the Sunday
before he began this trial journey:

> October 8: Service in the morning. I spoke on the
> Holy Spirit. In the afternoon—defeat. Evening, after
> service, shouting victory in the gully outside the city.
> Never knew James 4:7 to work better: "Resist the
> devil, and he will flee from you."

It was in this spirit, then, that Fraser left Tengyueh
with two companions, a Lisu man and his son having
come from Tantsah to help him. Traveling westward
in the direction of Tapu Pum, they came the second
night to a village in which the missionary was well
known. Talking and singing with the usual crowd
around the log fire, he was careful to avoid any appearance of urgency in giving the message so near his
heart.

"I have taught you the truth," was now his attitude. "It is all here in the Book of God. It is for you
to decide what you will do about it."

Next morning he was preparing to take to the road
again, when his companions ran in excitedly.

"Teacher, wait a little!" they cried. "This family want to turn Christian, if we will help them."

Wondering, Fraser gathered them together and explained more fully what it meant to "turn to God from idols." He had learned that anything short of the complete destruction of all implements used in spirit worship did not count as making room for Christ in heart and home. That was the dividing line; once it was crossed, faith could take possession in a real way. So it was with thankfulness he found that his hosts had come to the point of really making the clearance that meant so much.

It was a good beginning but, in the days that followed, no fewer than seven families destroyed their demonolatry amid scenes of rejoicing. It seemed too good to be true.

"Oh, yes," Fraser was tempted to think, "just this place or two! But it may end here."

Traveling grew rougher as they neared the Burma border, and the Kachin huts at night were deplorable. But the joy of finding open hearts continued. Only the briefest journal entries remain to indicate what happened, but the writer well remembers Fraser's face and voice as he recalled the moving story years later. At Melting Pot, high in the western mountains, ten families destroyed all traces of demon worship, even pulling down the spirit shelf in the little shrine perched above them on the mountainside. Farther on, Fraser and his companions came in pouring rain to Cypress Hill, where their stay included the eighth anniversary of his landing in China. That was a week of wonders, for no fewer than fifteen families turned to the Lord, burning every vestige of demonolatry. And so it continued, though not without opposition from the great enemy.

"Teacher, come quickly!" was the call in one Kachin village when five neighbor families had turned from demon worship, with bonfires in home after home.

"Why, what is the matter?"

"The devil is raging—trying to destroy my son!"

This was only too true, as Fraser found when he followed the distressed father. The young man was so violently possessed that he could hardly be restrained from throwing himself into the fire. United prayer prevailed and, before long, the power of the name of Jesus brought deliverance.

In the midst of these experiences, Fraser wrote to his mother:

> Please excuse pencil again . . . under the circumstances in which I am now living. The one and only bench this Lisu family possesses is not quite six inches high. They never go in for chairs. No such luxury—and this family has no table either. They have no other furniture except the mud stove, and I sleep on slats two or three inches above the earth floor. All around me, or around the log fire, rather, are Lisu, Lisu, Lisu! The good woman of the house

is sitting next to me, wearing such a quantity of beads and ornaments as would give you a neckache. A couple of girls nearby are watching me write and half a dozen boys on mats around the fire are learning to read the Lisu catechism. They are all interested in my writing, but I tell them to get on with their books.

But I am not going into further detail about the "comforts" of this Lisu home, high up amid mountains and forest, because the most important thing is that my good host and hostess "turned Christian" this morning, removing all sorts of things used in their former demon worship—bits of stick, pieces of paper, and much other trumpery—burning the whole lot in their center-room fire. They turned quite wholeheartedly. They told me that they had long prayed to the spirits to give them a child, but without result, and asked if they might now pray to the true God for a son. I remembered the experiences of Sarah, Rebekah, Hannah, and Elisabeth, and recommended them to go ahead. But they insisted that I must pray for them too. My prayers, they were sure, would be more effectual than their own!

Two other families in the village "turned" at the same time. Altogether on my trip so far—less than two weeks—fifteen families in four different villages have burned up all their idolatrous stuff and turned to God. I go to each home and gather the family for a good long talk, explaining the step they are taking. Then we all stand and I pray with them, after which they go around chopping and tearing down

all sorts of things and piling them on the fire. . . .
They seem glad to make a clean sweep while they
are about it. The boys rather enjoy seeing things
smashed up (boy-nature, you know!) and help to
ferret out suspicious objects. When they have swept
the place clean—soot, cobwebs, and all—they take me
to the next house where people intend to "walk the
way of God," as they put it.

Early in November, Turtle Village was reached.
It was to become the center of Fraser's western district. Here twenty-four families were ready to declare themselves Christians. Thirteen of these destroyed their demonolatry in one day, and Fraser remained on for two weeks, teaching and encouraging
the converts. By that time calls from a new district
turned him southward, where, in the mountains
above the Burma Road, they found an even more remarkable response. When only Mottled Hill and ad-
jacent villages had been visited, Fraser could write
of forty-nine families out of fifty-nine, which had
broken down their demon altars and turned Christian.

Faced with such a situation, the lonely missionary
was in difficulty. The year was drawing to a close.
He had been itinerating already for more than two
months and was feeling the strain of constant teaching and preaching in crowded hovels, around smoky
fires, living on the poorest of food, and getting little
sleep at night. He loved the work and the people,

but badly needed a letup. And there was all the rest
of his wide field to care for—right up to Tantsah,
eight days' journey away. Scores of new believers
needed teaching, and the older centers must not be
neglected if Christian leaders were to be raised up.
What could he do? How could he respond to this
new opening? The joy of harvest is not without its
cares, and Fraser could only look up for divine guidance.

"Before they call I will answer, and while they are
yet speaking I will hear." The need called loudly.
With what thankfulness Fraser found the promise
then and there fulfilled, and in the very way he could
most have desired! For in an out-of-the-way village,
most unexpectedly, he ran up against no less a friend
than Ba Thaw himself, in Lisu dress, up from Burma,
visiting among his scattered flock. The joy and surprise of both may be imagined, and the thankfulness
with which Ba Thaw listened to the story Fraser had
to tell. Yes, Ba Thaw would come, if Mr. Geis approved, and stay among the converts Fraser was so
loath to leave. He would do his best to shepherd
them and spread the knowledge of the truth in
Christ.

It was a wonderful provision, for Ba Thaw remained for months in that southern district, following
up and deepening the work. But first of all, he accompanied Fraser to Tengyueh for Christmas, joy-
fully carrying the tidings of this movement among

the tribes for whom they had prayed and worked so long. Fully 600 people in 129 families were won to Christ—rich fruitage of the journey which might have ended so differently!

And the letter Fraser had dreaded to write was never written.

Thou on the Lord rely,
So safe shalt thou go on;
Fix on His work thy steadfast eye,
So shall thy work be done.

Far, far above thy thought
His counsel shall appear,
When fully He the work hath wrought
That caused thy needless fear!

Chapter 15

"I SENT YOU TO REAP"

Just back from my Lisu trenches," wrote Fraser from Tengyueh that Christmas.

> I have been trying the last few nights to make up arrears of sleep. While at Husa (southern district) I think I did not get to bed before 2 A.M. for ten nights in succession.
>
> We are now enjoying our usual winter weather— clear skies, dry roads, and brown withering grass everywhere. This is *the* time for itinerating, so I am due for the road again, after a needed rest behind the firing line. I must revisit all these new centers with as little delay as possible.

But a higher Wisdom planned otherwise. After a few weeks in his northern district, Fraser was laid low with appendicitis. He had gone as far as Tantsah, where he had the joy of seeing people definitely turning to the Lord, and also at Cold Horse, the village of the Sword-ladder Festival. Happily he was back in Tengyueh when the attack came on. The Indian doctor at the consulate pressed the need for an operation. This, together with letters from Mr. Hoste

urging a visit to the coast, influenced Fraser to undertake the journey. It would mean a long absence just
when it seemed that he could least be spared. But a
second attack after he set out and a night of agony
alone in a Chinese inn made it sufficiently plain that
the operation was necessary. This was successfully
performed at the headquarters of the mission in
Shanghai, and the quiet days that followed brought
welcome opportunity for rest and prayer.

If I were to think after the manner of men I would
be anxious about my Lisu converts—afraid of their
falling back into demon worship. But God is ena-
bling me to cast all my care upon Him. I am not
anxious, not nervous. If I hugged my care to myself
instead of casting it upon Him, I would never have
persevered with the work this long—perhaps never
even have started it. But if it has been begun in
Him, it must be continued in Him. Let us all who
have these Tengyueh Lisu on our hearts commit
them quietly into His hands by faith. "He will perfect that which concerneth" us—and these Lisu converts too. And then let us give thanks for His grace
to us and to them.

When God sends His servants to reap, such a time
of special waiting upon Him is all to the good, even
if it seems to intrude upon the urgency of the task.

The days that followed were worthwhile and revealing for the convalescent as he came in touch with
the staff at headquarters and with fellow workers

from many parts of the field. The mission at that time numbered about a thousand members, stationed in fifteen provinces, and there was much coming and going in the home on Woosung Road—place of arrival for new parties and base of supply for the interior. Here Fraser met with many he had known only by name before, and in turn became the object of much interest. When he could be persuaded to talk about his experiences, or pour out his rich stores of music in informal social hours, impressions were made that resulted in helpful friendships through many years. Especially was this true in his personal touch with Mr. Hoste, whose practice of giving hours daily to prayer for all aspects of the work greatly appealed to Fraser. Both then and afterward it was among the most cherished privileges of his life to join in those intercessions and to learn, through hours at a time spent on their knees, what actual praying means in the life of one bearing great responsibilities. Mr. Hoste's favorable impressions of the young pioneer had much to do with the unexpected developments in Fraser's later service.

However, Fraser was unconscious of all this. He only rejoiced in renewed vigor, a strengthened prayer backing, and the companionship of a prospective fellow worker as he returned to Yunnan. To his prayer circle he wrote from Shanghai commending this young American to their interest:

I have just met Mr. Flagg, who is to be my colleague at Tengyueh. His home is in Boston, U. S. A.
He is a graduate of Harvard University and Moody
Bible Institute. He is twenty-seven years of age,
physically strong, and keen to get to work. He has
been engaged in city missions and street preaching
in New York, Boston, and other places, and is wholeheartedly for evangelistic work. I expect to see him
develop into a fine worker, and am sure we shall pull
well together.

The long journey to West China, by sea and over-
land, provided Flagg with varied opportunities of
coming to know his senior missionary. He found
Fraser to be as human, natural, and resourceful as he
was spiritual—essentially a man among men. Crossing the uplands of Yunnan they visited the tribal districts, north of the capital, to which Fraser had first
of all been designated. Hundreds of Meo and Lisu
Christians welcomed them. After inspiring days with
the Gowmans and Mr. Porteous, then in charge of
the work, they struck out cross-country for the west
of the province. Unaccustomed to horseback riding
for days and weeks together, Flagg could only wonder at Fraser's easy handling of the rough mountain
ponies on dangerous tracks.

Up hill and down dale, you never tire of it in beautiful Yunnan. I do all my traveling now on horseback, and have become so used to it that I do not
care where I ride, so long as the horse will take it.

In many places the road is literally as steep as your staircase and broken as well. Flagg declares I could ride down the steps of the Washington Monument! Only today my pony actually turned a somersault. It was in a place where the path runs between banks only a foot or so apart, and he had hardly room to walk. With unusual thoughtfulness he gave me notice by falling right forward with his head on the ground. I got off over his head, and he plunged and kicked around until somehow he was lying on his back with his head where his tail had been. His neck was twisted in such a strange way that I wondered whether he was going to get up at all. But he *did* and, after more kicking and struggling, began to eat grass as if nothing had happened. (Have you ever noticed how nonchalant horses can be?) Neither he, nor I, nor the Chinese saddle were any the worse, so I put on my right sandal, which had dropped off, got on the animal, and went on reading my Chinese newspaper as before.

All along the way, Fraser was at his one absorbing task. Whether in Chinese inns at night, or with fellow travelers by day, he lost no opportunity of making known the Glad Tidings. He enjoyed preaching in Chinese, especially to the Christians where any were to be found, and was conscious of added power in his testimony. Of this he wrote to his prayer circle on reaching Tengyueh:

If I am sure of anything, it is that your prayers have made a very real difference in my life and service. Preaching in many places along the way, I experienced power and blessing unknown in former years. My chief request is always for prayer for the Lisu, but much blessing and help have come to my own life as well.

Fraser's growth along with that of his work was indeed the story of the next few years. Outwardly it was a time of much pressure—traveling almost incessantly, caring for hundreds of new believers. Inwardly there had to be a constant regirding with the whole armor of God to stand against the wiles of the devil and be ready always for advance as the Lord might lead.

As far as I know my Lisu work was undertaken at His bidding, which gives me confidence in asking your continued prayers. All our work needs to be (1) in accordance with scriptural principles, (2) in agreement with the inward witness of the Spirit, and (3) in harmony with the providential working of God in our circumstances. Thus we shall have assurance within ourselves of His guidance, and shall find doors opening before us without our having to force them. Inward and outward guidance will fit like lock and key, and we shall be saved from rendering service which, to Him as for us, would be second best.

And so the young pioneer came again to all the joys and conflicts of the work he loved. Another winter was drawing near. After more than seven months'

absence he was eager to see for himself how prayer
had been answered, especially for the converts in his
southern district he had found so hard to leave.
Down the familiar Burma Road he traveled, following the river from Tengyueh to Bhamo, until the
plain was reached where the mountains stand back
to the east, full of Kachin as well as Lisu villages.
There he had left Ba Thaw, the friend so providen-
tially met almost a year previously, and from whom
he had not heard in the interval. Ba Thaw had already returned to his post in Burma, but as Fraser
climbed to Mottled Hill and revisited place after
place so much upon his heart, he found the young
Karen pastor warmly remembered and his work in
evidence.

The people here so took to Ba Thaw and he to
them that he remained more than four months
among them. The result is that not only have the
converts been greatly helped and strengthened, but
others have been won. So I have come back to find
fifty-one families in this district, instead of forty-
nine, all standing firm as far as demon worship is
concerned, and thirty-six additional families of Lisu
converts in places I had not previously visited.

This young Karen is quite an exceptional man. He
dresses like the Lisu, lives among them as one of
themselves, and wherever he goes is greatly loved.
He is a better speaker of Lisu than I am, and is more
capable in the shepherding of young converts. He is

thoroughly spiritual, and I have no better friend among the Christians, tribal or Chinese, than he.

Following up Ba Thaw's work, Fraser now gave himself to getting into touch with the Christians throughout that part of his field. And most interesting work it was, though attended by hardships which even he found severe. Living in the same mountain shanties that had entertained Ba Thaw, he too wore Lisu dress and made himself one with his hosts. From Mottled Hill, high above the Burma Road, he went around to all the neighboring hamlets, down to larger villages and markets in the plains, going southward, ever southward, to the Burma border and beyond. This lone journey kept him on the road for more than two months.

At Mottled Hill the first place of worship was being built to the true and living God—the first in the whole of western Yunnan to be put up by the Christians themselves at their own expense. It may have been Ba Thaw's influence that encouraged them to take this step so soon after discarding their demon worship. They were freely giving land, labor, and materials so that their chapel would be larger and better than any of their own dwellings. The roof, of course, was of thatch, the walls of bamboo matting, and the floor of earth trodden hard, to be covered with rushes to seat the congregation. For lighting, as winter was drawing in, resinous pine chips were

provided, and a big flat stone on the platform on
which to burn them. It was all beautiful and seemly
from their point of view, and the opening ceremony,
as Fraser described it, was a full-dress occasion. From
hamlets far and near the Christians came—over a
hundred crowding into the clean, newly finished
chapel, while interested onlookers stood outside.

It was not easy to get these new converts to understand regular and reverent worship. In fact, their apprehension of Christian truth was most elementary.
They only knew that they had turned to God from
demon worship, and that Jesus was the Saviour they
now trusted. The prayer most often used by begin-
ners at this time was:

> God, our Father,
>   Creator of heaven and earth,
>   Creator of mankind,
> We are Your children,
>   We are followers of Jesus.
> Watch over us this day;
>   Don't let the evil spirits see us.
> Trusting in Jesus,
>
> Amen.

The idea is that if the demons catch sight of anyone, they attack him; hence the continual effort to
outwit the evil spirits and evade them. Singing was
from the first a great attraction, though, as Fraser
wrote to his mother, "If you were listening outside,
you might think some kind of comic drama was going

on. It does not take much to amuse the Lisu—such a merry, jolly kind of folk."

Singing lessons were always looked forward to, and Fraser took no end of pains to train the younger people especially. He tells of one occasion when in a room full of people he was going over a new hymn with some young men and boys with musical voices. Girls, gay in feminine attire, were grouped behind him, to some of whom he turned, inviting them also to learn the tune he was teaching. This led to a bashful withdrawal, so precipitate that one of those addressed tripped over a doorsill and fell backward into an inner room—tinkling chains, ornaments, bangles, and all—nothing left to be seen of her but two bare feet over the wooden sill. This, of course, increased the giggling and general merriment. "Such is singing instruction among the Lisu!" Fraser concluded.

But the hymns impressed their spiritual lessons. "Jesus loves me, this I know" was usually the favorite, followed by one of Ba Thaw's translation: "I've wandered far away from God," with its frequent refrain, "Now I'm coming home." Already two Christian lyrics of many stanzas were taking shape, one outlining the Old Testament and the other, New Testament history. These conveyed scriptural truth in simple rhyme, easy to learn and remember.

Sometimes Fraser was startled to find how unawakened was the consciousness of right and wrong among these new believers. The government had

begun its nationwide campaign against the growing
and using of opium, both common in tribal districts.
Quite openly, the Christians of Mottled Hill told how
they had resisted this interference with their liberty:
They heard troops were coming into the mountains
to pull up and destroy the ripening crops. The Kachin, especially, took up arms to fight the troops. After preparing their knives and poisoned arrows, they
held a prayer meeting to ask the help of God. And
prayer had been wonderfully answered, they naively
assured their missionary, because the soldiers never
came, and they had been able to make more money
than usual out of their opium crops!

Happily Fraser understood his mountain children,
and had behind him not a few praying friends to
share the long patience and soul exercise that spiritual parentage involves.

Fraser wrote his prayer circle:

They know my position and I am telling them
plainly that I cannot baptize anyone directly connected with the growing, use, or sale of opium. Still
we must have broad enough sympathies to recognize
genuine *faith*, even when it is accompanied by an almost untutored conscience.

There is such a thing as exercising faith for *others*.
God may be calling us to stand with and for them in
spirit. He is able to quicken into life the very fee-
blest spark of desire for Him, or to use for their
blessing the smallest amount of truth they may have
apprehended. Indeed I have seen this before among

the Lisu. They may know next to nothing; yet if in any measure the grace of God is in them, they remember the little they do know and it seems to sustain them.

Let us all be imbued with the spirit of Paul, who, though he had never seen the Roman converts, truly longed after them that he might impart unto them some spiritual gift. Far from absolving himself from responsibility, he called himself a debtor both to Greeks and barbarians, to the wise and to the foolish.

Outwardly Fraser's work at this time was making progress. The cost, however, went far deeper than daily hardship and every kind of discomfort. Almost desperate at times from lack of privacy in crowded hovels, he would go out on the mountainside alone to fight inward battles with the powers of darkness, in order that captives of sin might be delivered.

The opening of that first chapel was a time of great rejoicing, but one of these times of testing quickly followed. Fraser spent Christmas Day at a village near the Burma border, where the heads of thirteen families met to discuss whether or not they should turn Christian. To his great disappointment, the decision was against it, influenced chiefly by two old men of whom he had hoped better things. How he had prayed for them, and now his discouragement was correspondingly deep. He simply had to be alone to wait upon God. So that afternoon he went

over to Kama, a neighboring hamlet, where he secured a little empty room for the time being. And
there the Lord met him.

It was through the record of Jehoshaphat's experience with the Moabites that renewal of faith came
to him: "The battle is not yours, but God's. . . . Ye
shall not need to fight in this battle: set yourselves,
stand ye still, and see the salvation of the Lord with
you . . . fear not, nor be dismayed; tomorrow go
out against them: for the Lord will be with you"
(II Chron. 20:15-17).

Challenged in this way, the missionary gave himself to prayer, alone in that little room. His journal
records that about midnight he was enabled to commit the whole situation to God:

> Seem distinctly led to fight against principalities
> and powers for Middle Village. Have faith for the
> conversion of that place, and pray as a kind of bugle
> call for the hosts of heaven to come down and fight
> for me against the powers of darkness holding two
> old men who are hindering their villages and per-
> haps three others from turning to Christ. Had a good
> fight of prayer, then slept in much peace of mind.

Early next morning Fraser was in the home of old
La-ma-po, who lived at Kama, and in a long friendly
talk persuaded him to a better mind. Together they
went over to Middle Village, where the leaders were
much more responsive. A wonderful day followed,
for eleven out of the thirteen previously undecided

families turned to the Lord. "Victory, just as expected—hardly striking a blow!" Fraser noted with
thankfulness. Next day was even more encouraging,
for at Kama and another village twelve more families
were brought in.

But deeper lessons had to be learned. Not so easily
is the great enemy displaced. His counterattack was
swift. At a place called Haitao the day ended in defeat. Late that night Fraser went to his knees again,
alone on the mountainside near Kama. There he
prayed as before, even claiming Haitao for Christ as
he had Middle Village. The result was painfully different.

Going over to Haitao early the next day, he took
old La-ma-po with him. Perhaps that was the mistake, or it may be he was too confident, as he came to
feel later. Bitter disappointment awaited him. Not
only was the attitude of the village coldly antagonis-
tic but old La-ma-po showed his true colors by turning utterly against both the missionary and his message. The defeat was complete, and at first Fraser
could not understand it. Deeply distressed in spirit,
he went back to the little room at Kama, and there
again the Lord met him.

> I find considerable peace in leaving the whole mat-
> ter in God's hands. But the rebuff of spirit has been
> very severe, and I shall walk more humbly before
> the Lord after this.

But the end was not yet. "Weeping may endure for a night, but joy cometh in the morning." Meeting some bright, steadfast Christians from Mottled Hill a day or two later, Fraser thanked God and took courage. Within the following week, twenty new families turned to the Lord, and he was more than busy teaching the rejoicing converts. In all, during that Christmas and New Year season (December 1, 1917 to January 10, 1918) no fewer than fifty-six families made open confession of Christ south of Mottled Hill, where that first little chapel had been built.

Chapter 16

LOVE AND PATIENCE

ON CHRISTMAS DAY a year later the first believers' festival brought together village leaders from all over Fraser's wide field. His bachelor hospitality was taxed to the utmost when they came trooping into the house at Tengyueh, from Tantsah on the north to the Burma border on the west and south.

Much of the year had been spent itinerating, for to evangelism was now added the pastoral care of more than two hundred families. These were scattered in remote hamlets hidden among the mountains, or in nearer Chinese market towns. Traveling on horseback where he could, Fraser had plenty of rough riding and weary climbing. But nothing daunted him.

I have been out just over a fortnight and am in Water Bowl Village, where there are fifteen Christian families. I expect to be out two months longer. In Lisu country, I seldom need to travel more than fifteen miles a day, since the villages are within a few miles of each other. The roads are steep: a day's journey will sometimes require a descent of three thousand feet to the plain, then a similar ascent up the other side. Cross-country roads can be just as precarious—you have to ford streams, jump from rock to rock, and venture over crazy bridges. Sometimes you cannot even see the road ahead. A horse is no use in this kind of country.

Yet he could add, "I enjoy few things more than tramping over these hills, and always like traveling days better than stopover ones." Some of the stopovers were full of interest, however, as a February letter to his mother tells in unusual detail. It was a wedding that detained him, nothing less than the first Christian wedding in his southern district. After accompanying the wailing bride with her relatives to the bridegroom's house, Fraser was pressed to act as master of ceremonies. This brought up the question of whiskey drinking. Fraser had to insist that there be no drinking, for the Chinese saying was all too true: "For a Lisu to see whiskey is like a leech scenting blood."

As a matter of fact most of these new converts waver on the whiskey question when it comes to weddings and funerals. They had brewed one big jar of whiskey (ten times that much would have been normal) and had hidden it in a neighbor's yard. I got wind of it through one of the young men who searched the village for any of the abominable stuff still remaining in their houses. (The younger people of both sexes will as a rule heartily support me in my temperance crusade. They are the Radicals, the old people the Conservatives!) I got them to mix a lot of pig food with the contents of the jar, to make it undrinkable.

At another village they told me of a big jar of whiskey in a household which was preparing for a betrothal feast. They badly wanted me to stay for the occasion, but I threatened to go away at once unless they consented to destroy the stuff. Finally the owner agreed and gave me the pig food to mix with it. Their whiskey is not liquid but a mash of fermenting rice—the liquid drawn off through a tube at the bottom of the barrel. I do not now destroy the mash, as it is a pity to waste what is really good fattening food for pigs. Neither do I tip it out on the ground, as pigs are worse drunkards even than the Lisu, and will drink themselves to death if you let them. I get the people to mix bran with the mash, then they can feed it to the pigs as needed, but would not touch it themselves. A novel form of temperance crusade!

But to return to the wedding. The only ceremony Fraser introduced was public prayer when the bride arrived, before she entered her new home. There was too much noise and excitement for anything more, except the inevitable handshaking. Still standing outside the house, all the company shook hands first with the bridegroom, then with the bride, half hidden from view.

The bridegroom came along and offered a big hand with a big smile on his good-natured face. No doubt the bride looked charming, but Lisu custom permits her and the two bridesmaids to satisfy their bashful instincts by covering their heads and shoulders with a large felt rug! She was told, however, to give me her hand. So a feminine hand appeared from under the rug, and I shook it heartily. Then a way was cleared through the crowd, and the big felt rug moved slowly into the house, with the three girls under it. Once inside, they made their way to the inner room and disappeared from the public gaze, not that there had been much to gaze at before—she was so, so bashful, you know!

But even before the bride reached the house, a strange excitement broke out. Everybody started pelting everybody else with carrots, potatoes, and other root vegetables—a kind of snowball fight with vegetables instead of snow! Fraser was taken by surprise and did not know what to make of it.

They told me all about it afterward and I had to veto it for a Christian wedding.

"These roots are hard and might hurt," I protested.

"Oh yes, they do hurt, if they hit you," was the reply.

"And you throw them so hard!"

"It is great fun," the young folks said, "but we don't keep it up for long."

"But surely you don't pelt the bride?"

"Oh, yes," they laughed, "it only makes her run into the house all the quicker!"

Reluctant though he was to interfere with established customs, Fraser realized that this one must be abandoned when he discovered that it had its origin in demon worship.

> The idea was, originally, to drive away the evil spirits and to make the union propitious—though they do not seem to think so much of that now, as much as the sport of the thing. When I told them (perhaps unwisely) of our custom of throwing rice or confetti after the bridal pair, they at once jumped to the conclusion that it must have been, originally, for the same purpose!

Of one thing Fraser was increasingly conscious on these itinerations, and that was the need for a deeper work of grace among the Christians themselves. Because they had so little hold on spiritual truth they were easily upset by rumors. One such rumor circulated at this time was that Fraser was an agent of the British government, and that everyone of military age who joined the Christians would be conscripted and sent to fight in the European war. Not a few who had given up demon worship went back to it for protection from this supposed danger.

What was to be done? With over two hundred families to care for in widely scattered hamlets, his own visits were necessarily few and far between. If only the people could be taught to read and be provided with suitable literature, a new understanding might be awakened, which would lead to better things. So far they were quite indifferent to anything beyond the first elements of Christian truth. If believing in the Lord Jesus meant protection from evil spirits and deliverance from the punishment of sin in the life to come, what need of anything more? It was hard to get them to observe Sunday or to see the need of regular meetings. Of these conditions Fraser kept his prayer circle fully informed, making no attempt to disguise the facts or the concern they caused him.

I am not painting a dark picture. I only wish to tell you the real position of things as candidly as possible. In some ways the Lisu converts are ahead of ordinary churchgoers at home. They are always hospitable. They are genuinely pleased to see me when I go to their villages. They are sincere as far as they go; we see very little among them of the ulterior motives commonly credited to "rice Christians." They will carry my load for me from village to village without pay, and give me hospitality. But with the exception of a few, very few, bright, earnest young people, there are not many who wish to make any progress or are really *alive* spiritually. Most of them cannot be tempted away from their warm fires in the evenings (these villages in the mountains are very cold in the winter) to come together and learn a little more, even though I am in a nearby house which also has a fire!

In time past I have often given way to depression, which always means spiritual paralysis, and even on this last trip have been much downcast, I admit, over the state of the people. When at a village near Mottled Hill, a month or more ago, I was much troubled over all this, but was brought back to peace of heart by remembering that, though the work is bound to be slow, it may be nonetheless sure for all that. My mistake has too often been that of too much haste. But it is not the people's way to hurry, nor is it God's way either. Hurry means worry, and worry effectually drives the peace of God from the heart.

Rome was not built in a day, nor will the work of building up a strong, well-instructed body of Lisu Christians, in the Tengyueh district, be the work of a day either. Schools will have to be started when the time is ripe. There will be need of much visitation, much exhortation, much prayer. It will not be done all at once. The remembrance of this has cast me back upon God again. I have set my heart upon a work of grace among the Tengyueh Lisu, but God has brought me to the point of being willing for it to be in His *time* as well as in His *way*.

I am even willing (if it should be His will) not to see the fullness of blessing in my lifetime.

One of the older workers of the mission—one of the most helpful—said to newcomers, "The Lord direct your hearts into the love of God, and into the patience of Christ" (II Thess. 3:5, A.S.V.). Now that will do for China! If you have the love of God and the patience of Jesus Christ, that will do for China. But the letters we are quoting were written by a

Patience in God's work
① in you 4/30/79
② in others

Love and Patience   221

young man, strong and eager, learning lessons in the
school of hardship and loneliness. A thinker, a student of the ways of God with man, he was arrested
by the patience as well as the power of infinite Wisdom and Love. "The God of all patience" was making Himself known to this ardent soul as the One
who "worketh for him that waiteth for him."

Preparation, delay, and growth are characteristic
of God's working both in history and in nature. Scripture and the facts of nature meet when James, exhorting us to patience, says: "The husbandman waiteth for the precious fruit of the earth, being *patient*
over it" [5:7, A.S.V.]. The same principle applies
to our own spiritual lives, and to our labor in the
Lord. A mature Christian is not the product of a day
or a month or a year. "It takes time," said the late
Dr. Andrew Murray, "to grow into Christ." We must
strike our roots down deep in the soil of the Word
and be strengthened by long, long experience. It is
a slow process, and it is right that it should be so:
God does not want us to be spiritual mushrooms. It
is true that in the Lord's work there is a place for
haste—the King's business requires it (there is a right
and a wrong haste). And there is assuredly a place
for diligence, for earnestness. James Gilmour said
he did not think we could be too earnest in a matter
for which Christ was so much in earnest that He laid
down His life. You know it was said of Alleine that
he was insatiably greedy for souls. While it is day
we *cannot* but be up and doing to the limit of the

balance of work and trust (rest)

1979
- 91

1888   1886

strength which God supplies. But the element of corroding care will enter into Christian work if we let it, and it will not help but hinder. We cannot press souls into the kingdom of Heaven; neither, when they are once converted, can we worry them into maturity; we cannot by taking thought add a cubit to our own spiritual stature or to anyone else's. The plants of our heavenly Father's planting will grow better under His open sky than in the hot-houses of our feverish effort. It is for us to water, and to water diligently, but we cannot give the increase, however hard we try. An abnormally rapid growth is often unnatural and unhealthy: the quick growth spoken of in Matthew 13:5 is actually said to be a sign of its being ephemeral.

In the biography of our Lord nothing is more noticeable than the quiet, even poise of His life. Never flustered whatever happened, never taken off guard however assailed by men or demons—in the midst of fickle people, hostile rulers, faithless disciples, He was always calm, always collected. Christ the hard Worker indeed—but doing no more and no less than God had appointed Him, and with no restlessness, no hurry, no worry. Was ever such a peaceful life lived under conditions so perturbing?

But we also, as He, are working *for* eternity and *in* eternity (eternity has already commenced for us). We can afford, then, to work in the atmosphere of eternity. The rush and the bustle of carnal activity breathe a spirit of restlessness. The Holy Spirit breathes a deep calm. *This* is the atmosphere in which we may expect a lasting work of God to grow.

Let us take care first of all that it *is* a work of God—
begun and continued in God—and then let us cast
our anxieties, our fears, and our impatience to the
winds. Let us shake off "dull sloth" on the one hand
and feverishness on the other. A gourd may spring
up in a night, but not an oak. The current may be
flowing deep and strong in spite of ripples and coun-
tercurrents on the surface. And even when it receives
a temporary setback from the incoming tide of evil,
we may yet learn to say, as Jeremiah once said under
the most distressing circumstances, "It is good that
a man should both hope and *quietly wait* for the salvation of the Lord."

The immediate task before Fraser that summer
was the completion of his translation of one of the
Gospels, that the Lisu converts might have some portion of the Word of God in their own language. He
had already made a beginning. Now, as the busy
farming season had almost put a stop to teaching
in the villages, he went down to Myitkyina to avail
himself of Ba Thaw's efficient collaboration.

He arrived in time for a happy occasion. Ba Thaw
was about to be married to a sweet little Christian
Karen girl. Received with hospitality by the American missionaries (and later by the Ba Thaws in their
own home), Fraser worked on month after month,
through the great heat, to finish not only Mark's Gospel but also a simple dictionary, a primer, and an enlarged catechism with a number of new hymns. He

was eager that the Lisu church should be a reading church, lovers of the Book, founded upon its teachings and able to impart them to others. With the co-operation of the American missionaries, who were working with Lisu on the Burma side of the border, he also perfected his script for the language, reducing it to the simplest form of writing, so that his manuscripts were ready for printing when he returned to Yunnan.

Rich with the spoils of summer, and refreshed by contact with fellow workers, Fraser set out for the highlands of Yunnan. Once before he had climbed that mountainous borderland to meet bitter disappointment at Tantsah, and even now he could not help being concerned about the state of things he might find among his large and scattered flock. Coming first to his western district, Fraser found himself at Turtle Village for the weekend, and the welcome with which he was received set his heart at rest.

When I left Turtle Village last there were fourteen families of Christians; now there are twenty-one. When I left Water Bowl there were twelve families; now there are nineteen. When I left Redwood Spur there were nine; now there are twenty. And this in spite of the fact that they have had practically no help of any kind for months. I hear that Melting Pot and Cypress Hill are the same as when I left them. They tell me that in the former village they have built a chapel, where they hold regular Sunday services.

In Turtle Village one of the elders of the place, a good old man, was seriously ill for many weeks. But he and all of them held on in faith and prayer, and he pulled through. These people are great believers in divine healing, and such an experience strengthens their faith considerably. Altogether I think they have increased in strength as well as in numbers since I was last here.

Their faith had been unexpectedly tested during Fraser's visit, but perhaps it was a needed lesson that prayer is not always answered in just the way we would have it. Fraser was glad that the loss was his, not theirs.

The Sunday I was at Turtle Village my horse fell. As soon as it was seen to be ill, the people came and asked me to come out and pray, for that is the first thing they think of in such cases. (Did I tell you of a group of dear little Christian Lisu girls I saw standing in front of their pigsty at Cup Village, last March, with hands over their eyes, *praying for the newborn litter of pigs?*) I confess I hesitated at first, not being used to that way of doing things. But the people seemed surprised at my attitude.

"Aren't you going to pray for your horse?" they questioned.

So I went with them. We stood around the animal as I placed it in God's hands for life or death. I was glad I had done so, though it died the next morning.

Before leaving Turtle Village, Fraser had the joy

of baptizing twenty-five, mostly young people, of whose faith in Christ there could be no question. To him as well as to the Christians it was a day of great rejoicing. Here is the picture:

> Each one promised solemnly not only to trust in the Lord Jesus for his whole lifetime but to abstain from any connection with heathen worship, whiskey drinking, immorality, opium smoking or cultivation, and to observe the Lord's day. I enjoyed the occasion immensely. We went down to their village stream that summer morning, the men and the women grouping themselves separately on the bank, as I commended them all to God in prayer, under His open sky. I then immersed them, one by one, in the swiftly running water, just below a big plank bridge. Will you pray that they may be kept true to their promises?

That first Christmas festival, when it came, was a step beyond all previous experience. Often Fraser had been the guest of Lisu hosts. But now, fifteen or more were to receive his hospitality at one and the same time! In lives that had so little contact with the world beyond their scattered hamlets, it was a great occasion. To them Tengyueh, with its city wall and gates, was a metropolis indeed, and a simple mission house a place of marvels. The men were housed on the premises, the women nearby at Mrs. Li's home —and how they enjoyed it!

Christmas Day was the climax, with a united service in the morning (Chinese as well as Lisu), games in the afternoon, when Flagg and Fraser appeared in a new light, followed by the crowning feast with more than eighty guests!

You would have been interested to see them when they first arrived. Very few had even been in the city before. When they came to our house (we let them roam all over it), the girls, going round in a bunch from room to room, kept up an involuntary murmur of admiration and delight. It was like Heaven to them! The men took things more calmly. Men with their big swords, gay satchels, leggings, and bare feet; girls with colored turbans, tassels, beads, necklaces, rings, bangles, and other ornaments —I wish you could have seen them!

Each day after morning prayers I had them all in our chapel, teaching them to read the script. In the evenings I led them in singing. Besides "Jesus Loves Me" and "I've wandered far away from God," which they knew already, I taught them "God be with you till we meet again" and one or two other hymns. They sang so well that Chinese people from the street came in to sit and listen.

One day our new consul came to call on us with the retiring consul, Mr. Eastes. The Lisu all crowded around them in the sitting room and outside, making all sorts of remarks and even feeling their clothing! We explained to the consuls that they must not mind, because our Lisu guests had little idea of Occidental proprieties.

"I should say not," replied Eastes, taking it all in good humor. "There is a fellow behind me stroking my back right now!"

Chapter 17

BLOOD OF HIS OWN

IN THE MIDST of his itinerations during 1918, Fraser had come to a spiritual experience which cannot be passed over. Back in Tengyueh that summer he was laid up with a badly infected foot. This gave opportunity for quiet and reflection, glimpses of which appear in his journal.

No one with any experience of the conditions under which he was working will wonder that in the crowding, clamor, and discomfort of Lisu homes, Fraser found it difficult to maintain the standard of spiritual life which alone could satisfy him. Perhaps the wonder was, rather, that he could not content himself with a lower level, or take refuge in excuses. To be alone for prayer he had to go out on the mountains or wake up at night when all around him were asleep. After long days of traveling, preaching, or teaching, he was weary and apt to sleep on until the household was stirring. Mist and rain at chilly heights often kept him indoors, with no chance of quiet for waiting upon God. This made it only too easy to lose the sense (though not the fact) of the divine Presence, and drift into a state of spiritual weakness and defeat. How was the situation to be met?

He had been thinking much of a saying of Stuart Holden: "I do not believe that any man is made victor except by blood of his own"—words easily misunderstood, yet how deep their meaning. What Hudson Taylor called "an easygoing, non-self-denying life" will never be one of power. When Paul wrote, "I can do all things through Christ which strengtheneth me," he disclosed the blessed partnership which alone secures spiritual victory.

> So often I have been unwilling to shed my own blood (so to speak) and have trusted with an armchair faith which has failed, as it always must. The whole cause of my defeat these two days is weakness of spirit. Under these conditions, any text you take fails to work. The spirit must be continually, constantly maintained in strength by unceasing prayer, especially against the powers of darkness. All I have learned of the other aspects of the victory life is useless without this.

It was drifting that Fraser dreaded most of all—slackness in spirit, sloth, prayerlessness, leading to defeat under trial. He well knew the meaning of the Master's word, "Men ought always to pray, and *not to faint*." He found it to be a choice between praying and fainting. For him, the good fight of faith lay right there. Such a life as his was only possible as long as it was inwardly victorious, renewed day by day. That meant the constant exchange, by faith, of the weak, ease-loving, often defeated "I" for Christ— "no longer I, but Christ liveth in me."

But the real Christ-life leads to the cross, and the cross does not get comfortable. "Blood of our own" must attest our faith in the precious blood of Christ if we are to share and to show forth the victory of the cross. Is not this the application of that great faith chapter in Hebrews, with its record of those who endured "as seeing him who is invisible"? "Wherefore . . . let us run with patience the race that is set before us, *looking unto Jesus* the author and finisher of our faith; who for the joy that was set before him endured the cross, despising the shame. . . . Consider him that endured . . . lest ye be wearied and faint in your minds. Ye have not yet *resisted unto blood,* striving against sin."

Armchair trust has no place in this battle and victory, as Fraser was proving. Shrinking from the cross was often his experience, but from his journal we gather something of his following on to deeper fellowship with his Lord:

Aug. 23, 1918: Considerable spiritual recovery. Enabled, practically, to clasp the foot of the cross.

Aug. 26: Thirty-two years old today. Quite conscious of Mother's prayers. I am sure she is praying for me. Good time of prayer alone in my room. Enabled to get to the cross and remain there. Have peace and rest of spirit. Preaching on the street in the evening.

Aug. 27: The cross is going to hurt—let it hurt! I am going to work hard and pray hard too, by God's grace.

Aug. 28: Reading through Thomas Cook's *New Testament Holiness*.

Sept. 1: Yesterday evening, prayer out in gully.

And a week later, when he was about to set out on a long itinerary:

Sept. 9: Reading Jowett's *Passion for Souls*. Very definitely and decidedly take my stand on I John 1:7: "If we walk in the light, as he is in the light, we have fellowship one with another, and the blood of Jesus Christ his Son cleanseth us from all sin"—Jesus Christ my Cleanser from all sin. Full of peace and blessing all the rest of the day. In the evening a Lisu man from Hochen signified his willingness to accept Christ and came for talk and prayer.

Sept. 11: Am proving I John 1:7 true these days. Faith becomes as natural as breathing. During the first few years I put forth too much self-effort with James 4:7: "Resist the devil, and he will flee from you." This verse probably has no connection with inbred sin, but rather with offensive warfare against Satan's kingdom in the world. In this, Thomas Cook's book has been a great help to me.

Sept. 12: My weapon these days against sin and Satan—or rather, sin alone—is *the love of God*. If "the love of Christ constraineth us," how can we do despite unto the Spirit of grace?

Sept. 16: Extracts from *Passion for Souls*:

"The Gospel of a broken heart begins the ministry of bleeding hearts."

"As soon as we cease to bleed we cease to bless."

"We must bleed, if we would be ministers of the Saving Blood."

Sept. 20: We should take up the whole armor of God before the "evil day" comes, so that when it does come we may be able to stand. We need to strengthen the defenses during every lull in the battle.

Four days later Fraser was in the villages again, rejoicing in the Lord.

Hudson Taylor wrote in the same spirit: "There is a needs-be for us to give *ourselves* for the life of the world. Fruit-bearing involves cross-bearing. 'Except a corn of wheat fall into the ground and die, it abideth alone.' We know how the Lord Jesus became fruitful—not by bearing His cross only, but by dying on it. Do we know much of fellowship with Him in this? There are not two Christs—an easygoing Christ for easygoing Christians, and a suffering, toiling Christ for exceptional believers. There is only one Christ. Are we willing to abide in Him, and so to bear much fruit?"

Chapter 18

A NEW CALL

IT CAME AT LAST—the call, "Come over and help us," from that group of Lisu far to the southeast of Teng-yueh, whom Fraser had met five years previously and left in the care of Moh Ting-chang. Fraser had often thought of them and prayed that the seed sown might take root in their hearts, but little or no news had come through to encourage such hopes.

The year 1919 had been marked by greater liberty in Fraser's own spiritual life and in labors more abundant in all his districts, especially among the Kachin.

His heart was drawn increasingly to this wild and lovable people, though it was difficult to gain a footing among them. More numerous than the Lisu, especially in Fraser's southern field, they were also more primitive, unkempt, and degraded, yet more aggressive. Living in larger communities, they were armed with old-fashioned guns and homemade gunpowder as well as daggers and swords.

Repeatedly Fraser was fired at as he passed through their villages, though, when he showed no fear, belligerence usually gave place to friendliness.

Robbed on journeys by Kachin highwaymen, he was even chased by one who was ferociously drunk and brandishing a drawn sword. Only fleetness of foot saved him. Yet there was a frankness and warmth of heart about them that made the missionary covet Kachin converts for his Lord. It appears that the attraction was mutual, in some cases at least, for all Fraser's dexterity was needed to escape the matrimonial intentions of one chieftain who was bent upon making him his son-in-law!

But though drawn into touch with the Kachin at this time, most of the year was spent in caring for the Lisu Christians in his widely scattered villages. Many were standing firm in the faith, though others caused grief by turning back to demon worship. At Mottled Hill, for example, Fraser was met by a double sorrow. The leader of the church there was a young Lisu of great promise. Fraser loved him and looked forward to his development as a much needed fellow worker. During his absence in Burma for translation work with Ba Thaw, however, the young man died in an epidemic of influenza. And that was not the worst of it. A heathen wizard in the district turned the occasion to his own advantage.

He announced that he had seen the soul of this young man all by itself—neither in Heaven nor in the place of their departed ancestors—holding a hymnbook that I had given him and weeping. Hence, he reasoned, Christians do not go to Heaven, and all we teach about it is a hoax!

The orphaned child of this same man was taken ill not long after the father's death, and they said that the spirit of the father had come back to "bite" (attack) his own child. Do not imagine that the converts hear these things with a superior smile as we might. No, they take them very seriously.

Many of the converts turned back, and even those who did not, have more uneasy misgivings on the subject than they are willing to acknowledge.

Sympathy with their point of view did not keep Fraser from feeling keenly the converts' defection. After some weeks in his northern district he was constrained to write his prayer circle a letter which reveals a conflict and victory that all true missionaries will understand. It reveals also the upholding that came to him through the prayer support of these faithful friends in the homeland:

Broadly speaking, God seems to have restrained the hand of the evil one. Mr. Flagg thinks it a miracle that after only two or three days of teaching, in some cases, so many of the converts have stood firm against all the temptations they have had to face.

I cannot insist too strongly on my own helplessness among these people apart from the grace of God. Although I have now been ten years in China and have had considerable experience with both Chinese and Lisu, I find myself able to do little or nothing apart from God's going before me and working among them. Without this I feel like a man who has his boat grounded in shallow water. Pull or push as he may, he will not be able to make his boat move more than a few inches. But let the tide come in and lift his boat off the bottom—*then* he will be able to move it as far as he pleases, quite easily and without friction. It is indeed necessary for me to go around among our Lisu, preaching, teaching, exhorting, rebuking, but the amount of progress made thereby depends almost entirely on the state of the spiritual tide in the village—a condition which you can control upon your knees as well as I. Sometimes I feel that a village is grounded like that boat at low water! In such a case you can no more get the people to hold together and strengthen each other than you could roll dry sand into a ball. They will be cold and unresponsive, and weeks or even months of teaching will not do much for them. Their "prayers" are not answered as when the power of the Holy Spirit is with them. I repeat, I feel powerless to help in such cases, except to do all that *is* possible and then commit them to God.

To change the figure, the preaching of the Word of God in these Lisu villages is something like vaccination. You apply the serum and the people are duly inoculated. But the result is different with different people and villages. In some cases the "vaccination" is successful. The people go ahead in numbers and grow in faith. In other cases the "vaccination" does not take, and the people revert to heathenism or to indifference. Does this apply to us also, on our plane and in our sphere? Have we not been inoculated by God's all-sufficient grace through the risen Christ (Rom. 6:1-14) against sin, that deadly smallpox of the soul? And what has been the result? Has it *taken*—in your life and mine?

"It is easier to get Israel out of Egypt than to get Egypt out of Israel," Fraser went on in this connection. Yet he could not help but touch upon the brighter side, which meant so much to him:

I do not want you to think I am discouraged about my Lisu work—far from it! I want you to know the truth, that is all. Much of what I say would probably apply to many places in the mission fields from which come rosy and optimistic accounts of the work —quite rightly, for it has that side. So has mine, and I am full of hope and really sanguine about it. I have quite a number of Lisu who are honest and faithful as far as they go, and some who are especially warmhearted and earnest. They are hospitable, generous, and comparatively guileless. I am quite aware that whatever difficulties we may meet in our Lisu work, there are difficulties in all Christian service. I rather suspect that you have them also at home. It was Dr. Dale, I think, who said that we may change our difficulties in Christian work but we can never escape them. I thank God with all my heart that I am just where I am and in the work I am now in.

Some of the Lisu converts, chiefly the younger people, give us much joy in the Lord. A boy of eighteen who was with me last winter is of this kind, always bright and helpful. He would pray aloud every evening before going to bed and was so fond of hymns that a missionary passing through our station called him "the singing boy." He is a hard worker and a good reader and penman. Two other young men from his village went with me on a two-week trip some time ago, carrying my loads and helping me in every way. When they went back home they refused to take a single penny for their work. Another man, in my southern district, stood firm in his village when all the rest turned back. I visited his village in the first instance, only because of his pressing invitation. Everyone there would testify to his being a total abstainer and keeping his family also from drinking liquor. No better testimony could be given of him than that he brings up his family to be of the same spirit as he. He could have given his eldest daughter, a bright, warmhearted girl, in marriage to a fairly well-to-do family, but rather than give her to a heathen people he got a much poorer husband for her, but a Christian. It is a joy to meet that family—they all have that charm which comes from wholeheartedness and absolute sincerity.

An interlude in this year of pastoral visitation came when news reached Fraser that the beloved Pastor Ting Le-mei, the Moody of China, was in Yunnan with the first party of the Chinese Home Missionary Society, and that he wanted to see something of the tribes in the west. This was an opportunity not to be missed, for Pastor Ting was a man of prayer, as well as one of the most spiritual leaders of the church in China.

Ting Li-mei's arrival at Tengyueh that summer was well timed, as far as the beauty of the scenery was concerned, though the frequent rains brought him a taste of discomforts to which his missionary companion was more accustomed. But Fraser found him ready to face every hardship. And Pi, the Chinese Christian who had come with Pastor Ting from Kunming, was a Greatheart of the most practical kind.

Those were memorable months to Fraser as well as to his companions. They traveled first through the Lisu country and afterward visited several stations in western Yunnan, holding conferences for the Chinese Christians. Ting's appreciation of the beauty of the mountains brought no little joy to Fraser, though their point of view differed somewhat when it came to the homes of the people. Ting Li-mei had never seen such poverty and squalor, and would have fared badly except for the food that Fraser had thoughtfully brought along. (Fraser never carried food for himself.) But the joy of finding little Christian communities in those remote mountain hamlets more than made up for all that was involved in reaching them.

One night they were overtaken by darkness before they could reach their destination on the way to Turtle Village. Dog-tired, they were stumbling along the dark and ghostly pathway through the woods, when they heard the sound of singing and recognized a sweet familiar hymn. A little farther on they came to a house Fraser had never seen, and found it to be the new chapel at Water Bowl, in which the Christians were gathered for evening worship. They were praying and singing in the dark because they could not afford oil for their tiny lamps, except on special occasions.

A Sunday spent at Turtle Village gave opportunity for Pastor Ting to speak by interpretation to the Christians, of whom there were over a hundred. His heart was drawn to them, but he asked Fraser whether he might venture to exhort them to practice a little more cleanliness in their persons and habits. This was done as tactfully as Fraser could wish, and to his personal enjoyment!

We must not dwell on the fellowship of those days except to give one picture of what it meant for the often lonely missionary to have a companion so human as well as spiritual in his outlook. After leaving Turtle Village, he took Ting and Pi up a neighboring mountain from which a wonderful view could be obtained.

> The frontier of Burma was only a few miles away, and we could see right down to the Irrawaddy valley and Myitkyina plain. Ting had never traveled far outside his own country. But he is one of those people I try to emulate, who find something interesting,

something to be pleased about, just everywhere. If it is not the scenery it is the costume of the people. If not that it is some new plant or tree or animal never seen before, or some interesting local custom or legend.

Up on the top of this range, he noticed a very peculiar tree—the strangest he or I had ever seen. It actually had six different varieties of leaf! One, and perhaps two, were parasitic growths, but not the others as far as we could see. It was fine to see the almost childish delight with which he gathered a specimen of each kind of leaf, and put them with some berries he was already saving. He was so pleased with the new things and scenes that he suggested we might have prayer together and thank God for it all. So then and there we three had a little prayer meeting, sitting on a big rock on that great, high, cold mountain overlooking Burma.

Indeed, it was in connection with his prayer life that Ting Li-mei's company was most helpful. The little book, drawn from Ting's pocket at any leisure moment to remind him of all those for whom he had undertaken to pray daily, became a very familiar sight.

I was sorry to see him go. He is a faithful intercessor. Every day you would see him on his horse, reading by the hour from his leatherbound notebook, in which he had a long list of names of Chinese and foreign friends. He remembers them all before God in silent prayer.

At Tali Pastor Ting and Pi left Fraser's escort, after three months of fruitful labor together, and there
Fraser welcomed the coming of one who was to mean
even more as a fellow worker and friend. The real
crises of life often come without observation. That
meeting between the pioneer missionary among the
Lisu of western Yunnan and the new arrival, who was
to be in so real a sense their apostle, was unmarked
by anything of special significance. Fraser only saw
a young recruit of whom he wrote, "I got to like
Cooke immensely.... You can love him as a younger
brother." And Allyn Cooke recalled his impressions,
long years after, in conversation with the writer:

> Fraser seemed young and strong physically. He
> was very sociable for an Englishman [Cooke was
> from the U.S.A.]. He spoke Chinese fluently, just
> like the people, though when occasion required he
> would use scholarly language. In his traveling out-
> fit—homemade and kept for the road—he was some-
> times taken for a coolie or even "a foreign beggar!"
> But he always had the dress of a teacher with him
> and, at his destination, would soon appear, to the
> surprise of strangers, as "a perfect gentleman."
> And what a fellow traveler he was! Well do I re-
> member his thoughtfulness and unselfish care of
> others. He was never in a hurry, and would stop and
> talk with people on the road, always ready to do a
> good turn. He was kind to the animals, the coolies,
> the innkeepers. And he was so practical! The pack-
> saddle was too heavy? He designed another. The

new worker was unused to riding on top of the load? Fraser insisted on his using the only foreign saddle. It was always like that. He was used to local conditions, he would explain, and did not mind them.

When we reached Tengyueh, I came to know more of his spiritual life and was much impressed by his talks from the Word. He took me to some of his prayer resorts outside the city, and I found that he often fasted, in a quiet way, before preaching. The influence of his life only deepened as time went on. Indeed, everything that I have as a missionary I owe to Fraser.

Fraser and Cooke had hardly reached Tengyueh before a call came from some Kachin Christians who were badly needing help. They were connected with the American missionaries over at Namhkam in Burma. As the Kachin could not speak Chinese, they had taken the long journey to find Fraser and bring him to the scene of trouble. The call appealed to him, backed as it was by urgent letters from the missionary friends he valued. For months he had been praying for some way of access to the Kachin of his own district, some definite opening among these people so much upon his heart. Could this be the beginning of the answer?

A storm assailed Fraser when he arrived with the returning messengers. The opposition of the Kachin chieftains was formidable, and some of the Christians had barricaded themselves in their houses to fight for their homes and lives. Blood had been drawn on both sides, and it was some time before Fraser could bring about a truce so that matters could be discussed more calmly. Finally, however, prayer and patience prevailed, and he was able to negotiate a hopeful peace.

Meanwhile he had been seeking to draw out the sympathies of the Christian community and their pastor for the thousands of wild, unreached Kachin up in his own district. He could not speak the Atsi dialect of Kachin, but they could. Would it not be possible to send some of their own number as missionaries, now that this trouble was over, to the Atsi villages of Pangwa, halfway to Tengyueh, where hundreds of Kachin were settled? A rumor had reached him that some among them wanted to hear the Gospel—but how could they, without a preacher?

The suggestion went home and, not long after Fraser had left, the Christians of the Longchuen valley set apart two of their number to go and test possibilities at Pangwa. They were good men, kind and prayerful, and God used them.

Fraser meanwhile was on a four-month tour of his district in other directions, leading up to the Christmas festival at Turtle Village. What a wonderful time it was—the first big rally of rejoicing Christians among the mountain people! Hundreds came in from the north, south, and west, from the wide field watered so faithfully by Fraser's prayers and tears. They brought their own provisions, enough for several days, and offerings to present to the Lord. It was a harvest festival and big camp meeting all in one, with singing and rejoicing that could be heard afar. And the greatest joy to Fraser was the arrival of the new contingent from Pangwa—twenty or more Atsi young people, awakened to the meaning of their newfound salvation. There they were with the Kachin teachers from Longchuen—dirty and shabby enough, with rough unkempt hair and the timid alertness of wild creatures, yet with an eager wistfulness to enter into all that was going on and to belong to the people of the true God.

And there, in the midst of that memorable gathering, came the call that was to open new and wider fields of usefulness to Fraser. How little he had expected it just then. He could little realize all it was to mean! It was only a postcard from Moh Tingchang, the pastry cook of Hsiangta, but the wayworn missive carried a message that went straight to Fraser's heart. It came from the Lisu of that district who had not been ready, five years before, to turn from demon worship to the living Saviour. But they had remembered Fraser's promise. The spiritual tide was rising and, over the mountains, four days' journey, they now sent the plea: "Come back again and help us. We want to become Christians!"

And, strange to say, Fraser could not go.

Chapter 19

GOOD GROUND

FRASER WAS PERPLEXED. Before him lay Moh's post-card with its urgent invitation. Around him were the happy crowds gathered for the Christmas festival, including the group of newly won Kachin who had come to take him back with them to their settlement, where many more, they told him, were ready to turn to the Saviour. How he longed to go at once to the Hsiangta district, in response to Moh's appeal! But here were duties and opportunities that could not be set aside. Was there anyone who could go in his place? Flagg was shortly to be married, and had a long journey to take in another direction. Cooke was there, it was true, having left his books and teacher at Tengyueh, to bring the mail and give what help he could. But he had been in the district only a few months and knew little of Chinese and nothing at all of the Lisu language. The call to Hsiangta might lead to great things. If only Fraser could go himself! And then the thought of what it might mean to his young colleague determined his decision. He would ask Cooke to go with the best Lisu he could find to accompany him, and would trust God to work through them. So the little party set out on their four-day journey to the east and south, wondering what had led to this new development.

Moh had not given any explanation. But the truth was that he himself had been doing what he could to deepen the interest of the Cold Country Lisu, who had heard the Gospel from Fraser five years previously. Moh's conversion at that time had been followed by steady growth in the Christian life, and he had made the most of the occasional visits of the tribesmen to the Hsiangta market. They loved to gather in the pastry cook's shop, sure of a welcome, and eager to hear more of the One they were beginning to regard with special interest.

Fraser had already discovered that the Lisu all through that Burma borderland had the tradition of a coming king. They cherished vague longings for a teacher and deliverer, a king who would bring books in their language and good news for their people. Moh listened with no little interest to their talk of this looked-for champion and made much of the fact that in Lisu the name of Jesus rhymed with the name of their own tribe—*Jesu* and *Lisu* sounding almost alike. Jesus of the Lisu—was He not their coming One?

But the tribesmen were undecided. Material things had more weight with them than spiritual, and it was

not until Moh struck another note that the appeal
went home. The photograph of Flagg and Fraser in
tribal dress, taken at their first Christmas gathering
in Tengyueh, had reached him. There they stood,
large and lifelike, complete in every detail of Lisu attire, from turban to bare feet and leggings. Taking
up the photo, he handed it to his visitors. "Here is
your Lisu king," he said, "and he has books for you
and much good news."

The tribesmen gazed in wonder. Yes, it was Fraser.
Some of them remembered him, but he had not been
in Lisu dress when he came to their villages. Now
he looked different! Could he indeed be their Lisu
king? That picture decided the issue. After talking
it over with their people at home, they hastened back
to beg Moh to write for them, asking Fraser to come
at once and help them to turn Christian. Their ideas
about turning were very hazy, as Cooke and his companions were soon to discover.

It was just before Chinese New Year when the little party reached Hsiangta, and Moh was too busy in
his shop to go with them up to the Cold Country. A
Lisu inquirer who had taken the name of Paul had
come down, however, to escort them as they set out
for his home village. At a market town on the way
they stopped to pick up provisions for the New Year
feast. That was to be expected. But Cooke was concerned to see them load up with gallons and gallons

of whiskey. What could this mean if they were preparing to become Christians?

Although he was not in Lisu dress, Cooke was warmly received in the four villages and soon felt at home by the smoky fires, winning the confidence of his hosts in his quiet, kind way. In spite of preparations for the New Year feast, he and his helpers had good opportunities for pressing home the importance of making a clean cut with all idolatry and demon worship, drunkenness, and opium smoking, if they were to turn to the living God. Paul was able to speak Chinese, in which language Cooke had made some progress, so they could talk things over to some extent.

"Yes," he explained, "we want to turn Christian. But we must worship our ancestors once more, to send them away respectfully, and offer sacrifices to the demons, so that they will not injure us. And there is this whiskey—which of course we must use up."

More and more the young missionary was distressed as he saw preparations going on for the regular idolatrous feast. There in the middle of the room, the spirit-shelf was being dressed with new red paper, the incense bowls were made ready, and the food was spread out before the ancestral scrolls and dreaded demons. Could it be that the family was about to worship as usual, with all the accompaniments that were so degrading? Cooke and his Lisu companions knew well what it meant—an orgy of feasting and drunkenness—seeing who could eat the most fat pork and other dainties, and drink the most whiskey, until men and women alike were utterly debauched. How they dreaded the dancing and singing that went with it all, and the drunken stupor that would follow the night of dissipation! And all this in the home where they had spent such happy hours, talking and singing of better things.

At last, when all the family, old and young, gathered and went down on their knees before the spirit-shelf, and began to bow and knock their foreheads on the ground in worship, Cooke was overwhelmed with grief and disappointment.

"I sat there weeping as I watched them," he said to the writer years later, "thinking that they were not going to turn after all."

"Why do you weep, teacher?" broke in the voice of Paul, who alone had noticed his deep concern.

"Because you are sinning against the true and living God."

"But do you really care so much?"

"Care? How can I help but care for your poor souls?"

Something struck home to the young Lisu's heart. Something opened his eyes to see as he had not seen before. Preaching had not done it. "We must drink the whiskey we have bought," had been his attitude. "We must feed our ancestors and demons for another year, or vengeance will come upon us." But now—

"Do not weep, do not weep," he cried. "We will pour out the whiskey! We will truly turn, as you have taught us."

Then and there the scene was changed. With one accord the whole Fish family followed the lead Paul was giving. The spirit-shelf was torn down, the food put to better uses. The bowls and incense-holders were smashed, and all the twigs and trumpery used in vows and worship were thrown on the bonfire lighted in the courtyard.

Neighbors ran in to see what was going on. Whiskey flooded the pig troughs and overflowed the ground—yes, the whiskey they loved above all else! Soon the pigs were reeling drunk, but the rejoicing people were sober. Never had there been such singing, such gladness!

Cooke said later:

Paul led the way to the spirit-tree—just an old stump, too big to cut down. Incense and bowls for food stood on the shelf attached to it. He broke the bowls, tore out the shelf, burning everything that could be burned. A little hut stood nearby, with incense for spirit worship. They tore it down and carried it all to the bonfire.

"Now come to my house! Come to my house!" the neighbors began calling.

We went with Paul, and throughout the village the same victories were repeated.

What a day it was! "Weeping may endure for a
night, but joy cometh in the morning." God's hour
had struck and nothing could stay the incoming tide.
Cooke and his Lisu lads were small enough and weak
enough for God to use. They inspired no fear, aroused
no suspicion, and wherever they went the movement
spread. Within the next two weeks, thirty families
in that neighborhood had come out boldly for Christ.
And when Cooke had to return to Tengyueh to continue his studies, the two young Lisu remained to
strengthen the converts and carry on the work.

Fraser meanwhile, knowing nothing of all this, was
having a similar experience among the Atsi Kachin of
his own district. The welcome he received at Pangwa was a big surprise, the whole community turning
out with drums and music to do him honor. The Kachin evangelists from the south had done their work
so well that little more was needed to help forty
families to decide to become Christians. Settling
down among them, Fraser began at once to learn
Atsi, making such progress that within a month he
was preaching his first sermon in the language of this
once unfriendly tribe for which he had prayed so
long.

The joy of bringing the Gospel in all its saving
power to such darkened hearts helped him to bear
the poverty-stricken squalor of their way of life. He
found them to be a strong, independent people, harder to influence than the Lisu, but more fearless and

steadfast after they became Christians. But the work and privations so told upon him that he had to take a brief respite in a nearby market town, where a dilapidated Chinese inn afforded what seemed to him, by contrast, as good as "a holiday at the seaside." His graphic picture of this Chinese market with its abundance of good things was written to cheer his mother:

For lodging only, including firewood, water, and coverlet (if you care to use it), we pay the equivalent of twopence a day each, borrowing pots and pans from the landlord. The Lisu I have with me go out each morning to buy food. Sometimes I go myself and you would smile to see me with a basket of vegetables in one hand and a string of Chinese cash in the other, or a bit of fat pork dangling from a slip of bamboo, as I walk along the cobbled street of the market between the thatched stalls of the vendors. I take a positive delight in doing just what the Chinese do.

This is market day and the street is just beginning to hubbubify. You can see no less than seven races—Chinese, Shan, Palaung, Achang, Lisu, Jinghpaw Kachin, and Atsi Kachin. *I* would make race No. 8, wouldn't I? You can tell all of these races apart—except the two tribes of Kachin—by the dress of the women. They bring in all sorts of produce, carried either in two baskets with a pole over the shoulder, or else in one on their back, dump it down by the side of the street, then sit there and wait for buyers.

The shopkeepers put their stuff outside the shops on stalls, displaying a hundred and one different kinds of foreign and native articles—lamps, lanterns, kerosene, mirrors, perfume, woolen socks, boots, shoes, quinine, patent medicines, soap, pocketknives, handkerchiefs, pencils, etc., etc., together with a lot of cheap jackery, frippery and fruppery, janglery and banglery, around which you see the maidens and youthful matrons of the various tribes—their hearts entirely set on it all, and with a big-eyed wish-I-could-afford-to-buy-it look on their faces.

If you were to see the Kachin women and girls, you would pronounce them the wildest specimens of humanity you had ever met. You might even be as afraid of them as they would be of you! The Kachin is a straightforward, blunt kind of individual, without any of the abstruse ways of the Chinese. He does not always appear to be saying, "I wonder what that foreigner has up his sleeve, anyway?" The Kachin girl is most in evidence, for the men do not go to market much, and the older women not so often as the younger. You are free to chat with her anywhere and everywhere. She looks you straight in the face with an expression of mingled indulgence, delight, and amusement, as you try to stumble out your meaning in broken Atsi. She is an impulsive, demonstrative creature: you can just watch the progress of her thoughts, for she does all her thinking on the outside of her face.

Last market day I met some Lisu from the Upper Salween on the street. They were carrying tremendously heavy loads of betel nut to sell. "Come up to our village and teach us," one of them said. His village is about sixteen days' journey away. "We will give you food—as much rice and pork as you want." The invitation was sincere, but he was too busy to stop and talk. That district *must* be evangelized, but I want to find the right Lisu Christians to go first.

A pretty Lisu girl, petite and pleasant, asked me if I didn't remember her. It turned out she was from Mottled Hill, from a family who were formerly Christians. She is now married into a heathen village near here.

"Do the people in your village want to study the Christian books?" I asked her.

"I don't know—you had better ask them," she said.

"Do you want to?" I continued.

"Yes, ever so much!" she replied with as bright a smile as shyness would permit. Of course the younger people cannot do as they like: they have to obey their elders.

So much for the market. It is at its height now as I write—people haggling over petty little bits of prices and beating each other down by tenths of a penny at a time.

But very different were the thoughts which chiefly occupied Fraser's mind—for it was from this comfortless Chinese inn that he wrote to his prayer circle with special urgency. Recent experiences had deepened his conviction as to the vital part God has assigned to intercessory prayer in the work of His king-

Deeper conviction of the vital part
of intercessory prayer.
Kept intercessors informed

Good Ground   257

dom. Repeatedly he had noticed the difference between people and places that had been much prayed
for and those that had not. In the former, half the
work seemed to be done already, as if an unseen ally
had gone ahead to prepare the way. This made him
not only persevere in prayer himself, whether he felt
like it or not, but also impelled him to induce and
encourage Christians at home to pray.

He longed for a larger prayer circle behind his
Lisu work. He sent maps of all his districts, wrote
personal letters to the members, answered questions,
and sought in every way to make the needs real to
his prayer helpers. His pleasure was great when one
lady wrote that she was praying daily for the demon-
priest of the Sword-ladder Festival, and when another said that the Lisu were so real, through his letters, that it seemed to her as if they were living
"just across the street." That was what he wanted.
During this time in the noisy market town he got to
grips with his prayer supporters about it, pleading
the momentous issues involved:

> There are many things I wish to tell you about.
> I want to give you as good an idea of the people,
> their habits, their dress, their food, their language,
> their ideas, their peculiarities, as I possibly can. I
> want to tell you all about my plans for the self-sup-
> port of the work—a subject on which I feel very
> strongly indeed. But I want to distinguish between
> temporal self-support and spiritual self-support. The

Heathenism a stagnant pool
attempt to quench H.S. fire if not
for prayer

258   *Behind the Ranges*

former is eminently desirable and practicable, the latter is almost impossible, perhaps, for generations to come.

The Lisu and Kachin converts would be easily able to support their own pastors, teachers, and evangelists by well-advised cultivation of their own ample hillsides, and it is fitting that the mountains should bring forth supplies for the needs of those whose feet are beautiful upon them. But spiritually they are babes, and are as dependent upon us as a child upon his mother. They look to us out here for instruction, guidance, and organization; but they are dependent on the home churches in England and America in a deeper sense for spiritual life and power. I really believe that if every prayer by the home churches on behalf of the infant churches of the mission field were removed, the latter would be swamped by an incoming flood of the powers of darkness. This seems to have happened in church history—churches losing all their power and life, becoming a mere empty name, or else flickering out altogether. Just as a plant may die for lack of watering, so may a genuine work of God die and rot for lack of prayer.

One might compare heathenism to a great pool of stagnant water always threatening to quench the flames of Holy Spirit life and power in the infant churches, and only kept in check by the power of God. God is able to do this and much more, but He will not do it if all we out here and you at home sit in our easy chairs with our arms folded. Just why prayer is so indispensable we cannot say, but we had better recognize the fact even if we cannot explain it. Do you believe the Church of God would be alive today but for the high priestly intercession of the Lord Jesus Christ on the throne? I do not. I believe it would have been dead and buried long ago. Viewing the Bible as a record of God's work on this earth, I believe that it gives a clear, ringing message to His people—from Genesis to Revelation: "You do your part!"

Have you ever thought it strange that God allowed nearly eighteen centuries to pass before opening the Gospel door to more than half of the human race—India, China, and Japan? Though the church cannot shirk responsibility for the fact, I still believe God had a purpose in it. I believe that He tried the evangelizing of the heathen (if I may reverently say so) many times in former centuries, but His Church did not rise to the occasion. She was too encumbered with error and corruption, too powerless to nourish the children to which she gave birth. And such sporadic efforts as were put forth by earnest men in past centuries to form churches in what we now call the foreign mission field never resulted in anything live and permanent. At the time of the Reformation the Church was just beginning to come into her own, and it was not until after the evangelical revival of the eighteenth century that God, it seems, deemed her fit and strong enough to bear and nourish children in the midst of the great heathen systems of the world. It is rather striking that Carey's departure for India, which we regard as the birth of

260 *Behind the Ranges*

the modern missionary movement, took place just two years after the death of John Wesley, the central figure of the great evangelical revival.

And now the mother church of Protestant countries is well able to nourish the infant churches of the Orient, not only with men and money but also with a steady and powerful volume of intercessory prayer. Applying this to the work among the Tengyueh tribespeople, I am assured that you and those whom God will yet call to join you in this work are well able to sustain the spiritual life of the Lisu and Kachin converts, as well as to increase their number manyfold. And just as I feel that God has waited until the home church attained strength enough to nourish her children before giving her a large and growing family on the foreign mission field, so He has been preparing you for the spiritual parenthood of these Lisu converts, however many thousands of miles may separate you from them.

You may perhaps say, "Do you get the converts themselves to pray as they ought to?" This is a very natural question and I can best answer it by saying yes—and no. I try to get them into the habit of prayer, but it is only the cry of the babe, not the strong pleading of the adult. They only know how to pray with anything approaching intensity when they or their friends are sick. Their prayers in such cases seem to be remarkably effectual, but they know nothing of pleading for the salvation of souls. Unfortunately not many see that it matters much whether others are saved or unsaved. Their prayers are almost entirely selfish, just as a baby's cries are. One does not think less of a baby for that reason! Large numbers of converts do not realize what salvation means, even for themselves. They will do so later on, given time, instruction, and something in the nature of a revival, but at present their knowledge is very elementary and their attainment small. They have not yet grown to military age in this spiritual warfare. They are babes in God's nursery, not warriors in God's army. But you have centuries of Christianity behind you, you have been brought up under Christian influence, with an open Bible, devotional helps, and many other things to help your *I wish* growth into spiritual maturity. So now you belong to those of full stature in Christ who are able to "help . . . with power against the enemy." The vast difference between you and them is that you are "grown up" in Christ, while they are babes and sucklings. The work of pulling down Satan's strongholds requires strong men, not infants.

I am not asking you just to give "help" in prayer as a sort of sideline, but I am trying to roll the main responsibility of this prayer warfare on you. I want you to take the *burden* of these people upon your shoulders. I want you to wrestle with God for them. I shall feel more and more that a big responsibility rests upon me to keep you well informed. The Lord Jesus looks down from Heaven and sees these poor, degraded, neglected tribespeople. The travail of His soul was for them too. He has waited long. Will you not do your part to bring in the day when He shall "be satisfied"?

We talk of intercession's import
Let's prove it.

Anything must be done rather than let this service of prayer be dropped or even allowed to stagnate. We often speak of intercessory work as being of vital importance. I want to prove this in actual fact by giving my first and best energies to it, as God may lead. I feel like a businessman who perceives that a certain line of goods pays better than any other in his store, and who purposes making it his chief investment; who, in fact, sees an inexhaustible supply and an almost unlimited demand for a profitable article, and intends to concentrate on this line more than anything else. The *demand* is the lost state of these tens of thousands of Lisu and Kachin—their ignorance, their superstition, their sinfulness, the need of their bodies, their minds, their souls. The supply is the grace of God to meet this need which will be brought down to them by the persevering prayers of a considerable company of God's people. All I want to do is to bring the supply and the demand together.

Chapter 20

A HUNDREDFOLD

IT WAS SOME WEEKS after Cooke's return from the Cold Country before the sequel to his visit became known. One of the Lisu companions he had left behind turned up in Tengyueh, eager to find Fraser, with a big order for Gospels, hymnbooks, and catechisms.

"But who are they for?" was the natural question.

"Why, for all the converts in our Christian villages."

"All the converts! Are there so many?"

"Yes, scores of families. And more are coming in."

The young messenger would have come before, but he and his companion had so many inquirers on their hands that neither of them could be spared. Now the need for books was urgent and he had left everything and had taken the six-day journey alone to procure them.

"But the inquirers cannot read, can they?"

"Oh, yes, we have taught them!" came the eager answer. "And many of the younger people can write as well."

And so it dawned upon Fraser and his colleagues
that this work of God was a new development, almost
apart from their own efforts, yet the fruit of years of
prayer. With what joy the remembrance came to
Fraser, then and later, of his "prayer of faith" in Burma, five years previously!

> I believe it was January 12, 1915, that I was definitely led to ask God for "several hundreds of families" from the Lisu. Some may say, "Your prayer has at last been answered." No! I took the answer *then*. I believed *then* that I had it. The realization has only now come, it is true, but God does not keep us waiting for answers. He gives them at once (Dan. 9: 23).

How wonderful it was now to listen as, bit by bit,
the young Lisu told his story! After Allyn Cooke had
left the Hsiangta district to return to Chinese study,
the converts themselves went on with their joyous
testimony even beyond their own clan. It was the
middle of the New Year season, the one general holiday of the year. People were more or less at leisure,
and the dry, sunny days made it easy to be out of
doors. From village to village and from house to
house the Lisu lads ("teachers" they now called
them) were escorted as interest spread.

The turning of the Fish family when Cooke was
there was only the beginning. It was the surrender,
the test case, so to speak. Paul, who had come out
then so strongly, continued to take the lead, and the

*Answer taken then, believed he
had it. Realization seen now.*

Lord used the Lisu lads from Tengyueh as if they
had been mature Christians. Wherever they went
there was blessing.

Recalling it all, Allyn Cooke commented:

> It is marvelous—the people God uses! Before long
> the new Christians were able to teach others, and so
> the work went on and on. They sent in to Tengyueh
> for loads of books, the money for which had been
> paid to leaders out there, appointed by the two who
> had been with me.

Fraser was eager to see for himself just what was
going on, but it was some time before he could be
free to revisit the district, and then it was by way
of a route he had not taken before. He found it
necessary to go down to Rangoon to see about the
printing of their Lisu literature. The work was being
held up for lack of Gospels, hymnbooks, and catechisms for which people in the new district were
clamoring. He could not leave Tengyueh until the
return of Flagg from his wedding journey, but as
soon as the newlyweds were established in charge
of the city work, Fraser set out on the sixteen-day
journey, taking with him Cooke, whose eyes needed
skilled attention.

The Rangoon business completed, Cooke returned
to Tengyueh by what is now the Burma Road, but
Fraser struck cross-country to the east, reaching the
China border where the Salween makes its great
bend around the Hsiangta district. There to the

north of him lay the scene of the new spiritual movement, but Fraser's thoughts were focused on a nearer point just then—a village only a few miles away,
across the river and up the mountain rampart beyond. He had been burdened in conscience about
that place for more than five years because of a lost
opportunity at the time of his previous visit. Hastening homeward after a long absence from Tengyueh,
he had been stopped by a Lisu woman at her door in
that particular hamlet.

"Where are you going, stranger?" she inquired with
the easy friendliness of the mountain people.

"Just going on up north."

"And what is your business?"

"I am a preacher."

"A preacher! What's that?"

"I tell about the Good News," he replied, moving
on.

"But stop, if it is good news, and tell us about it."

"I am on a long journey and cannot stay."

"But you *must* stay!" she persisted. "What is the
use of being a preacher if you have not time to
preach?"

The shot went home, but Fraser hastened on. A
lost opportunity—how he had regretted it! He had
prayed about the place for years. Was he now to have
another chance?

The ferry came and Fraser crossed the river, but
the Lisu who was carrying his load would go no

farther, and he was stranded on the northern bank until another could be found to take him on up the mountain. Waiting there hour after hour, he was interested in two men who came down to the shore he had just left and seemed to be calling for the ferry. They were very persistent, waving their arms and shouting for a long time, but he could not hear what they said. The river was wide, and no one paid them any attention. It was not until months later he discovered they had been calling for the foreign teacher. Sent from a group of Lisu villages, they were to bring him back with them in order that they too might hear his message. The breath of God was stirring hearts all through that remote region so long without the Word of life.

Somewhere in the mountains before him, Fraser was expecting to run across his two young evangelists in the midst of their work. It was a great joy to find them in one of the first stopping places above the Salween. How much there was to hear and to ask! They had already been some time in that locality, which though they little realized it then, was to become the chief center of the whole movement. Quite a number of villages on these mountain slopes were already more or less Christian—and yes, that place about which Fraser seemed specially interested was among them. The woman who had called him was the wife of Pa Tsong-si. Both were among the first to believe. Just beyond their hamlet lay Sinchaiho, the larger village to which Fraser was soon taken. Between the two places he must have passed the ridge—silent then and unaware—on which the central station of Muchengpo was soon to stand, shedding broad beams of light both near and far. Of this part of the journey he wrote to his prayer helpers:

> I wish you could have been with me as I went from village to village, to see the royal reception they gave me! And you would have shared in it too. What with the playing of their bagpipes, the firing off of guns, the lining up of all the villagers, men and women, young and old, to shake hands with you (they use both hands, thinking it more respectful), you have a feeling of being overwhelmed—an "overweight of joy."

In that district and in the Cold Country district farther north, Fraser stayed on for weeks. Indeed there was no getting away until he went down with fever, through overstrain, and had to return to Tengyueh for a time. "The people," as he put it, "were all tumbling over themselves in their earnestness." They could not learn enough or read enough or, above all, sing enough, by day and night, with their "Elder Brother Number Three." (Fraser had two older brothers, so to the Lisu he was not only "Elder Brother" but "Elder Brother Number Three"—a more cumbersome appellation, but from their point of view a more courteous one.)

It was the rainy season but, in spite of frequent downpours, often wet through and weary, Fraser tramped from hamlet to hamlet, living on such food as the little homes could provide, sleeping on a bamboo mat at night by some log fire, with all the household around him, and scarcely ever without a crowd by day. It seemed as if the people never left him. The young folk especially would go on singing the hymns he had taught them, long after he had fallen into an uneasy slumber. There seemed no limit to their vitality and friendliness. Almost the whole village would stay with him all day long, crowding the room to suffocation around the fire. And many were the hearts the Lord opened.

Some things specially please me about this new eastern district. In the first place, the work was practically begun and has been almost wholly carried on by the Lisu themselves, however raw and poorly trained they may be. They have not only passed on the little they know but have taught others to teach in their turn. So many of these young people and children had learned to read and write, in an elementary way, that I was flooded with little notes and have not yet found time to read them all.

Another matter for thankfulness is that the proportion of Christians to heathen is so large. In some vicinities scarcely any heathen families remain. There is a great advantage, as it considerably lessens temptation and complications. Last but not least, practi-

cally all the converts agree not to plant opium. This
will pave the way for baptisms and the formation of
churches in due time. They want to have a large
gathering at Christmas. Will you pray that it may
be a time of much blessing?

"If this is not an answer to prayer," Fraser asserted,
"what is it?"

Up to the present I find that in this new district
alone there are over 240 families professing to be
Christian. The total number of converts in the districts previously worked, of which I have sent you
maps, is over 180 families of Lisu and more than 20
families of Kachin. So there are now, in all, about
450 families of tribespeople for whose teaching and
shepherding we are responsible. This represents
over 2,000 people, young and old, for the average
family out here numbers about five persons.

"Rejoice with me," Fraser briefly concluded, "and
pray on for them all, in every phase of need you can
think of."

Chapter 21

THE END IN VIEW

THE MISSION HOUSE at Tengyueh was a different place now that Fraser's bachelor housekeeping was again exchanged for the life of a family. Mrs. Flagg was a great acquisition, not only to her husband—now in charge of the Chinese side of the work—but also to Allyn Cooke, whom she relieved of household cares, and to Fraser, whose letters frequently refer to her efficiency and kindness.

Mrs. Flagg came from Buffalo, U.S.A., expecting to go straight into work in the interior of China. But being an expert accountant, she was asked to remain in Shanghai to give help in the treasurer's department of the mission.

After six years in that important service, she is now glad to be set free for this inland province, and we are glad to have her. She knows little of the language yet, but is quick and capable and will soon be able to make herself understood.

Mrs. Flagg was also an excellent housekeeper and made the best bread Fraser had ever tasted in China.

But her helpful spirit meant far more to the sometimes lonely pioneer.

She is certainly very kind to me and does not at all encourage my going out to live among the Lisu. She wants me to make this my headquarters, where I can be reasonably comfortable. That makes her your friend forever, doesn't it!

But Fraser's point of view was different. He saw in the new arrangement the possibility of his fulfilling a long-desired opportunity to leave the Chinese work entirely to his colleagues and to go out himself "to live in the wilds." He wanted to be in closer touch with his Lisu and to share their life more completely. And this desire was realized some weeks later.

It was a poor little home in the heart of his western district to which Fraser was welcomed. Turtle Village, lying six thousand feet up in the mountains, was now almost entirely Christian. Placed at his disposal was a little house of bamboo matting with a thatched roof, a hollowed-out fireplace, in the middle of the floor, and a bamboo bedstead, table, and stool. At the back of the room a long broad shelf was fixed up for him—made of a coffin-plank borrowed for the purpose—on which to place his belongings: a few books, medicines, supplies such as cocoa and milk, and a can of cookies sent as a gift from Ba Thaw's young wife in Burma. (Once again generously spared from Myitkyina, Ba Thaw had come up to give help

love for children

in the translation of a second Gospel, which was urgently needed.) The bamboo shed was divided into a central room and two side rooms, one of which was the kitchen and the other the bedroom.

Here then, with much thankfulness, Fraser made himself at home with young and old, entering into all the life of the village. He had a real love for children and welcomed their informal visits. They ran around him at all hours, learning when they must keep quiet so as not to disturb his work.

Seated at his rickety table one day that summer, Fraser was writing to his prayer helpers, when he heard whispers and the shuffling of little feet outside his door. Timidly at first, six or seven children appeared, and the charming sequel was incorporated in his letter:

The leader of this afternoon's party wanted a piece of soap. Now a piece of soap for one child means, of course, a piece for each and all, so I suggested that she might wash her hands in my washbowl and with my soap. The desire to be clean is such a laudable one that we must not discourage it, must we? So she prepares to start in but, her hands being innocent of previous washings, she is a little in doubt of the *modus operandi*, and looks at me inquiringly. There is some lather in the soap dish and I tell her to use that first, whereupon she scrapes some gingerly and spreads it on the back of her left hand—just as you would spread butter on a piece of bread. No, I tell

her, she must *rub* it in, not just spread it on, so she
tries again. However, it soon seems evident that a
practical demonstration is necessary. After I wash
my hands to show her the approved method, she
starts in again. She warms to her work this time, and
washes both hands and face with more vigor, more
splashing, and more blowing than I thought I had
included in my demonstration. There is nothing like
erring on the right side, is there?

Of course by this time all the others have discovered that the thing they want more than anything
else in the world is to wash *their* hands too. They
never thought of it before, but sometimes discoveries
are made on the spur of the moment. So very soon
they are all squatting around the little galvanized
washbowl, not without some edging and pushing—
to say nothing of differences of opinion as to who had
the soap first—and are reveling in their newly found
amusement. As there were not more than two or
three cups of water in the bowl to begin with, and
as their hands were scarcely snowy white when they
came in, the color of the water when they have been
at it five or ten minutes need not be described. Some
of them seem to think it necessary to present their
hands to me for inspection after washing. One very
small boy comes along with such a solemn face
(washing is a very serious business to him) and
holds both hands out in mute inquiry. I smile ap-
proval, pat his head, and away he toddles as sol-
emnly as he came.

Of course they all succeed in getting their sleeves
wet up to their elbows, and part of their tunics and

dresses wet too. Moreover, they do not seem as anxious to remove the soap from their hands and faces as they were to put it on. They smell of soap for hours afterward and go about with soapy-shiny faces.

One little girl comes to present herself for inspection, and I seat her on the stool beside me. She is not at all afraid, but she looks up out of the tops of her eyes with a kind of awe, as if I were a mile instead of a foot or two above her. It is a pure pleasure to get children's confidence, is it not? They finish, as you might guess, by spilling all the water on the floor—but we will not blame them.

Little Miss Kung, about ten years old, was one of Fraser's chief friends in Turtle Village. Introducing her, he wrote:

She has big brown eyes, round and full like a deer's, a bright face, and an eager childish smile. She has her head shaved (like all other Lisu girls and women) except for a circular patch about four inches across at the back of her head, the hair of which is braided into a short queue. She wears a rainbow-colored cap, on the top of which is fastened a little tuft of fur about four inches long. Her dress is held together by a woven-pattern-cloth belt about two inches wide. And her apron, which is separate from the dress, comes down nearly to her feet. I wish you could hear her eager childish prattle. You would realize two things: that these children are not lacking in quick intelligence, and that they are just flesh-

and-blood children like ours in England. How she will chatter!

These children live such natural lives. They know all their hills and valleys as well as the palms of their hands. They can name all the animals, birds, and insects to be found there, and understand their habits. They are familiar, too, with the trees and shrubs. While tending cattle they will sit and make necklaces of red berries or bracelets out of wild grass.

My little friend will talk about these and many other things. She will tell you all the affairs of the village—how so-and-so lost something, and then his mother scolded him, at which he got sulky and ran up and slept in the hut on their buckwheat field. Then how his sister saw him and told his uncle, what the uncle said, and then what someone else said, and how they had a quarrel about it—all of which details do not interest me half as much as the charming vivacity of the child who is telling them. She will close her story by looking straight up into your face with an eager smile as much as to say, "Isn't that interesting?" Then she will suddenly look serious and gaze off into space for a moment's reverie—just as you see eager, demonstrative children do at home— but her reveries last only about two seconds, after which she will suddenly start up again on a new tack, as bright and eager as before. And so she prattles on.

She can write a little, though she usually contrives to get her *n*'s and *s*'s the wrong way around. Once, when I was sitting at my table writing to one of my prayer partners, it struck me to ask her (she was standing at the other side of the table watching me) to put her name at the head of the sheet. She complied with alacrity, and was just going to write when she suddenly pulled herself up and said, "I haven't yet asked God to help me," whereupon she bowed her head on the table and asked God to help her write her name! I think I can see her now, with her head in her hands, her rainbow cap on, and the tuft of fur flapping forward onto the table in front of her.

To win the love of the children was one of Fraser's chief joys in his Lisu wilds, but he did not often succeed with the very little ones. "They usually give me a doubtful, suspicious look," he confesses, "and then decide in the negative."

Such was a tiny little girl at Water Bowl Village. She was about two years old, but able to walk only by holding onto the bamboo partition as she went around the room. She would not come to me. But, do you know, she could sing "Jesus Loves Me" with scarcely a false note! I could hardly believe my ears, for she was little more than a baby. I recalled the words, "Out of the mouths of babes and sucklings thou hast perfected praise." Did you ever wonder why God has set so high a value on the praise of little children? Whatever the reason, their praise is "perfected," and we can never be better than perfect, in spite of all our poetic and musical accomplishments! Oh, yes, we grown-up people know a great deal, or think we do. We may indeed do many things in God's service better than children can. We may preach better. We may pray better. But there is one thing we shall never do better than children— and that is to praise God better. There is no sweeter music in the ears of our heavenly Father than His praises sung by the innocent lips of a tiny child.

There was something about the singing of the Lisu converts that brought Fraser himself much pleasure. He rarely mentioned, even to his mother, any sense of privation in his strangely primitive surroundings, but the hunger for music—real soul-stirring music— was always there.

Cooke is musical with real taste and feeling. He has a good violin and puts his soul into his playing in a way that makes it a pleasure to accompany him. But a portable organ such as mine is a poor accompaniment to a violin.

When I dip into real music, I often have the feeling that a part of myself has been more or less undeveloped—I do not mean in regard to execution, but in regard to general musical education and culture. Not that I would have my life different in actual practice, if I had the choice of making it so. One has sometimes to prune a tree in one direction that it may develop better in another. But if I ever dream —and I do sometimes—of golden ages and existences, the golden age to me is that of a century ago, more or less, and the golden existence, the swim of the musical world in Continental conservatories. I dream of bathing my soul in the creations of Beethoven, Mozart, and other great masters; of drinking in opera music; of living in the world of the Rubinsteins, Sarasates, Paganinis, and the great singers. I know very well that all this never is nor ever can be wholly satisfying, and I deliberately relegate it to its own place. It is not, and I do not wish it should be, more to me than a dream. My natural longings, however, do go out in that direction.

So Fraser loved the singing of his young Lisu and took great pains to train them in a method of his own, by which they could read simple music and even copy out new tunes for themselves. The value of hymns was so great in imparting truth and developing Christian experience that, with the help of Ba Thaw, he constantly added to their supply of both original hymns and translations. Two special favorites set forth Bible history in many verses, easily remembered by reason of their tunes, rhymes, and repetition. These two long hymns of the Old and New Testaments were eagerly learned and sung by the young converts, and went far to supplement the fragmentary portions of Scripture as yet available.

The days at Turtle Village were largely devoted to the translation of the Gospel of John, and to thought and prayer over the practical problem of self-support in the growing Lisu church. How easy it would have been to slip into the too-frequent custom of paying out of foreign funds the larger part of the expense

280 *Behind the Ranges*

incurred in the work! But the more Fraser lived in touch with the people the more he was convinced that they were really able to do for themselves all that was necessary. And he did not regard them as Christians of another type from himself. The greatest joy and privilege of his life lay in service and sacrifice for the Lord he loved. Fellowship with Christ was indeed precious in the realm of spiritual gain and gladness, but fellowship with Him in suffering brought yet deeper revelations of His love. Were these spiritual children, for whom he so truly travailed in birth, to be denied their right to this deeper fellowship? Were they to be excluded from free, self-propagating life as believers? Was the Lisu church to become a parasitic body, dependent on foreign money and control? Fraser had seriously considered these questions. As he looked upon the problem of the mountain people—the need of tribe after tribe in darkness throughout that great borderland—he saw the possibility of a growing, indigenous church, unfettered by foreign funds and methods, carrying the name of Jesus far afield by its own zeal and devotion. He saw voluntary, unpaid preachers, guided by the Spirit of God, going out in faith to make the Gospel known and attesting by self-sacrifice the reality of their love to the Saviour. He saw in faith the blessed possibilities so largely to be realized in the Lisu church, by the grace of God. And for *that* church, beloved of his soul, he was ready to deny himself, as

*allowed them the joy
of giving*

all wise parents must. He was ready to endure and
to let them endure, that they might "grow up into
him in all things."

But it was not easy. The extreme poverty of the
mountaineers was always there before his eyes. Was
he not sharing it, living for months on end in their
primitive homes? No aspect of their hard, bare life
was unknown to him. Yet he loved them well enough
not to make their way as Christians too easy or a one-
sided receiving. The joy of giving must be theirs too,
and there was much they could give. For this reason
Fraser did not pay the young men who volunteered
to carry his loads from village to village. When chapels were needed, he did not take the initiative, but
left it entirely to those who would use them. The
principle he inculcated was that those who enjoyed
the benefit should bear the labor or expense. He let
them pay for their Gospels and catechisms, notebooks
and pencils, which came to be in great demand as the
young folks learned to read and write. He let them
supply the food for their Christmas festivals and the
oil for lighting the chapels at night. He refrained
from paying the voluntary preachers who went out
from time to time. He left even the two young teachers still working in the eastern district to the care of
the warmhearted converts over there. How much
easier it would have been to go ahead and do things
at his own expense or at mission expense! But no—

he held on in the apostolic spirit: "I endure that they may obtain."

In this connection Fraser had written to his prayer helpers a few months previously:

One thing about which I am much exercised and want to ask your prayers is the matter of self-support. I could write much more than you have time to read on the subject, but will at least say this—that the Lisu converts, if wisely organized for the purpose, are well able to support their own evangelists and teachers, and to put up their own chapels and schools without the help of a single penny of foreign money. At the beginning it may be best for us to help them a little, but I regard entire self-support as a goal to be reached as soon as possible. It is not at all pleasant for us missionaries to insist on such poor people giving for the support of their work, when we are so wealthy by comparison. Nevertheless it has to be done, unless we want them to become parasite Christians.

On my last journey I was up against the problem in the village of City Hill. A young convert wished to join me in order to learn as much as he could while helping in evangelistic work among the heathen Lisu. As he could be of considerable use to his fellow villagers on his return, I put it to them that they might help his wife and children while he was away. I calculated that five rupees a month would be sufficient to provide for the family. And, as he was willing to give eight months to the work, a sum of forty rupees would be needed. It would have been far easier to provide the money from my own funds, but I had determined upon principle not to do so. When I broached the matter to them, the converts said they would think it over and give me an answer the next evening.

That next evening the villagers announced that they were prepared to give two annas a family, not for a month, but for the whole time the young man would be away—a total of one rupee for the eight Christian families. No doubt they expected Fraser to give the remaining thirty-nine.

There was a time when I should have been hesitant to press the subject any further with people living in such poverty. But I know the Lisu better now, and so proceeded to give them a good sound reproof for suggesting such a meager contribution. They did not like it much, naturally enough, and some of them grumbled and argued against me vigorously. But I stood my ground.

I pointed out that they were proposing to give to the work of the Lord, who had given His life for them, just about one-sixtieth part of the money they usually spent on tobacco and betel nut. I reminded them that there was more than one among them who had not yet broken off opium, and that a single opium smoker would burn away enough money during eight months to meet the entire need! They could not deny that for a single marriage they would spend eight hundred times the amount they had suggested each family should give—if not a thousand or two thousand times as much!

"Yes," they argued, "but we *have* to get wives. That is a necessary expenditure."

"Very well," I answered. "If you think so little of preaching the Gospel, perhaps it is not necessary for the young man to go at all."

And there I left the matter, begging them to reconsider it. The lad himself was disappointed, and so was his young wife, a nice, true-hearted girl, who really wanted her husband to go and learn more. I myself felt saddened, more than any of them, and made it a special matter of prayer that they might be brought to a better state of mind and heart.

The next evening they seemed to have come round a little, and eventually they made the following arrangement: Three of the eight families concerned promised to take the wife and two children into their homes and support them for a month at a time. Two other families gave a rupee each outright. This amounted altogether to a contribution of seventeen rupees instead of one. It was not all they could have done, by any means. But, not thinking it wise to press the matter further, I paid the balance of twenty-three rupees myself. I made it quite clear, however, that I did not want them to give anything at all if they did it grudgingly.

"No, Teacher," they instantly replied, "we are *glad* to give."

How different a spirit from the evening before! The Lord had been working in the meantime.

<u>Fraser was learning to depend more and more on prayer and the work of the Holy Spirit.</u> He longed to see the Lisu church a missionary church from the beginning, and spared neither prayer nor effort to make it so.

Now is the time to commence self-support among my Lisu, now while the work is still in its formative stage. I want you to pray very earnestly that it may go forward on wholesome, self-sustaining lines.

"Do not be afraid of burdening the people," was advice which had sounded strange to Fraser some years previously. "It does them good," the experienced and truly devoted missionary had asserted.

The advice was needed. We do not consider ourselves rich as compared with other Europeans out here, but we are rolling in wealth compared with these poor tribespeople, and are tempted to feel mean when we burden them in any way. But I am convinced that we ought to do it. Really, the people themselves expect us to. So I let them carry my baggage on their backs from village to village, sometimes as far as twenty miles, and never offer payment. They do not expect it any more than they expect to be paid for the hospitality I always accept when staying among them. They *expect* to do these things for their foreign teacher as well as for their own evangelists. Would I then be doing them a kindness to encourage a mercenary spirit where there is none to begin with?

As to paying converts to preach the Gospel, Fraser had reason to feel that for the foreign missionary to do so was "a vicious system" with grievous results.

> It is the line of least resistance, but something like the broad road that leads to destruction. It is far better to let our work go slowly, and tread the narrow way of self-support. We shall never regret it.

> What I want to see everywhere is the spirit of sacrifice for the Lord who bought us with His blood—a desire to prove not what we can *get* but what we can *give*—and my heart burns as I write it.

Shortly after this Fraser returned to Tengyueh. For a limited time he taught English in a local school two hours a day, carefully refunding the mission the amount of his salary in excess of the normal mission remittance. It was at this time that he picked up much valuable information to help the Lisu grow better crops on their mountain slopes. He also taught a group of Lisu converts who were preparing to be missionaries to their own people. Besides this the British government at Rangoon had commissioned him to compile a handbook on the Lisu language. This he completed and, with the help of Ba Thaw, eventually finished translating the Gospel of John.

Fraser was so well occupied that he might have stayed much longer at Tengyueh, but tidings reached him of a new movement of the Spirit of God out in his eastern district, which soon sent him back to the hills.

Lao-luh, one of the two young Lisu whom Cooke had left behind in the Cold Country, appeared in Tengyueh. Though suffering from an ulcerated eye that badly needed attention, and shabby and way-worn from his long journey, he was overflowing with gladness as the bearer of good tidings.

Listening to all he had to tell, Fraser was carried back in thought to the banks of the Salween and the day he had crossed it, coming from Rangoon the previous summer. He had not forgotten the men who had gesticulated on the far bank and then had finally turned back and disappeared. Now he heard the unexpected sequel.

Lao-luh had just come from those villages across the Salween, bringing with him two of the many tribespeople over there who were earnestly inquiring about the way of salvation. They had sent for this Lisu lad of whom they had heard, and he had gone willingly from village to village and from home to home, telling all he knew of the saving power of Christ. The joy in that remote region was great as demon altars were destroyed and whole households turned from darkness to light. Lao-luh was overwhelmed when more than a hundred families had declared themselves Christians and were asking for books and further teaching. All he could do was to hasten back to Tengyueh, a week's journey over the mountains, to find Fraser and at the same time seek help for his sore eyes.

Fraser deeply felt the call of the new development and, though tied down for the time being by his commitments in Tengyueh, took upon his heart the burden of seeking souls. Mr. Flagg, who was more at liberty, returned before long with Lao-luh to the Lisu hills.

Mr. and Mrs. Flagg had been drawn out to the Lisu and they felt with Fraser that the time had come for them to move into the eastern district and follow up as fully as possible that manifest working of God.

With a deep sense of his own insufficiency Fraser turned to his praying friends at home. He now had the tremendous responsibility for five or six hundred families who looked to him as father, mother, teacher, shepherd, and adviser. "I went in for big things when I took up tribes work," he admitted, "and I do not regret it. To a large extent we get what we go in for with God—though we may have mistaken ideas about how and when He will work it out."

Chapter 22

LOVE'S ENDURANCE

FRASER AND HIS COLLEAGUES were facing this new situation. April, 1921, had brought the stirring tidings from the Salween. Now, early in May, permission from Shanghai reached them to move out and make their home center in that southeastern district. Funds were in hand to build a simple bungalow sufficient for their needs, and plans they had long been making could now be put into execution. Fraser turned instinctively to his prayer circle as he thought of all the help and guidance that would be needed.

It seems increasingly clear that God is pointing us to this new field, rather than to the older districts of which you have particulars already. The number of converts in this eastern district is still increasing. The 150 families which have already turned to God this year added to the 250 last year make a total of about 400 households gathered in during the past 16 months. Our western, southern, and northern districts combined have barely half this number, nor are the converts as promising. So we feel distinctly led to open our main center among the eastern Lisu, working the other districts chiefly through native evangelists. After all these years of what I feel have been guerilla warfare, we are to have a permanent mission station right among the people. For this we have long been praying, and at last the way seems open. You will join us, will you not, in praying over all phases of this new development.

There were seven voluntary Lisu preachers in the new district by this time, and Fraser was anxious to give them much needed training. He was still teaching in the Tengyueh high school but arranged with the principal to lengthen his summer vacation to include the whole month of August. Ba Thaw was still with him for translation work, so they went together and conducted a regular Bible school at Sinchaiho—the first of the great gatherings for which that locality (Muchengpo) was to become famous. And what an enthusiastic, happy crowd it was, in the bamboo chapel on the mountain slope, high above the river! For two weeks the meetings continued, morning, noon, and night. Such fellowship had never been known in Lisuland before. If at times the unaccustomed students showed signs of weariness, the singing of a hymn or chorus quickly restored interest.

The home of Moh Ting-chang at Hsiangta was always open to the traveler, and Fraser was especially thankful for it on the return journey. He had not been well for some weeks, but had put it down to the damp heat of the season. Was this what caused his uncertainty about a detour he wished to make on his way back to Tengyueh? Moh and Ba Thaw were hoping to go with him to the town of Mangshih, down on the great Shan plain, where the copy of Mark's Gospel which led to Moh's conversion had been picked up. But the more Fraser planned for the journey, the more he felt uncertain about it. Difficulties of all sorts cropped up, and at last he felt sure that he was being guided to return home at once.

A week later, in Tengyueh, he knew the reason. He had resumed his classes at the high school and, though far from well, was teaching as usual, when he suddenly collapsed with what proved to be a serious attack of typhoid fever. For weeks his life hung in the balance, for malarial complications caused repeated relapses, but by the middle of October he was able to write to his mother:

I have any amount of things to be thankful for ("Count Your Blessings!") and the first is that I got back to Tengyueh just in time. If I had gone down to Mangshih, the fever would have caught me two days' journey away from here, with no place to stay, no one to look after me, no proper food or facilities for nursing in such serious illness. As you know, I have scores of times put to the test the simple plan of waiting upon God for guidance in perplexity, and have never yet been disappointed. Decisions so made have invariably proved to be wisest and best.

The kindness and care of his colleagues had been beyond telling.

> Flagg came down from Paoshan specially to look after me, and has been nursing me ever since. Mrs. Flagg moved out of their own room (the best in the house) to put me in it. They have given me the use of anything and everything they have. I am wearing Flagg's bathrobe as I write this. Naturally I feel very grateful to them, and I am sure you will too.

This almost fatal illness, and the fact that he could now leave his work in competent hands, led Fraser to apply at last for furlough, years overdue. His English teaching was not resumed, but the translation of John's Gospel was continued and was to be finally completed with slowly returning strength. Meanwhile came the move to the Lisu home Flagg had prepared in the Cold Country, with willing help from the local Christians. Bright autumn days were before them, and Fraser was eager to be back in his itinerant work again. Hundreds of converts were looking forward to the Christmas festival, which would have to be celebrated in the new center as well as at Turtle Village.

But again the unexpected happened. The grassy uplands of the Cold Country proved too exposed for the convalescing missionary. The unseasoned boards of the mission bungalow let in the wind almost as freely as the bamboo walls of the chapel. After the second Sunday (when Moh Ting-chang came over for the services) Fraser went down with a sharp attack of pleurisy. Recovery was slow, retarded by painful swelling of his legs, which made walking out of the question. Christmas Day was spent in bed instead of among his Lisu children, who felt for the first time the shadow of coming separation.

Fraser was now in his fourteenth year in China. The rugged strength and endurance he had brought to his task were perceptibly failing, but not so the brave spirit. His heart went out not only to the hundreds of converts around the new home and across the Salween River but also to the Lisu of all the regions to the north, and to other unevangelized tribespeople right out to the Tibetan border.

Mr. Lewers, a pioneer missionary on the Upper Mekong (twin river to the Salween), sent to Fraser for a couple of Christian Lisu to come to his help. He was alone up there, three weeks' journey to the north of Fraser's field. He had as yet little knowledge of the language, and there were tens of thousands of Lisu to be reached.

Spare two of these evangelists, at such a time, to go so far away? A smaller soul could not have faced it. But Fraser had grown with his work, had grown into a leader of wide vision and great faith. "Look not every man on his own things, but every man also on the things of others" surely applied to this situation. Two of his best voluntary helpers were willing to go without payment of any kind, leaving their farms and families for an indefinite period, to face hardship and danger for love of Christ and in obedience to His command. As Fraser let them go, he gathered strength to go on in the work without them only through waiting upon God.

Now began another long itineration before he could leave for furlough. Flagg had gone up to the Mekong to escort the Lisu evangelists, and Mrs. Flagg with little Ruth—not yet a year old, but a fast friend of Fraser's—would have to be alone for six weeks at least, several days' journey from the nearest white people. Bravely Mrs. Flagg faced it, the first woman missionary to the Lisu. And the converts rallied around her, including Paul and his family and neighbors, in the spirit Fraser recalled when he said some years later:

> The Christians of three out of four of these Cold Country villages have been among the most satisfactory we ever had—so loyal, so hearty, active, and intelligent. God will reward them.
>
> I think of one or two men, leaders in nearby villages, who have done almost everything they could possibly do for us, refusing any payment, and who say, "Teachers, by right we ought not only do what we have done but support you in food and clothing as well."
>
> They remind me of what the Apostle Paul said of Aristarchus, Mark, and Justus: "men that have been a comfort unto me" (Col. 4:11).

So Mrs. Flagg was well surrounded in her husband's absence, and would not hear of Fraser's journey being delayed. Two objects were before him now. In the villages throughout this eastern district there were many cases of real or supposed persecution to look into, and troubles to settle among the Christians themselves. And beyond, across the Salween, hundreds of new converts who had never yet seen a missionary waited his coming. It was the middle of February, 1922, when he left the Cold Country for Mangshih and the great plain stretching southward, and summer was well advanced before he came back, having had little if any news of his colleagues or of the outside world for three and a half months. "I never made a more needed journey," he wrote on his return, though the cost to himself had been great.

It was a new experience, on this trip, to find himself a traveling magistrate as well as missionary; but there seemed no escaping the double role.

I do not relish these affairs. Too often a wrong spirit is manifested by the converts themselves when trouble of any kind arises, and frequently the right is not all on one side. There are, of course, some cases of pure persecution, where the converts suffer undoubted injustice. In two of the cases I have had to attend to, the sufferers told me that in their opinion the best way to settle the matter would be to get their swords, go in a body, and kill their persecutors! It is not easy to teach them to love their enemies.

Yet these same young converts were so loving and hospitable to their missionary, with all his Christian ethics, that Fraser found it hard to pass on and leave them. A Chinese shopkeeper in the market town of Chefang undertook to mail a letter sometime, somewhere, for the passing traveler. So, standing at his counter, Fraser wrote in pencil to his mother, giving some details:

> The Lisu converts I have been staying with at Palien the last few days are so very kind and hearty that it is a pleasure to be in their home. You love them and hate to leave them.
>
> One of the cases we have investigated was that of the kidnaping of a Christian girl by a heathen Lisu. We went to "rescue" her (my Lisu and I) over across the Salween, but it turned out a kind of fiasco, for, when we found her, she did not want to be rescued after all! So we had to leave her—and this after walking I do not know how many hours by night with a lantern, to surprise them before they could run off with her again. We must have walked thirty miles each way. The matter was settled by the payment of a fine.

But as a rule, young women who had been abducted were only too glad to be set free again.

> A case has just come up which I am having to settle. A Christian girl was carried off by some heathen of the same locality. They tried to get her to recant and consent to be the wife of a heathen man,

but she stuck to her guns bravely. Being afraid of getting into serious trouble with us, they let her go again. But, returned or not returned, we cannot let our girls be abducted with impunity, and are taking steps to protect them.

Many of the cases to be settled were across the river among the most recent converts, and there also Fraser found the same warmth of heart and welcome. The custom of handshaking had come even to these villages, and men, women, and children would flock out at his approach, line up on both sides of the pathway, and greet him with singing—each one in turn gripping his hand in both their own, often with eyes shut and teeth clenched in their earnestness. They were so glad to see him and to have someone, at last, to teach them more about how to be saved from the power of demons and the fear of death.

But over here, across the Salween, Fraser found himself faced by conditions more trying than any he had previously met.

The country is poor and barren. The mountains are high and rocky, and the poverty of the people terrible. Most of them are in rags and tatters, and the squalor of the hovels in which they live makes it a trial to the flesh to be among them.

Yet these were the homes he shared, day and night, for the next two months. The frequent rains of the wet season made it difficult to be out of doors. But, with all their poverty, the people had already built

eight little chapels, which were put to good use. Two
hundred and more families in forty villages—how was
Fraser to help them all? To make the most of his
time in the district, he arranged to hold a Bible
school in a central place, and invited all who could
to come together for half a month of teaching. This
was a new thing indeed, with all the thrill of a festival
for these backward people, and willingly they gathered about him, making their own arrangements for
food and shelter.

Of course it was all primitive in the extreme. The
bamboo chapel might be full for a meeting, but in-
quiries yelled from outside would be answered in the
same strident tones from within. And if a herd of cattle were driven by, the whole audience would stam-
pede to the door and out on the hillsides to take stock
of them, leaving the teacher, meanwhile, waiting
with what patience he could muster. But it was a
beginning in placing these new believers on the rock
of revealed truth. It made them feel that they were
people of the Book—and many of the younger folk
became eager to learn to read and write.

Fraser too was learning. He had been inclined
to be impatient at first with the extreme ignorance
and backwardness of the people. They were so taken
up with externals, rules and regulations as to how to
be a Christian: whether, though not growing opium
himself, one might work for a heathen on his opium
fields; whether pickled beans might be eaten (they

are pickled in liquor), what to do when your son is
engaged to a girl in a heathen family who insist on
liquor being given at the wedding; whether you may
wash clothes or hunt game on Sunday, etc., etc.

And their slowness in learning to think for themselves! Question and answer might proceed a little
way, for example:

"Who were the sons of Adam and Eve?"

"Cain, Abel, and Seth" (for the lesson had been
carefully taught).

"Good! Now who were the parents of Cain, Abel,
and Seth?"

"Don't know. It isn't in the catechism."

Impatient with them? Well now, let me whisper
to you. Yes, I am afraid I do get a little impatient
sometimes. But, remembering the dense ignorance
these people have been brought up in, the absolute
lack of Christian nurture or advantages of any kind,
I feel sorry ever to have been impatient with them.
They mean so well. You see them sitting there—men,
women, boys, and girls—in all their poverty and ignorance; you remember One who was never impatient, never harsh, even with sinners and outcasts,
and your heart goes out to them. You have a new
understanding of what this means: "He had compas-
sion on the multitudes, for they were as sheep having
no shepherd."

Yes, Fraser was learning. The best food that his
mountain hosts could give him at this time was so

poor that there were days when he simply could not
eat it. It would not go down any more, and he had to
fall back on his old plan of going without food altogether until his hunger compelled him to eat just
what they ate. And yet, comparing the conditions of
comfort and civilization down on the plains, in the
Chinese cities with their culture, where Christ was
not wanted nor His truth received, he could rejoice in
"coming right away up to these mountains, amid the
rocks, mists, and forests, to find ourselves in little
Lisu chapels of bamboo and thatch, put up by simple
Christian folk for the worship of God."

The people shiver in their rags. They are poor,
dirty, ignorant, and superstitious, but they are God's
gift to us. You ask God for spiritual children and
He chooses them out for you. You shake hands with
the brothers and sisters and mothers He has found
for you, and sit down with them, the boys and girls
all around you if possible. I would far rather teach
Lisu children to sing "Jesus loves me, this I know,"
than teach integral calculus to the most intelligent
who have no interest in China. [Remember, Fraser
was an engineer.]

In this spirit Fraser came very near to these new
believers. After Bible school was over he went with
them to their villages.

I have never traveled with people whose company
I have enjoyed more on the road than these Lisu
converts. They are so obliging, so good-humored,

so simple-minded, and so easily pleased. They never grumble at hardships. They will perhaps get drenched in a heavy downpour of rain, get little but dry rice to eat at the end of a long day's journey, but still seem as happy as ever, to judge by the peals of laughter you hear from their smoky campfires at night.

When you have been with them so many days—chatting, walking, eating, living, and sleeping with them—you feel when you come to shake hands and say good-bye that you know them better and have helped them, imparting to them something of yourself.

Fraser was much impressed at this time by the thought that "not many wise men after the flesh, not many mighty, not many noble are called" to follow Christ.

Two things stand out clearly in my mind: how "foolish" and "weak" our new converts are; and how God has *really* chosen them. The words of I Corinthians 1:27-28 are fulfilled before my very eyes! If you could come out here and see how useless mere preaching and persuasion are among these people, you would understand this better. One feels so helpless in face of their ignorance and need! But the Lisu work in our present district, with over 250 families on either side of the Salween River (400 families and more in all), has been spontaneous from the beginning.

They will take you to a village you have never set

foot in or even heard of before, and you will find several families of converts there, some of whom can read and write after a fashion, and a chapel already put up! They just teach one another—inviting converts over from neighboring villages for the purpose. They just *want* to be Christians when they hear all about it, and then turn Christian, missionary or no missionary. Who put that "want-to" in their hearts? If they are not God's chosen, God's elect, what are they?

Chapter 23

LOVE'S REWARD

BUT FRASER'S STRENGTH was giving out. Rumors had reached him across the Salween that made him anxious to get back to his colleagues, and great indeed were the changes that he found. The Flaggs were no longer living up in the Cold Country. A serious earthquake had taken place there, leaving Mrs. Flagg with an overstrained heart which could no longer bear the altitude of seven thousand feet. They had therefore moved down to Muchengpo, two thousand feet lower and more in the center of their eastern district, where, to his surprise, Fraser found them when he came up from the river.

Hardly could he believe his eyes! There, close to the spot where the wife of Pa Tsong-si had hailed him the first time he passed that way, a new settlement was springing up—right on an inviting lower ridge, running out into a great circle of protecting mountains. The level site had often attracted him, and now he found it a veritable hive of activity, for the local Christians had come to the help of the missionaries and were doing all in their power to make the new place habitable. To Fraser's joy he found that they were doing it voluntarily, without payment of any kind, in a spirit of loving indebtedness.

> The people have been most kind. They have put up a bamboo and thatch house for us, just like their own, though a little larger—without asking a penny in payment. They have also plotted out a garden (we can occupy as much land here as we want). They have ploughed up the ground and are digging it for us. They have put up a goathouse, a kitchen, and sleeping quarters for the servants, and have dug a trench a mile long to bring water to the place—all without a penny of payment. They are still bringing us presents of eggs and vegetables.

More than this, the Christians were cutting wood and putting up a fence around the mission station.

> Here we are on a ridge protected on both sides by the slopes of a big deep valley covered with forest. The vegetation is luxuriant and the effect superb as the clouds roll up over the hilltop or hang suspended halfway up the mountains. I like it here; we all do. The Flaggs are thinking of putting up a permanent home next dry season.
>
> After a shower such as the one just over, the streams rise high. As I write I can hear the roar of the river down in the valley below us. The climate is wonderful for crops and gardens. The soil is so fertile that things seem to spring out of the ground almost by magic. Ferns and grass grow luxuriantly,

and the trees stand high. We are hoping for great things from our experimental garden, having planted seeds from India and America, as well as yours from Letchworth.

Best of all, they were in the midst of the people, not far up the hill from Sinchaiho. Hundreds of believers had already confessed their faith in Christ at this quiet spot in the valley where the baptisms were held. A chapel had been built beside the river, a tributary of the Salween, and Sinchaiho was fast becoming the center of the Lisu church.

Here Fraser made his home with the Flaggs in the new mission bungalow, while the Christians from all sides gathered about them. Even from across the Salween they came, as Sunday by Sunday Fraser led the large gatherings on the leveled space around the house or down in the Sinchaiho chapel. They were memorable days, especially the Sunday when he witnessed the baptism of 240 more believers amid scenes of great rejoicing. He did no baptizing himself, standing aside in favor of the colleague to whom he was handing over the care of all the work. But his joy was as great as the long travail of soul before had been deep. It was of this time he wrote: "I never was loved so much in my life before."

Looking back over the years of his Lisu work, Fraser was more and more impressed with the large part that praying friends had had in it all. His chief desire in going home on furlough was that he might make personal contact with every member of his prayer circle and be greatly prospered in adding to their number. Some time before, he had written them a letter which fully expressed his mature thought, regarding both the work and their part in it. With sincerest humility it began:

> Perhaps I ought to apologize when writing to you on the prayer life, for most of you are older Christians than I am and have had longer and perhaps deeper experience of it than I have. At the same time I have opportunities to observe the working of prayer that some of you have not, so you will forgive me if I try to pass on thoughts which have come to me in connection with my work.

He then went on to speak of a promising center in his field, a place where he himself had spent much time teaching the Christians, where through various causes the work had gone back and was now discouraging. Among those who had reverted to heathenism were two or three of the best instructed young people in the district, certainly the best readers and penmen. While this caused deep sorrow and led him to revise his methods, it emphasized the fact that it is not human instruction or influence that we have to depend upon, but the grace of God working in the heart.

> Some missionaries question whether my methods are the best. They feel that I am trying to cover too

much ground, and that it would be better to go in for "intensive work," as it is called. What is the use, they wonder, of spending two or three days in a village and then going on elsewhere and leaving them for perhaps a year? What can you expect of them? Why, they know practically nothing! Yes, I admit that it is not ideal. I believe in instructing my converts as much as anybody. Yet I can show numbers and numbers of Lisu Christians, with no more knowledge than two or three days' instruction could impart, standing firm *with the grace of God behind them* (that is what makes all the difference), trying in their blundering way to observe the Lord's day, to pray, and to sing—while those you give weeks and months of attention to, in other places, fall away.

Instruction, especially in the Scriptures, is a good thing. It is essential if a man is to grow in grace. We are to be "renewed unto knowledge after the image of him that created" us. Paul prays for his converts that they may be filled with knowledge. Knowledge is good, wholesome, needful. If a man is already a Christian, knowledge—spiritual knowledge—will help to establish him. I intend to do all I can to impart spiritual knowledge to my converts. I do not despise secular knowledge either, for it is a help rather than a hindrance to the apprehension of spiritual truth. But it is possible to overemphasize almost anything however good it may be. That the Apostle Paul believed it possible to overemphasize knowledge, his first letter to the Corinthian church shows, in more than one passage. They say that "knowledge is power"; but this, I feel, needs to be qualified. In the spiritual realm it is certainly not true that knowledge always imparts power to keep a man from falling away.

As a matter of fact there is much knowledge which has no life-giving power in it at all. It is possible to preach dead sermons—full of good, orthodox truth, but dead because the power of the Holy Spirit is absent. It is possible to read a dead Bible, for the same reason. There is no magical charm about the letter of God's Word. Apart from the power of God's Spirit, the best instruction we can give our converts is as dead as the dry bones of Ezekiel 37. With the "breath of God" breathing upon it, it may become as powerful as "the exceeding great army" the bones were turned into. The power came from the breath of God, not from the dry bones. The dry bones were all right, but they were absolutely useless without the breath of God. And so are education, teaching, instruction of any kind out here on the mission field, if of the dry-bones variety. Some people go so far as to say that the problem confronting the church on the mission field is fundamentally an educational one, and too many put that belief into practice. It seems to me like constructing costly artillery, firing big shells—and doing no damage to the enemy. And I can imagine Satan laughing up his sleeve.

Then follows a yearning plea for prayer, much prayer, more prayer for those emerging from spiritual darkness into the light of life. How Fraser's heart went out for these babes in Christ—that, the eyes of their understanding being enlightened, they might "grow up into him in all things."

I used to think that prayer should have the first place and teaching the second. I now feel it would be truer to give prayer the first, second, and third places, and teaching the fourth.

These people out here are not only ignorant and superstitious but they have a heathen atmosphere all about them. You can actually feel it. We are not dealing with an enemy that fires at the head only, to keep the mind only in ignorance, but with an enemy who uses "gas attacks" which wrap the people around with deadly fumes and yet are impalpable, elusive. What would you think of a soldier who fired a gun into the gas, to kill it or drive it back? Nor would it be of any more avail to teach or preach to the Lisu here, while they are held back by these invisible forces. Poisonous gas cannot be dispersed, I suppose, in any other way than by the wind springing up and dispersing it. Man is powerless.

And from this allegory Fraser stressed the place of prayer, intercessory prayer, even at a distance.

In answer to your prayers the breath of God can blow away all those miasmic vapors from the atmosphere of a village. We are not fighting against flesh and blood. You deal with the fundamental issues of this Lisu work when you pray against "the principalities, the powers, the world-rulers of this darkness, against the spiritual hosts of wickedness in the heavenly places" (Eph. 6:12, A.S.V.).

I believe that a work of God sometimes goes on behind a particular man or family, village or district, before the knowledge of the truth ever reaches them. It is a silent, unsuspected work, not in mind or heart, but in the unseen realm behind these. Then, when the light of the Gospel is brought, there is no difficulty, no conflict. All one has to do then is simply "stand still and see the salvation of the Lord."

This should give us confidence in praying intelligently for those who are far from the Gospel light. The longer the preparation, the deeper the work. The deeper the root, the firmer the plant when once it springs above ground. I do not believe that any deep work of God takes root without long preparation somewhere.

On the human side, evangelistic work on the mission field is like a man going about in a dark, damp valley with a lighted match in his hand, seeking to ignite anything inflammable. But things are damp through and through, and will not burn however much he tries. In other cases, God's wind and sunshine have prepared the tinder beforehand. The valley is dry in places, and when the lighted match is applied, here a shrub, there a tree, here a few sticks, there a heap of leaves take fire and give light and warmth long after the kindling match and its bearer have passed on. And this is what God wants to see, and what He will be inquired of us for: little patches of fire burning all over the world.

We have seen how true this had been in his own experience, and Fraser was the first to acknowledge the efficacy of the help of his prayer circle. He now pleaded for the continuance of their intercessions on the part of his colleagues, Mr. and Mrs. Flagg.

It had been a sore trial to him, some months previously, when Allyn Cooke, on his marriage with Miss Leila Robinson, had been appointed to Tali to relieve Mr. and Mrs. Hanna, who had to go home on furlough. The station was a central one and could not be left without missionary supervision, but Fraser had so hoped that the Cookes would come into tribal work. Prayer and thought had reconciled him to the situation, however, and when he had to leave the Tengyueh Lisu, it was a relief to know Ba Thaw would have them in his care. Fraser was thankful for the cooperation of this godly man and of the American Baptist Mission, who released him for this work. He had planned to revisit many of the old centers in the west on his way to Rangoon, but was able only to take in the Atsi Kachin at Pangwa and the district of Mottled Hill, spending a Sunday in each.

It had been a hard parting, when Fraser set out from Muchengpo to pay a farewell visit to Moh at Hsiangta. But there a glad surprise awaited him, a token for good as he went on his homeward way, for Moh had kept his recent mail, and there was a letter from Lewers on the Upper Mekong, telling of the work of the Lisu helpers Fraser had spared from his own field to go to one still more needy. He had missed them, but great was his joy now as he learned of the blessing of God upon their labors. More than a hundred families up there had already turned from drunkenness and demon worship to Christ, and the missionary wrote begging Fraser to come and help them with the many inquirers.

The Lisu church a missionary church already! And for himself how great the reward: "never loved so much in my life before." But more precious even than the love of thousands who, through him, had come to know the love of God was the deeper fellowship with that dear Lord Himself, whose call he had obeyed in all the freshness of youth.

Truly, "whosoever will save his life shall lose it; but whosoever shall lose his life for my sake and the gospel's, the same shall save it" (Mark 8:35).

Chapter 24

MARRIAGE AND WIDER
MINISTRY

AFTER A FURLOUGH of almost two years, Fraser returned to China by way of North America. His chief
concern at home had been to call forth prayer for
the neglected tribes of southwest China. His ministry
was used of God beyond the scope of his own work,
and it set the pattern for the Prayer Companionship
in England. Fraser's appeal for definite, intelligent
prayer—real partnership in the work—led to the
grouping of prayer companions in circles of ten, each
group to surround one individual missionary and his
work with prayer support and detailed interest.

Returning to Shanghai in September, 1924, Fraser
was faced with one of the greatest and most unexpected trials of his life. Eager to be back among his
beloved Lisu, he was quite unaware that the leaders
of the mission had other thoughts for his future. A
serious situation in the province of Kansu, northwest
China, called for firm and judicious handling. Fraser's
personality and experience fitted him to deal with it,

and no one else was available at the time. Though the Flaggs were at home on furlough, the Lisu work was comparatively well cared for, with Mr. and Mrs. Carl Gowman and the Allyn Cookes in charge at Muchengpo. Blessing was still spreading from that center, where more than a thousand Christians were longing for Fraser's return. What it cost him to leave them and turn away to other service, words could never tell. "Yunnan was my first love, my Rachel," he said long after, "but Kansu became my Leah." For the wider fruitfulness of his life grew out of that painful experience.

So for the next three years the northwest claimed him instead of the Burma border—and more contrasted spheres could hardly be. But Fraser came to love the great wide spaces, the bracing desert air and mountain ranges, and the nomad peoples of the Gobi and Tibet. He responded to the strong character of the northern Chinese and Muslims in the opportunities that came to him through educational work and Bible teaching.

Visiting all the stations of the mission in Kansu and many in Shansi, he came to know their problems firsthand. It was a time of great and increasing difficulty. A threatening wave of antiforeign feeling was sweeping over China. This led to the general evacuation of Europeans and Americans from all but the treaty ports. By consular orders missionaries had to come down to the coast as their lives as well as those of other foreigners were in imminent danger. Fraser and his fellow workers in Kansu were shut up to a perilous journey by raft down the Yellow River. It was largely due to his leadership that they were brought safely through the attacks of bandits and the dangers of sandbanks and whirlpools by the way— especially after the tragic drowning of the most experienced member of the party, Fraser's beloved friend and fellow worker, Dr. George King of the Borden Memorial Hospital at Lanchow.

From that time on, Fraser was more and more drawn into the central executive of the mission. This meant being detained in Shanghai, where office routine and correspondence naturally were a sore trial to his spirit. But there also was the urgent need to exercise faith, prayer, and endurance at the very heart of the mission.

When at last Fraser was set free to return to Yunnan, it was as superintendent of all the CIM work in that province. That journey back to the west was a pilgrimage indeed—a coming home after five years of heart hunger. And little as he expected it, it was a homecoming in another sense, as he was to discover. Only a few days before his arrival in Kunming another traveler had reached that city at the close of a longer journey. Knowing nothing of Fraser, she had come out from England as a missionary to join her parents in Kunming, the Rev. and Mrs. Frank Dymond of the United Methodist Mission. Talking with a fellow worker soon after his own arrival, Fraser heard of her coming, and the name of the young lady impressed him—Roxie Maud Dymond. Immediately a quiet voice said in his heart: "That is your wife— the one I have prepared for you." To one who never sought his own had indeed come God's best earthly gift. He was no longer to be what he had once called himself: "the loneliest man in China." Disparity in years—for she was a young student fresh from college—was lost sight of in a union of heart so deep that it made them one in all their outlook.

Before this friendship could ripen, Fraser spent a year visiting all the stations of the mission in eastern and western Yunnan. This took him back to his own loved Lisuland on the Burma border. He did not go alone, for younger workers were coming to the province. He had brought the Harrisons and John Kuhn with him in January, 1928. And in March he returned to Haiphong to meet the Fitzwilliams and Castos and bring them around by sea to Rangoon, then through Bhamo to Tengyueh. Having settled the young couples into language study, Fraser set out with the Lisu men who had come down from Muchengpo to escort him. Back over the familiar road they traveled to Moh at Hsiangta, and finally to the big welcome at Muchengpo.

Many were the changes during his five years' absence. First the Allyn Cookes had come, when the Flaggs went on furlough, and with their loving hearts had nurtured the growing Lisu church. Then the Gowmans had returned to the Tengyueh district, bringing all the experience they had gained in tribal work elsewhere during the interval. Gowman, with his great energy and wide outlook, had found the Lisu converts ready to reach out to the regions beyond. He had encouraged them to organize bands of volunteer preachers to go into all directions, exploring possible openings for making known the Glad Tidings. In this way the Gospel had spread eastward and northward to new fields, reaching even to the valley of the Upper Salween, which Fraser had visited with Mr. Geis and Ba Thaw long years before. To hear of these developments was a wonderful experience for Fraser. For three full weeks he stayed with the Christians at Muchengpo, and was thrilled when they gathered to read letters from their own "volunteer missionaries" and to pray for them.

From there he went down to join the Paynes at the anniversary services of the Chinese church at Paoshan which he had founded some twenty years earlier.

Soon after Fraser reached Kunming again in the spring, his duties as superintendent took him down to Shanghai to attend the quarterly meetings of the field council of the mission. He was there for Easter, with its many opportunities of fellowship with others in special meetings as well as personal interviews with leaders of the mission and hours of prayer and conference with Mr. Hoste. The result was that in April he set out with a large party of new workers for Yunnan.

His marriage on October 24, 1929, was the crowning blessing on a life so fully outpoured for others. There was no provision for home or outward comfort, the bride being more than willing to join her husband in his journeyings throughout the province. He was due to visit the western stations, so they set off after a few days on the strenuous two-week journey to Tali. By this time there were new developments on the Burma border that took them south to the tribal region, where Mrs. Fraser was introduced to her husband's former field.

Christmas at Muchengpo was a great experience for, in addition to meeting all the hundreds of Lisu Christians who gathered for the services, Mrs. Fraser enjoyed fellowship with the largest group of foreign missionaries ever assembled in the mountains up to that time. The bride made the acquaintance not only of Mr. and Mrs. Gowman and their children but also of the Castos and Fitzwilliams, two young couples from Tengyueh who had joined them.

The Cookes had by this time returned from furlough, but they were six days farther on, over the mountains, at the newly opened station of Fuhinshan, to which the Frasers continued their journey. A Bible school was in progress when they arrived, so they were introduced at once into stirring scenes.

A thousand Christians formed the family Mr. and Mrs. Cooke had taken over with the new center, and the house perched high on the ridge overlooking great distances was the hub of much activity. Fraser at once threw himself into all that was going on, reminding Allyn Cooke of the old days at Turtle Village, except that now he was "a very happy bridegroom."

Too soon the fortnight fled away, and their journey had to be resumed. The way was now more difficult, stretching into a wide expanse of territory east of Fuhinshan where there were no mission stations. To face it alone would have been to Fraser an everyday experience, but to take his young wife with him thirty-five days across to the Red River was quite another thing. It was an exploratory journey that had to be taken in the interests of the work, however, and there was no hesitation.

Out in that wide territory so devoid of Christian witness were many cities of importance, besides countless towns and villages they passed as day succeeded day. "In one place," wrote the bride, "the people brought out an old stool on the hillside for me to sit on, while they crowded and crowded around the first white woman they had ever seen." It was a foretaste of what lay before her with her husband in the years to come. "In east and west," she wrote, looking back upon many journeys, "we traveled among Lisu, Lahu, Liti, Meo, Nosu, Kopu, Laka,

Palaung, Woni, Kachin, Wa, Lolo, and Shan, besides Chinese."

Back in Kunming, after coming up from the Red River through the field of their colleague, Mr. Allen, the Frasers had a couple of months to give to correspondence and other duties before setting out again for Shanghai to attend the council meetings in June, 1930. Then followed a whole year during which Fraser's duties detained them at the coast in executive work. Their first child, Catherine, was born in March, 1931. She was only three months old when they returned to Yunnan for their next period of inland service.

This included a visit to the Upper Salween, where important developments were taking place. Carl Gowman was gone from Muchengpo, his lamented death having deprived the work of a great leader; but others were being raised up to strengthen the Lisu evangelists who were penetrating farther and farther up the gorge of the Salween. From Paoshan on the east, Mr. and Mrs. Talmage Payne had come to the evangelists' help, living with them for months at a time in nothing but a small tent at Pine Mountain, their first settlement. There a number of Christians had been gathered out, and the evangelists had gone farther afield with the Glad Tidings. The Paynes, broken in health through those pioneering experiences, had been obliged to go home on furlough before Mr. and Mrs. Fraser came west again, wanting to see for themselves something of this new field.

Knowing the journey out to the Salween would be incredibly hard, the Frasers left little Catherine with Mr. and Mrs. Booth, who had succeeded the Paynes. With some of the Lisu pioneers they traversed the mountain passes and dropped down into the mighty canyon of the river, making their way painfully northward to Deer Pool. Here a Sunday was spent with the first group of Christians won to the Lord on the Salween, Fraser speaking to them in their Lisu language.

The next Sunday found them back at Pine Mountain, staying in one of the hovels of the village clinging to the mountainside. And there also they found Christians to rejoice their hearts with promise of a coming harvest. Over three hundred gathered at the midday service and could scarce disperse at night for the joy of having the teacher who could speak in their own tongue come to them.

Three months later, after the birth of their second child down in Burma, Fraser settled his family at Muchengpo while he himself went northward on needed visits. In an ordinary Chinese inn, at the town of Chenanso, he was taken ill and could go no farther. Happily a lady missionary with some knowledge of nursing was there. When she saw that the illness was serious, she sent for Charles Peterson from the nearest CIM station.

Week followed week, and still the traveler did not
return to Muchengpo. When at last they heard that
he was down with typhoid fever, Mrs. Fraser, taking
the baby with her, went to find him. The five-day
cross-country journey gave opportunity to prove the
wonderful keeping power of the peace of God.

Two weeks later friends from Muchengpo came to
carry the patient back over the mountains. This illness had lasted two months and it soon became evident that furlough was needed. This was Fraser's
second long term of service—nine years on the field.
Letters from the General Director in Shanghai urged
them to go home without delay by way of Burma.
Before leaving, Fraser wrote the following letter to
the writer, who, with her husband, was in Kunming
at the time.

Mr. Cooke, now on the Upper Salween, has just
sent an S.O.S. for more volunteer evangelists from
this district—fourteen days' journey away—as they
have more and more families turning from demon
worship all the time. You will be interested to know
that for the very first time in the history of this work
we are about to send out three young women to
teach in the villages near here. They are 16, 20,
and 21 years of age. They volunteered together and
are so thoroughly in earnest that Fitzwilliam and I
and the local deacons have decided to give them a
trial. We are placing them under the direction of
one of the regular Lisu evangelists and his wife.

I would like you to have seen them come into my study so bashfully and girlishly—two of them coming only on the excitedly whispered persuasions of the boldest of the three. And they all sat there for some time, mildly squirming before saying what they had come to see me about. But they were nevertheless in earnest. Perhaps you will pray for them sometimes: Tabitha, Sarah, and Ruth.

You will know, doubtless, that the Lisu work is entirely self-supporting. All the money for our regular evangelists, with their food and the food for their families, is provided by the Lisu themselves, from their harvest festival offerings. The volunteer evangelists are not paid at all, nor their families, but they are fed by the people in the villages where they stay.

The work is also largely self-governing. Important matters are settled by the deacons of the whole district at their annual meeting each December. There is also an annual meeting of the deacons of this district, usually presided over by our ordained Pastor Paul. This often partakes of the nature of a legislative assembly—they make rules, take minutes of the meetings, etc., whether the missionary is there or not.

I would love you to hear our Lisu sing. Mr. and Mrs. Cooke, our missionary musicians, have always taught them to sing in parts—and that without an organ. I have heard very few congregations at home, either in England or America, whose singing is so moving. The Lisu themselves love it. How you would like to go to bed on Sunday night to the

strains of some sweet hymn which they are still singing, and in parts, in one of their homes in the village nearby. How I love to hear them sing "When
my lifework is ended, and I cross the swelling tide"!
I must not seem to boast—but I know one poor missionary heart that has swelled with emotion and
praise on listening to the hearty and tuneful singing of these aborigines of the Burma-China border.

Chapter 25

FULFILLMENT AND
TRANSLATION

IT WAS A VERY HAPPY FURLOUGH, spent in England and North America. The Frasers reached London and Letchworth early in February, 1934. After a period of rest in his mother's home, Fraser bought a car to take them from place to place for their many meetings. Quickly the summer sped, bringing helpful contacts with friends from Bristol to Aberdeen, as well as snatches of rest and family reunion. One of these was to celebrate Fraser's mother's seventy-ninth birthday—that dear mother whose prayer life meant so much to her son.

Christmas was spent in North America, on their return journey. Well does the writer remember the arrival of the little family in Philadelphia, the strong, genial personality of the father, the sweet dignity of the mother, and the charm of the children. Many were the hours of conversation on that visit that left the writer not only in possession of the main facts of the story told in these pages but also with a strong

impression of the bright and prayerful spirit of the
man himself.

It was March, 1935, when they arrived in Shanghai, eager to return to their beloved field before the
summer. But long delay awaited them. The situation
in Shanghai was such that Fraser's presence was
more needed there than in Yunnan. One of his own
sayings was, "There is the flame of a burning bush in
everything that is a work of God." That flame was
there, burning in his own life all through the months
that followed, when—restricted largely to office work
—his heart went out in prayer especially for the
young workers of the mission, with whom he was
corresponding all over the inland provinces.

There was one break in the absorbing claims of
Fraser's position when, in July, he went up to Shansi
to take part in the Yutaoho Convention. In that lovely valley, on the banks of the stream that turned the
wheels of mill after mill, the summer community was
gathered. They occupied the millhouses rented to
them for the season and, whenever possible, met in
the open air.

Mr. and Mrs. Frank Houghton had come from
Szechwan to take part in the conference, which he
addressed in the morning, Fraser taking the evening
meetings. The blessing given in answer to prayer on
their united ministry was so great that the testimony
meeting at the close was prolonged until well after
midnight.

Mr. George Gibb had been appointed that summer to succeed Mr. D. E. Hoste as general director of the mission. By the end of the year Fraser could again be spared from Shanghai. In his journal for the last day before sailing for Hong Kong, he recorded the fact that made it significant: "Nov. 21, 1935: Walked with Mr. Hoste in the morning to Kiaochow Road Park." It was Fraser's last walk with the beloved leader to whom he owed so much.

Christmas in Kunming was the cheery season that marked the homecoming of the missionaries' children from the faraway school at Chefoo, North China. Once each year, as many of the parents as were able would come to the city to spend this brief holiday with their boys and girls, crowding the houses of the mission to overflowing. Mr. and Mrs. Allyn Cooke came down this year from the Salween to be with their sons and, incidentally, to welcome the Frasers. Following the departure of the children for Chefoo, the parents stayed on in Kunming for three days of devotional meetings. Fraser, having dearly loved little ones of his own, understood the hearts of his fellow workers at such a time and entered into the meetings with special sympathy. Most of the speaking was left to him, and none of those who were present would ever forget the depth and tenderness of his messages. His subject was the Holy Spirit, whose personality, presence, and power came home to some of his fellow workers as never before.

"He spoke about a life in the Holy Spirit," wrote Mrs. Cooke, "as a blessing we should claim. He showed how in life after life in the Old Testament an added blessing was given, lifting it to a higher plane. So there is ever new and deeper blessing for us as we definitely appropriate the Holy Spirit's power. It has been so with me since then—daily victory that I never knew before."

"It was Fraser's zenith," wrote another. "He was a Spirit-filled man."

And then, as if it were the most natural thing in the world, Fraser set out from the conference with his wife and children, to go back with the Cookes and Mrs. Fitzwilliam to their remote tribal districts in the southwest of the province. Mr. Fitzwilliam was already there, prospecting for a new center among the Kachin, who were much on Fraser's heart. To open up work among them, he and Mrs. Fraser were keen to settle for a time in a Kachin village. Mrs. Fraser longed for the opportunity to have a definite part in the work herself and, already proficient in the Chinese language, she was ready to learn Kachin by living right among these people.

We cannot enter upon the full story of this development now. Fraser himself summarized it in a letter to the writer when absent from his family on superintendent's work:

Mrs. Fraser and the children are with the Fitzwilliams. It would interest you very much to see them all living as they are in a bamboo house, single-storied, with a bamboo floor and thatched roof. They have a large garden in a most beautiful spot on the mountains, with Kachin villages all around (also Lisu, Palaung, and Chinese) and the plain of Chefang some six miles below. Longchiu in itself is an Atsi-Kachin village, about ten miles from the border of Burma. The headman and all his family are Christians, as are also several other families. It is a small beginning, a door ajar rather than wide open, yet sufficient to give us a good entrance.

I will not go into detail as to how the Lord made the way plain before us—how we found the framework of a house exactly the size we had wished, all ready and waiting for us; how it was in the best open site in the village and belonged to the Christian headman, who at once granted us permission to use it and live there; how we prayed in the thatch for the roof (we were too late to get thatch in the ordinary way); how the Christian Lisu in the village of Palien, three miles away, came and thatched our roof without charge; how we found carpenters and finished all the necessary work in an unusual spell of fine weather just before the rain set in; etc., etc. All this is the romance of missionary life to those of us who are in it, small though the details may seem.

All through the summer, this little home was Fraser's headquarters, he and his family occupying one of the side rooms, and the Fitzwilliams the other, while the central space was used as a living room for them all. Once he came back from a journey to find Mrs. Fraser and the children quite alone among the people. His fiftieth birthday was spent with them in these surroundings, where his knowledge of the Kachin language came in so useful. When, after four months, the Frasers were called to Paoshan, Mr. and Mrs. Fitzwilliam remained to carry on the work.

And now a congenial task had to be taken up. Mr. and Mrs. Cooke, who had been gradually completing the translation of the New Testament into Lisu, had finished their long undertaking and were ready for a final revision. (The entire cost of the first edition of this Lisu New Testament was borne by the freewill offerings of the Chinese Christians in Manchuria.) It was to help in this work that the Frasers had moved to Paoshan, and he was now ready to join them on the Upper Salween. Moses, their Lisu translator, was there. It would be a long task and one for which quiet was needed.

Much had happened on the Salween since Fraser and his bride had been there five years previously. Soon after that visit, the Cookes had been transferred from Fuhinshan to Oak Flat (Pade) to follow up the work of the Lisu evangelists who were reaping a harvest of precious souls. A year later they had to move still farther up the great canyon, a week's journey to the north, to the district of Luda, where the converts already numbered over a thousand. Mr. and Mrs. John Kuhn had come to Oak Flat, so the Cookes were free to devote themselves to the more remote field, where the Christians were suffering much persecution. Conditions had improved by the time of Fraser's second visit, and the Cookes were in the midst of a large and growing work. They had been joined by Charles Peterson, who shared with Fraser his two-room shack near the simple mission house.

At Luda, then, in the winter of 1936, Fraser found himself engrossingly engaged with these beloved colleagues on the task of revision. Years of work had been put into the translation, by themselves and others, and unnumbered prayers were reaching their fulfillment. Meanwhile, the fellowship of that little group was most precious.

Fraser was at his best. "He was in excellent health," Peterson recalls, "able to do a long day's work and enjoy it. Morning devotions were most helpful as he brought thoughts from the Word, fresh and warm. He was always that way. Whenever he went to a station, he had messages from God for everyone who was prepared to receive them."

Mrs. Cooke said:

Our homelife was greatly enriched through his coming. He had read widely, and his conversation was rich and varied. He would sit, between times, and play on our little organ—a polonaise from Chopin or treasures from Beethoven—bringing such glorious music out of it! The Lisu would crowd in to listen.

The thing that impressed me as the months went on was his firm control over every part of his life. He was completely master of himself. He not only wanted to live a self-denying life, enduring hardness for Christ's sake, but he did it. To bring his daily life up to the level of his highest thought seemed to be quiet natural with him. And he was so practical about it.

His correspondence, for example, was very heavy. I have known him to sit up all night answering letters, but he would not let that extra work interfere with regular hours of revision work during the next day. When the mail came in, he would put the letters to be answered into envelopes addressed to the senders, and keep them on his table ready for attention.

Mr. Cooke put in:

He was very sociable. When he wanted to write letters or study, he would come down and do it with us, rather than stay up in his room alone.

Mrs. Cooke resumed:

No matter how busy he was, he never cut short the morning time of family worship. He would often continue with us in prayer and Bible study until nine or ten o'clock. Mr. Cooke and I were alone with him for a while, before Peterson and Carlson joined us. But Mr. Fraser was just as willing to impart his precious messages to us as to a larger company. How we did enjoy them, for we had been long away from such ministry in our own tongue.

Hymn-singing was always part of these times of worship. Mr. Fraser always chose the grand old-time hymns, and seemed so in his element—playing the little organ and leading us in song. His favorite hymn was "The Lord's my Shepherd, I'll not want," and he would announce it by saying, "Let us sing a hymn written three thousand years ago."

But it was in work together on the New Testament that these friends chiefly enjoyed one another. Fraser was argumentative. He liked nothing better than a good tussle over some point under discussion, but always in a perfectly friendly spirit. He said of Moses, their language informant, that what he did not know of Lisu tones and grammatical phrases was not worth knowing; his own knowledge of Greek was scholarly. In the open air, on the veranda of the mission bungalow, they would sit and work in the sunshine, moving indoors to the fireside when a chill came into the air at that altitude of six thousand feet.

Fraser wrote the following to his mother:

> Oh, what fascinating work it is. How I love Bible translation and Bible teaching—and how both seem to water my own soul!

From early November until after Christmas this was the order of the day. Then the exigencies of correspondence brought them down from Luda to Oak Flat, a week's journey nearer to their post office. The Kuhns had gone home on furlough, so their house could accommodate the Fraser family. Mrs. Fraser planned to come up with the children to join her husband for the last month or so. This was a great joy to Fraser who, before he knew that they were coming, had written to his mother:

> I would love to see my babies again, if only for ten minutes! It is a real denial for me to be away from them, for they will never be the same age again. I do not want them to grow older. I want them always to put their little hands in mine when I walk with them and I want them always to prattle to me.

It seemed strange that just at that juncture an accident should have been allowed to cut them off from their accustomed source of supplies. All their provisions coming up from Burma were kept at the railhead in the house of a trusted business friend until messengers could be sent for them. Imagine their distress, shortly before leaving Luda, to hear that their friend's house had caught fire and its contents burned to ashes. All their supply of groceries and other provisions was cut off without warning, just as they were expecting a considerable addition to their numbers at Oak Flat! But a moment's reflection assured Mrs. Cooke that it must be among the "all things" that work together for good to them that love God. Faith did not fail, and they were helped and carried through in wonderful ways. Mrs. Cooke recalled:

People began sending us things. Butter, tea, and other supplies seemed to hold out. We found that we could get some things locally. And Mrs. Fraser, when she came, brought provisions, knowing nothing of our special need.

It was touching to see the joy of that family reunion. Fraser changed the subject at devotions that morning, and took the beautiful story of Ruth: her love for Naomi and how they came into the line of David's ancestry.

We took our chairs out of doors into the sunshine at the back of the house. They sat together, those two lovers. I can see them yet.

Fraser had given much time to prayer during all those months in the Salween. Week by week he took one or more services with the Lisu, who loved to hear him speak in their own language. And when Mrs. Fraser came, leaving the children in Mrs. Cooke's care, she would go up with him to the chapel, where they spent hours together, waiting upon God.

The completion of the Lisu New Testament was a crowning joy in Fraser's life. All through the years of work upon it, he had been in close correspondence with the Gowmans, the Cookes, and others who had taken part. He had watched its progress with the keenest interest, doing all he could to forward it. And now he rejoiced with the large company of Lisu Christians who were longing for its appearance.

It was a joy to him also to arrange for a series of

conferences in the following year, when Miss Anna Christensen was to come again to Yunnan.

Mr. Peterson wrote:

Miss Christensen came in the spring of 1938, with the hope that God would bring blessing to the Chinese church. This was granted. Souls came into a new relationship with God, wrongs were righted, sin confessed, and many received assurance of the new birth. Great blessing came also to the Lisu who heard her. Of the four hundred who attended the meetings in Paoshan, the number who understood Chinese was small—possibly only Job and Titus. But Job's heart was greatly stirred. He was certainly born again before that time, but the truth had not gripped him. After that it was different. He returned to Oak Flat and, during the April Bible study week, urged all the teachers to make sure that they had the new birth. The blessing did not stop there but was carried into the Rainy Season Bible School. During that time the evening services for an entire week were concentrated on that subject, and each of our students was required to take it in the practice preaching class. Their hearts were full of it, and through them the blessed truth has been taught throughout all the Oak Flat district.

Six days south of Paoshan, blessing came to the Lisu at Mengka [where Mr. and Mrs. Payne were stationed] through another of Miss Christensen's series of meetings. At least thirty Lisu were there, and all of them received help. Teacher Luke's experience is typical. After hearing a message on covered sin, he got a huge piece of paper and made a list of all the sins he had ever committed, as far as he could remember. Then he wrote at the bottom: "But I have confessed them all to Jesus. He has forgiven them and washed my heart. I know that I am born again."

Through these meetings blessing was carried to most of our southern Lisu districts, and more than six months later our Lisu are still speaking of Miss Christensen and the blessing they received at the meetings she conducted.

By that time Fraser and his family were again settled at Paoshan. More and more his heart was drawn out in prayer. He had found and rented a room in a Muslim neighbor's house, where he could be alone for prayer—just a bare attic room, unfurnished, with no window, but with a few boards that could be lifted out to let in light and air. There were many coming and going in the mission house, and he would go over to his rented room before breakfast and sometimes remain there in prayer for hours.

"Is there any special burden on your heart that you could share with me?" his wife asked.

"No," he answered tenderly, "just the many and great needs of the mission. And I want to be wholly occupied with my Lord Jesus." This had been his life attitude. And it was in this spirit after only a few days of sudden illness that on September 25, 1938, the call came: "Come up higher."

That mortality might be swallowed up of life.

Chapter 26

FAREWELL

W{\small HEN} F{\small RASER} {\small FIRST CAME TO} Y{\small UNNAN} he had taken an evangelistic journey to Paoshan, then called Yung-chang. It was his first preaching trip, quickly followed by another in the same general direction. And, remarkably enough, each resulted in a friendship which was a strength and blessing to the very end of his life. The first was with Chao Ho, the friendly tanner of Paoshan; the second with Moh of Hsiangta, though that developed later. The paper-covered Gospel picked up in the crowd, which led to Moh's conversion, was carried to him by his little nephew at that time.

And now, in the desolation of Mrs. Fraser's bereavement, it was this long-tried friend in Paoshan who came to her help. Chao Ho could never forget an act that had touched him deeply in a time of sorrow. At his Christian mother's funeral, Fraser had taken the place of a filial son, wearing full mourning and walking beside him, next to the coffin. For well-nigh thirty years they had maintained an unbroken friendship, and now it was Chao Ho who came forward to give expression to the loving sympathy of all the Paoshan Christians. During the last day or two of Fraser's illness, they had come in sorrowful succession to see him—kneeling for a few moments at his bedside in silent prayer. And now their hearts were one in the desire to show due respect to his memory. And so it came about that Paoshan witnessed a memorable procession on the day of interment. A single figure in white (the garb of deep mourning) walked immediately in front of the coffin through the streets of the city. Chao Ho had claimed the privilege of acting as chief mourner.

The reader will remember how Fraser in early years delighted to play with Winifred, baby daughter of Mr. and Mrs. Embery, at Tengyueh. Now back in China as a young missionary herself, Miss Embery wrote the following account of the funeral:

For a long time, Paoshan Christians and others have asked and wondered about a Christian funeral, so we all felt that the arrangement should be a worthy example and glorifying to God. Silk banners were carried, bearing texts of Scripture in velvet or embossed gold paper, such as "Forever with the Lord," "I am the Resurrection and the Life," and "His works do follow him." Beautiful wreaths of flowers had been made, also a red silk banner in the form of a cross, bearing the words "He bore our sins in His own body." And, in place of the usual photograph of the deceased on its stand, a cross of red and white flowers was framed in a wreath of greenery.

In the chapel full of flowers a memorial service had been held the day before, led by Mr. Chao, who told many touching incidents of love and faithfulness in Mr. Fraser's life, during the many years in which they had known each other, often working together through times of difficulty and persecution. He closed by applying in a Christian sense the words of Sun Yat-sen: "Comrades, the Revolution is not yet completed—we must put forth fresh effort." Many present signified their desire to yield themselves afresh to the Lord, to carry on the work of the Gospel.

The following morning fifty or sixty Christians preceded the coffin as it was carried out. As we passed through the city streets on our way to the West Gate, the silence and respect of those in the procession seemed to inspire quietness among the onlookers. Mr. Chao had insisted on wearing the white of the chief mourner, as the "son" of the deceased. It certainly was not an easy thing to do in the streets of his own city.

Ground had been secured for a cemetery on the hills outside the West Gate, and there they laid him, overlooking the plain that had been the last scene of his labors, even as it had been almost the first.

But the farewell that comes nearest to our hearts was that earlier one, when the Lisu from the Salween River who had come down with young Peterson and

Christianson had to go back, carrying the sorrowful tidings. They had been just in time to help with the last days of nursing, and had almost witnessed the passing of their beloved leader and friend. They had borne him afterwards to the chapel on the mission premises, where a simple service had been held. The prayers were in Lisu, the hymns sung were in Lisu, the love and tears were from Lisu hearts—a little company of the thousands drawn, through Fraser's life, into the love that is eternal.

About the arrival of the news at Oak Flat on the Salween, Isobel Kuhn wrote a little later:

> After the first shock, there was a desolate feeling as regards *human* fellowship, that there was no one now to work for. "How Mr. Fraser will enjoy hearing about this," was always a first reaction to any joy or blessing. There was no one else on earth who had such a complete knowledge of the details of our problems, no one who could share so perfectly in our joys and sorrows.
>
> And he never disappointed us in the sharing. He was more than Superintendent to us—he was our missionary ideal, a continual rebuke, challenge, and stimulus to maintain at any cost the apostolic methods of missionary work. His brilliant gifts, united with unfailing humility and a sympathy motherlike in its tenderness and thoughtfulness, made him our refuge at all times of perplexity and need. And to win a smile of approval from him was worth any extra effort. It is one thing to be praised by a person

who has no experience of your task; it is quite different to win a "well done" from one who is himself a master in that very line of things. We have lost a great stimulus, as well as an indispensable counselor. I say "indispensable," for no one can ever take his place. Life can never be the same to us without J. O. Fraser.

But life does not stop for heartache. Away to the west, eight days' journey from the mission shanty on the Salween, many Lisu were waiting, waiting for the Word of life. Once and again they had sent over the mountain ranges to beg for teachers; once and again Christian Lisu had responded, "biting their way through the snow" of the pass eleven thousand feet high. And now there was a little company of believers at Goo-moo, longing for a visit from the missionaries. John and Isobel Kuhn were ready to face the perilous journey, when arrested by the shock of their great loss.

But what could be more in keeping with Fraser's own life and spirit? "My heart is on it," said Homay, the young Lisu woman who was to accompany Mrs. Kuhn. "I can hardly wait to start for Goo-moo." And so said the other volunteers—six men, all of them ready for all the rigors of the way and for evangelism at the other end.

So they set out, asking nothing but the joy of carrying the name of Jesus farther afield into the darkness—but not before they and the other Christians at Oak Flat had themselves contributed no less than twenty dollars toward the cost of preparing their beloved leader's last resting place.

Moody Press, a ministry of the Moody Bible Institute, is designed for education, evangelization and edification. If we may assist you in knowing more about Christ and the Christian life, please write us without obligation to: Moody Press, c/o MLM, Chicago, Illinois 60610.

182- What is lost through temporary lapse can be regained

182- occupation of superficial concerns- workaj reports

219 very few will come to meetings to study

260- remarkably effectual prayers for the sick but not for lost